Regulation, Institutions and the Law

Books from Social Science Press

Globalization and the Millennium Development Goals: Negotiating the Challenge (HB)
Edited by Manmohan Agarwal and Amit Shovon Ray

Cultural History of Medieval India (PB)
Edited by Meenakshi Khanna

Religious Division and Social Conflict: The Emergence of Hindu Nationalism in Rural India (HB)
Peggy Froerer

The Enigma of the Kerala Woman: A Failed Promise of Literacy (HB)
Edited by Swapna Mukhopadhyay

Cultural History of Modern India (PB)
Edited by Dilip M. Menon

Delhi: Ancient History (PB)
Edited by Upinder Singh

Unbecoming Modern: Colonialism, Modernity and Colonial Modernities (HB)
Edited by Saurabh Dube and Ishita Banerjee-Dube

After the Iraq War: The Future of the UN and International Law (HB)
Edited by Bernhard Vogel, Rudolf dolzer and Matthias Herdegen

Social and Economic Profile of India (HB)
(In full colour)
Peeyush Bajpai, Laveesh Bhandari and Aali Sinha

India and China in the Colonial World (HB)
Edited by Madhavi Thampi

Everyday Politics of Labour: Working Lives in India's Informal Economy (HB)
Geert De Neve

Viramma: Life of a Dalit (PB)
Viramma, Josiane Racine and Jean-Luc Racine

Lived Islam in South Asia: Adaptation, Accommodation and Conflict (HB)
Edited by Imtiaz Ahmad and Helmut Reifeld

Tamil Nadu Human Development Report
(Text in two colours)

Reforming India's Social Sector: Poverty, Nutrition, Health and Education (HB)
Edited by K. Seeta Prabhu and R. Sudarshan

Human Security in South Asia: Energy, Gender, Migration, and Globalization (HB)
Edited by P.R. Chari and Sonika Gupta

Middle Class Values in India and Western Europe (HB)
Edited by Imtiaz Ahmad and Helmut Reifeld

Religion and Personal Law in Secular India: A Call to Judgment (HB)
Edited by Gerald James Larson

WTO Agreement and Indian Agriculture (HB)
Edited by Anwarul Hoda

Sikkim Human Development Report 2001
Mahendra P. Lama

Trade, Finance and Investment in South Asia (HB)
Edited by T.N. Srinivasan

The Everyday State and Society in Modern India (HB)
Edited by C.J. Fuller and Véronique Bénéi

Children's Lifeworlds: Gender Welfare and Labour in the Developing World (HB)
Olga Nieuwenhuys

FORTHCOMING

Mansions of Music: Pedagogy, Performance and Criticism
Lakshmi Subramanian

Making the Past Work: Writing History in the Soviet Union
Arup Banerjee

Regulation, Institutions and the Law

Edited by
Jaivir Singh

Social Science Press
NEW DELHI

Published by
Esha Béteille
Social Science Press
69 Jor Bagh, New Delhi 110 003

Distributed by
Orient Longman Private Limited
Bangalore Bhopal Bhubaneshwar Chandigarh
Chennai Ernakulam Guwahati Hyderabad Jaipur
Kolkata Lucknow Mumbai New Delhi Patna
www.orientlongman.com

ISBN-13: 978-81-87358-28-2
ISBN-10: 81-87358-28-9

Set in Giovanni Book 10/12
Typeset by Eleven Art, Delhi 110 035
Printed by Yogesh Pracashan
at Ravindra Printing Press, Delhi 110 006

Contents

Preface and Acknowledgements xi

List of Contributors xiii

1. Introduction 1
   Jaivir Singh
   Regulation: Institutional and Legal Concerns 1
   Conceptualizing, Evaluating and Describing Regulation 4
   Connections 8

2. Structuring Regulation: Constitutional and Legal Frame in India 10
   T.C.A. Anant and Jaivir Singh
   Introduction 10
   The Constitution 12
   Separation of Powers and Regulation 15
   Case Studies 16
   Conclusion 25
   Postscript 26

3. Potential Problems in the Implementation of the Competition Act, 2002 28
   Aditya Bhattacharjea
   Introduction 28
   Features of the Competition Act 29
   Institutional Capacity Building 36
   Conclusion 40
   Postscript 42

4. Compacts Conventions and Codes: Initiatives for Higher International Labor Standards 43
Kaushik Basu
Introduction 43
The Issues and the Historical Background 44
Existing Initiatives and Their Shortcomings 47
Recommendations 51
Restructuring International Organizations 53

5. Globalization and the Politics of International Corporate Taxation: A View from India 60
by Rahul Mukherji
Introduction 60
Source-based versus Residence-based Taxation 67
Permanent Establishment 75
Governing International Corporate Taxation 79

6. Investigating Social Norms: Towards an Understanding of 'Embeddedness' in Regulation 87
Shailaja Fennel
Introduction 87
Role of Social Norms 89
Regulation, Evolution and History 91
State, Society and Changing Regulatory Regimes 93
Exploring the Need for Regulation in the Provision of Services 97
Conclusion 101

7. Electricity Market Regulation in Germany: Response to Common Norms and Specific Interests 105
Enrico Schöbel
Introduction 105
Electricity Network Regulation due to Normative Principles 107
Electricity Network Regulation in Response to Specific Identifiable Interest 108
Specific German Institution of Negotiated Network Access Conditions 110
The German Green Electricity Regulation 114
Conclusion 116

8. Lessons from Regulation of Post-reform Power Sector: A Case Study of Orissa 120
Mohamed Zakaria Siddiqui
Introduction 120
Method of Regulation 122
Making a Tariff Order 127
Issues Underlying Tariff Orders 127
Alternative Strategy to Regulate in the Current Scenario 141
Conclusion 148
Appendix 150

9. Small Investor Protection and Issues in Corporate Governance: An IT-enabled Approach to the Decision Making Process of Firms 153
Murali Kallummal
Introduction 153
Capital Market-based Financial Intermediation in India: A Brief History 157
Information Technology-enabled Approach and Effective Firm-level Decisions 170
Conclusion 176
Appendix 178

10. An Enquiry into Insurance Regulation: The Interaction of Investment and Price Regulation 184
Ajit Ranade and Rajeev Ahuja
Introduction 184
A Simple Model 187
Simulation Results 190
Justification for Price Regulation 191
Conclusion 193

11. Telecom Liberalization: A Case Study of India's Experience with Regulation 195
Rajat Kathuria
Introduction 195
The National Telecom Policy (NTP) 1994 197
Initial Years of the TRAI 200
The Telecommunications Tariff Order 1999 203
The TRAI (Amendment) Act 2000 206

Wireless in Local Loop and Limited Mobility 207
Question of Legitimacy 210
Conclusion 212
Annex I 214
Annex II 214

12. Issues in Government Intervention, Black Economy and Governance in India 218
Arun Kumar
Introduction 218
Need for Government Intervention in the Political Economy 219
Cause of Black Income Generation: Illegality around Laws 227
Possible Solution 236
Conclusion 240

LIST OF TABLES

5.1: Comparison of Types of Corporate Taxation 75
5.2: Standards for Taxing Digitized Trade 81
8.1: Power Purchase Requirements with Actual and Normative Multiplier 130
8.2: Normative and Actual Tariff Structures 133
8.3: Power Purchase of the DIST COs for 2002–03 134
8.4: Metering Status of the DIST COs (Percentage) 138
9.1: Geographical Incidence of Shareowners in India 165
9.2: Size-wise Distribution of Firms 169
9.3: Age-wise Distribution of Firms 169
9.4: Diversification of Share of Small Shareholders and Extent of Influence in the Process of Decision Making 172
A9.1: Changes in Financial Assets of the Household Sector (Percentage Share) 178
A9.2: Distribution of Outstanding Credit of Banks According to Interest Rate Range 178
A9.3: Distribution of Firms Based on Operation as Private and Public Limited Companies 179
A9.4: Size of Firms and Firm Allotments in a Public Issue 180
A9.5: Age of Firms and Firm Allotments in a Public Issue 180

LIST OF FIGURES

8.1: Process of Restructuring of OSEB Assets 121

8.2: Distribution Losses of the DISTCOs 137

8.3: Vicious Circle of Low Quality of Power Supply 144

8.4: Demand for Reliability for Different Categories 145

9.1: Flow Chart Showing Various Organs of Financial Market 159

9.2: Flow Chart Showing Constituents of Capital Market 159

9.3: CRS Approach to Decision Making in Firms 174

A9.1: Growth of Primary Market in India: Debentures vs Equity 181

A9.2: Corporate Financing and the Trends in the Primary Market in India: (1970–2001) 181

A9.3: Relationship between Secondary Market and Primary Market in India 182

A9.4: Saving and Investment Related Activities in India: 1960–2001 182

10.1: Expected Utility and Proportion of Investments in Safe Asset: $U(X) = \sqrt{x}$ 189

10.2: Expected Utility and Proportion of Investments in Safe Asset: $u(x) = \ln x$ 190

10.3: Expected Utility and Proportion of Investments in Safe Asset: $u(x) = 1 - e^{-\rho x}$ 191

Preface and Acknowledgements

Many people have contributed to this book, both in its inception as well as production. In 2003, shortly after I joined the Centre for the Study of Law and Governance, JNU, taking cognizance of my ongoing research on regulation (jointly with T.C.A. Anant), my colleagues Professor Kuldeep Mathur and Professor Niraja Gopal Jayal encouraged me to organize a conference around the issue of structuring regulation. As a consequence, Dr Ram Singh, a colleague at the Centre at that time and I jointly organized a conference in November 2003 entitled, 'Regulation: Institutional and Legal Dimensions'. Dr Singh put in a good deal of effort in organizing the conference; he saw to not only many of the organizational details but also dealt with the most onerous task of keeping and submitting accounts to the JNU administrative authorities. I believe without his active involvement the conference and therefore, this volume would not have been possible.

Though I intended to publish the proceedings soon after the conference was over, one thing or another inhibited me from finishing the job expeditiously. At that point Professor Niraja Gopal Jayal took on the task of encouraging me to put the proceedings together as a book—thus, she is responsible for the fact that the volume has been ultimately produced. I thank her for her persistent encouragement.

While editing the various papers for this volume, I was obliged to read all of them (along with the comments of anonymous referees) very carefully and gained an appreciation of the multiple perspectives that they offer on regulation—each paper has a valuable insight. I take this opportunity to thank all the contributors. I do feel that this volume is able to raise questions on 'structuring regulation'. The definitive answers of course, are awaited.

The conference which led to the compilation of this volume would have been impossible without financial support. The organization of the conference drew on a grant provided to the Centre for the Study of Law and Governance, JNU by the Ford Foundation. I am indeed very grateful for the support provided by the Ford Foundation in this regard.

Jaivir Singh
August 2007

List of Contributors

Rajeev Ahuja
The World Bank, Washington D.C., U.S.A

T.C.A. Anant
Professor, Delhi School of Economics, University of Delhi, New Delhi, and Member Secretary, Indian Council of Social Science Research (ICSSR).

Kaushik Basu
C. Marks Professor of International Studies and Professor of Economics and Director, Programme on Comparative Economic Development, Cornell University, U.S.A.

Aditya Bhattacharjea
Reader, Delhi School of Economics, University of Delhi, New Delhi.

Shailaja Fennel
Lecturer in Development Studies and Fellow of Jesus College, University of Cambridge, U.K.

Murali Kallummal
Consultant, Centre for WTO Studies, Indian Institute of Foreign Trade, New Delhi.

Rajat Kathuria
Professor, International Management Institute, New Delhi.

Arun Kumar
Professor, Centre for Economic Studies and Planning, Jawaharlal Nehru University, New Delhi.

Rahul Mukherji
Associate Professor, Centre for Political Studies, School of Social Sciences Jawaharlal Nehru University, New Delhi.

Ajit Ranade
Chief Economist, The Aditya Birla Group, New Delhi.

Enrico Schöbel
Dipl.-Volkswirt Public Finance and Fiscal Sociology, University of Erfurt, Germany.

Mohamed Zakaria Siddiqui
Doctoral Student at Centre for Economic Studies and Planning, Jawaharlal Nehru University, New Delhi and currently Visiting Doctoral Student at Centre for Operation Research and Econometrics, Université Catholique de Louvain, Belgium.

Jaivir Singh
Assistant Professor, Centre for the Study of Law and Governance, Jawaharlal Nehru University, New Delhi.

1
Introduction

Regulation: Institutional and Legal Concerns

In the first instance to introduce this collection of papers on regulation, it is helpful to try and fix a frame within which we can understand the term 'regulation'. One cannot quite find a universally static definition of regulation, though for our purposes regulation can be functionally thought of as the use of legal instruments to implement a set of social-economic policy objectives (Den Hertog 1999). Such legal instruments are most often constructed as penalties (sometimes as subsidies as well) imposed on economic agents to make them comply with prescribed behaviour. Thus for example, regulated firms are expected to charge a specified price and/or supply a specified quantity, apply particular technology, pay minimum wages etc.; the failure to do so could mean that the firm in question will face penalties that could range from adverse publicity, fines or imprisonment, injunctions to orders decreeing closure of business. This functional understanding of regulation, while possibly failing to capture the complexity associated with regulation, is useful in that it points to an intimacy between law and regulation—law which is always present, both, as a source of legitimacy to wield the instruments of regulation and more broadly, to provide legitimacy to the act of regulation itself.

However to approach regulation entirely through a legal frame may be too partial, presumably the law is often enough, only an instrument to effect the 'set of social-economic' policies of the state. Economists have traditionally had much to say about regulation and possibly an admixture of appropriate elements of the law approached with some economic sense produces the *juste milieu* to approach regulation. The standard taxonomy associated with the theoretical study of regulation in economics is to distinguish between positive and normative theories of regulation, where positive theory explains and describes the consequences of regulation while normative theory aims to pronounce on which type of regulation best fulfils the standard economic efficiency criterion. Within the category of positive theory, it is common to broadly identify two approaches—the public interest theory of regulation and the private interest theory of regulation. The public interest theories look out and discern varieties of market failures that give rise to non-optimal allocation of resources and see the act of regulation as improving allocation by facilitating, maintaining or imitating market operations. While private interest theories may admit to an ostensible public interest impulse at the start of a regulation, they emphasize the point that as time goes on, 'capture' of both the wider state processes (legislative as well as executive) and the regulatory agency by the regulated industry come to characterize regulation.

Whether regulation is approached as a normative or positive issue or understood in terms of public or private interest, the large corpus of received economic literature on regulation tends to be typically quite thin in providing approaches to come to grips with either the kind of regulation that has unfolded in a country like India or to confront certain regulatory issues that have emerged from increasing trans-national interaction in the era of globalization. This statement should not be misinterpreted as an attempt to deny the universality of standard analysis of regulation, but rather an attempt to be sensitive to the nuance that often enough, there is a symbiosis between academic output and outcomes in 'applied' areas of study. A good amount of the standard regulation literature has grown organically in response to events in the United States and more recently, in Western Europe. While both theoretically as well as empirically, this literature can help conceptualize many aspects of regulation, it has to be realized that the bulk of the analysis of regulation assumes a North American or at best, a European institutional setting. To the extent that institutions matter, it follows that the questions one raises in relation to regulation would have to be sensitive to the wider institutional context within which they are raised. In other words, it is being suggested that since individual historical trajectories mould the context within which terms like 'regulation' come to have meaning, the difference in contexts may imply that the analytical frames within which critical questions are raised may also be required to be different from the modes employed by standard analysis. To illustrate the point, consider the advent of regulation in a market that has been either unregulated, informally regulated or is being subjected to 'reform' (as is the case with many instances of regulation in India). One could, in such cases, proceed by drawing on a corpus of existing literature, to analyse the effectiveness of the regulation, possibly attempting to understand the interests it serves, and follow the resulting ramifications. However this may provide an incomplete picture because outcomes created by such regulation may not be determined solely by the instruments defined in the statutes governing the regulation as such, but rather may be influenced by the manner in which the regulation has been structured both in relation to temporal (past institutions and past practices that may persist) as well as spatial considerations (complementary, competing or hierarchical agencies may stall the effectuation of regulatory intent). The regulation question in such cases, needs to be minimally framed keeping in mind the wider institutional context, which need not necessarily follow the North American or West European trajectories.

The institutional history of India has been such that the issue of regulation—at least as a clearly enunciated category, was rarely, if ever, a part of the policy discourses before the 1991 liberalization. While the predominant policy instrument that characterized the first 30 years or so of the Indian economy—licensing, was clearly a regulatory act of sorts, the terms 'regulation' and 'regulator' emerged in economic documents only after liberalization. The liberalization process means many things in different contexts, but to the extent the term is associated with restructuring unviable public enterprises and creating conditions that allow markets to function efficiently and as far as possible equitably, both regulation and the law have been put out upfront as the instrumental devices in the liberalization endeavour. This is in contrast to the pre-liberalization phase when regulatory control was largely administrative.[1] About a decade or so after the liberalization process was initiated, it is clearly important

[1]An early representation of this can be seen from the following quote: 'The Government's role should shift increasingly to restructuring unviable enterprises, ensuring fair business practices, safeguarding consumer interests and minimising the adverse effect of industrialisation on the environment' Government of India, Ministry of Finance (1993).

to see what regulation has come to mean and achieve in India. However, often enough, such attempts run into the problem of framing the conceptual framework that can help in posing appropriate questions, and if one uses standard models to grapple with questions of regulation, they remain somewhat incomplete. Apropos the point raised earlier, this disquiet is largely on account of the fact that the critical issues surrounding regulation often need to be analysed less as a problem of achieving professed ends and more in terms of contexts associated with the structuring of institutions that achieve the 'professed ends'.

This then, was the broad impulse behind the call for a conference on regulation at the Centre for the Study of Law and Governance, JNU, setting out an agenda to raise questions as to how can one conceptualize regulation innovatively in the contemporary context, particularly asking what the institutional frameworks are within which regulation is constituted and what insight the analysis of such institutions provide in grappling with regulation. The backgrounds of the many individuals who contributed to the conference in November 2003 and thus to this collection of essays, are diverse—some of them have a mainstream economics orientation while others do not; some are actively involved in the practice of regulation; a few have a legal background while others have more technical specializations. The collection of essays taken as a whole, then, is quite eclectic; some essays attempt to conceptualize regulation, others evaluate ongoing regulation, and a few provide basic descriptions of the regulatory structure.

Conceptualizing, Evaluating and Describing Regulation

The first paper 'Structuring Regulation: Constitutional and Legal Frame in India' by T.C.A. Anant and Jaivir Singh, aims to look at the design of regulation by asking how regulatory decisions should be taken and where they should be located in the wider structures of constitutional governance of a liberal democracy. Emphasizing the doctrine of separation of powers as a crucial element of the constitutional structure, it is pointed out that if regulation is designed with weak exercise of the doctrine, substantial social costs tend to be generated from the consequent 'over/under delegation' of authority. While the key case studies discussed in the sections, Insolvency Tribunals and Competition Commission as well as Autonomy of Central Banks in this paper provide immediate illustrations of the problem on hand, the analytical frame could be potentially harnessed to dissect other regulatory institutions in India.

Aditya Bhattacharjea's paper 'Potential Problems in the Implementation of the Competition Act, 2002', while acknowledging the structural concerns discussed in the previous paper in relation to the Competition Commission focuses primarily on the problems associated with the substantive content of the Act. Since the Act has not been legislated at the time this volume has been put together, Bhattacharjea is obliged to confine himself to the language of the Act rather than any 'real life' implementation of the law. While the new law, at least in comparison to the Monopolies Restrictive Trade Practices (MRTP) Act, exhibits some positive features, there appear to be a lot ill-conceived components, largely structural in nature. Apart from framing various aspects of the law with little or no cognizance of basic economic principles, there are very few provisions to build institutional capacity to process the kind of information regarding merger review as well as discerning intricacies of market structures, so very vital for a competition law to function well. It is significantly pointed out that the persistence of such flaws could very well lead to a loss of political support for competition law and regulation.

Kaushik Basu's paper 'Compacts, Conventions and Codes: Initiatives for Higher International Labor Standards', raises questions of politics and the appropriate design of regulation in relation to international labour standards.* Drawing extensively on his formal work on child labour he points to the welfare reduction that follows even the most well-intentioned laws legislated by developed countries restricting imports, or subsequent to moves that seek to organize voluntary boycotts of produce manufactured using child labour. Far more effective devices to raise labour standards include moves to raise the demand for adult labour from the South and possibly the more important device is to create equal spaces for countries of the South in international organizations—those that can act credibly to co-ordinate labour standards across the South as per need and ability. It is a democratic space that continues to elude countries of the global South.

Rahul Mukherji's paper 'Globalization and the Politics of International Corporate Taxation: A View from India' talks of the need for setting international standards in relation to corporate taxation in the era of 'digitization driven globalization', failing which, unilateral attempts to determine tax rules could imply problems of tax base erosion as well as double taxation. He points to a distinction between source-based rules, which allow for taxation at points where

* The original American spellings have been retained in this paper.

value is created and residence-based rules, which encourage taxation at the point where the economic enterprise is situated. While the broad and established global norm appears to be source-based taxation, Mukherji documents and critiques the desire of capital-abundant countries to establish residence-based rules, which would not only act to the detriment of the countries of the South but in the long run, move business to tax havens.

Turning from trans-national regulatory problems to the global flow of ideas on regulation, to the extent genealogies are germane to understanding how regulation comes to be structured, Shailaja Fennel's paper 'Investigating Social Norms: Towards an Understanding of "Embeddedness" in Regulation' is noteworthy for the survey of the literature on the role of reciprocity and mutuality that informs moves towards encouraging participatory forms of regulation of industry as well as services. Among other things, she visits certain sites of participatory regulation such as NGO involvement in the provision of education and housing in India. She finds that many of these 'new' forms of regulation, while no doubt influenced by their generic use as models in certain western institutional settings, are not able to address barriers of social equity adequately to function as robust models of regulation. In this context, Enrico Schöbel's paper 'Electricity Market Regulation in Germany: Response to Common Norms and Specific Interests', documents precisely the failure of the kind of self-regulation surveyed by Fennel—the attempt by Germany to regulate the electricity sector by getting industry-level associations to negotiate market access conditions among themselves.* While Schobel analyses the regulation of the German electricity market by posing the problem within the frame provided by the private interest, theory of regulation—the coagulation of 'green' and 'new entrant' interests—leading to the formation of an overarching regulator in the form of the Federal Network Agency, the paper also provides interesting details that have resonance with the issues raised by Fennel. It is pointed out that over the phase of self-regulation, the industry lobbied to turn negotiated outcomes into law—a move stalled by the anti-trust authorities. This bespeaks of the inherent intimacy between law and the act of regulation—a point that resonates explicitly or implicitly across many of the papers in this volume that seek to engage with the structuring of regulation.

* The German style of referencing has been retained for this paper.

Mohamed Zakaria Siddiqui's paper 'Lessons from Regulation of Post-reform Power Sector: A Case Study of Orissa', unlike other papers in this volume that cover specific sectors, does not approach problems associated with regulation of the sector at large, but looks at them specifically in the context of the state of Orissa. Siddiqui investigates post-reform regulation by looking into the structure contained within tariff orders issued by the Orissa Electricity Regulatory Commission to discern locations of opportunistic behaviour by the various actors involved. Among the various disincentives structured into the rules that govern regulation, he finds that grid suppliers end up bearing most of the risk both from distributing companies as well as the power generating units, while the lack of adequate metering gets reflected in losses claimed by distribution companies. Inadequate metering also constrains the ability of the regulator to process vital information. This description causes Siddiqui to call for changes in the incentive structure determined by the manner in which the tariff orders are set, in effect, implicitly demanding a restructuring of spatial configurations within the overall regulatory structure.

The following paper by Murali Kallummal 'Small Investor Protection and Issues in Corporate Governance: An IT-enabled Approach to the Decision Making Process of Firms' provides a detailed background of the history and institutions associated with the lack of confidence of small investors in the Indian stock market. Kallummal points to the fact that the small investor has traditionally been a major source of savings in the Indian economy, which he combines with evidence that a good amount of stock market funds find their way to 'small' firms, to demand that suitable regulation should be ascertained to sustain these beneficial relations. In particular he prescribes changes in the Companies Act to allow for greater use of information technology to create a more democratic mode of governance that would be favourable to the small investor.

Yet another dimension of financial market regulation is explored in the next two papers that look at the regulation of insurance markets. The paper on insurance regulation by Ajit Ranade and Rajeev Ahuja 'An Enquiry into Insurance Regulation: The Interaction of Investment and Price Regulation' looks at two instruments of insurance regulation—control of risky investments and price floors, as devices used to ensure the solvency of insurers. They use a simple model to demonstrate the redundancy of separate price regulation in the face of coeval regulation that seeks to ensure that insuring companies hold minimum levels of safe assets. Nevertheless they point to the utility of price regulation in a developing country context because there might not be adequate information and therefore, at least in the initial stages of regulating the market, there may be a need for the regulation of premium rates and contract standardization.

Rajat Kathuria's paper 'Telecom Liberalization: A Case Study of India's Experience with Regulation' provides an account of the challenges of establishing an 'independent regulatory authority' in India—a task which he accomplishes by looking at the key legal disputes across various stakeholders, which has in a sense, determined the trajectory of telecom regulation in India. He uses the insights gathered by looking into these disputes, to normatively comment on the impediments on the expansion of the telecom sector—the fractiousness hopefully resolving with the passage of time and the ability to effect regulation better.

The paper by Arun Kumar 'Issues in Government Intervention, Black Economy and Governance in India', attempts to take an overall look at government intervention. It is maintained that Indian elites manipulate rules and regulations to further their own interests, which act to perpetuate a 'black' economy. He sees a solution to such breakdown of the law by calling for the instatement of voluntary compliance of rules and regulations. It is argued that such a state can only come about if both democracy and social justice are able to take root more strongly. Though obviously open to challenge from mainstream rational view of social interaction, perhaps Kumar's point could be rephrased in a more nuanced rational paradigm that admits to multiple social equilibriums—where greater social equity is able to weigh the scales towards creating a milieu that breaks the current social equilibrium and causes society to move towards an equilibrium that rewards overall compliance to rules and regulation.

Connections

While all these papers taken together may appear diffuse, one way to build a connection across such eclectic content is to view the regulation problem as a set of questions that attempt to explore the links between regulatory outcomes and internal constitutions of regulatory institutions and/or the national as well as trans-national constitutions. The term 'constitution' is being evoked here in the sense of the constitutional political economy literature, which distinguishes between constitutional and in-period choice, with the former term being associated with choice of rules in contrast to the latter, which is associated with choice under rules, the realm of standard economic analysis (Brennan and Hamlin 2001). With the exception of the first paper, which makes a direct reference to this literature, the other papers are written with no conscious reference to this literature. Nevertheless they all take up 'constitutional' issues in one form or the other, for example, whether in terms of the tussle around international conventions on labour standards or how rules governing the power sector in Orissa need to be set, the generic set of questions are in a primal sense, the same. The similarity lies in the acknowledgement that where rational actors are able to design rules independent of coercion—rules that all would agree to, immune to political whim but adaptable to changing times, the acts of regulation would be performed with greater simplicity and efficiency than otherwise. This is a perspective worth taking in relation to regulation—a viewing lens that is more expansive than the more mainstream outlook on regulation, certainly an important advantage in the contemporary world where we strive to constantly build anew.

References

Brennan, Geoffrey and Alan Hamlin, 2001, 'Constitutional Choice' in William F. Shughart II and Laura Razzolini (eds.), *The Elgar Companion to Public Choice,* Edward Elgar, Cheltenham.

Den Hertog, Johan, 1999, 'General Theories of Regulation' in Bouedewijn Bouckaert and Gerrit De Geest (eds.), *Encyclopedia of Law and Economics,* Edward Elgar, Cheltenham and University of Ghent. Also available at *http://encyclo.findlaw.com/0740book.pdf.*

Government of India, Ministry of Finance, 1993, *Economic Reforms: Two Years After and the Task Ahead,* Department of Economic Affairs 33.

2

Structuring Regulation

Constitutional and Legal Frame in India

T. C. A. Anant and Jaivir Singh

Introduction

As the Indian economy transforms itself successively towards a more market-oriented economy, one of the key moves has been to create institutions that regulate various sectors of the economy—for example telecommunications, insurance, finance and banking. The genesis of such regulatory institutions gives rise to problems of design that are depicted by the following quotes,

> The Supreme Court today heavily came down on the appointment of a bureaucrat to head a quasi-judicial body, [The Competition Commission] terming this as an attempt to usurp the powers of the judiciary.
>
> *The Economic Times*, 1 November 2003.

> An independent central bank focused exclusively on price stability has become a central part of the mantra of 'economic reform'. Like so many other policy maxims, it has been repeated often enough that it has come to be believed. But central banks make decisions that affect every aspect of society, including rates of economic growth and unemployment. Because there are trade-offs, these decisions can only be made as part of a political process.
>
> J Stiglitz, Project-Syndicate, June 2003, *www.project-syndicate.org*

These two quotes illustrate the central dilemma inherent in the problem of designing effective regulatory institutions—keeping

This paper was first published in *Economic and Political Weekly*, Vol. 41, No. 2, 14 January 2006.

Earlier versions of this were presented the Annual meetings of the Canadian Law and Economics Association in 2004.

in mind the aims of regulatory decisions, how should such decisions be taken and, notably, where should they be located in the wider structures of governance? Traditional analysis of regulation often aims to evaluate the efficacy of the mechanisms or instruments used to achieve professed ends, or it seeks to evaluate objectives and the functioning of regulatory agencies. While such analysis is widely practised, and is undoubtedly important and essential, it is critical to realize that the choice of instruments and their use takes place within the wider construct of governance and in particular, constitutional governance. One way of confronting the issues raised in the quotes is to seek an answer to the question—how and where should one locate regulation within a constitutional schema? In this paper we seek to analyse regulation in terms of the appropriate location of the institutions that comprise and effectuate regulation within the constitutional paradigm.

In attempting an institutional analysis of this kind, we are obliged to conceptually represent the state. This is an essential task because regulatory commands emanate either directly from the state or a body delegated by the state. Mainstream economics does not, by and large, engage significantly with the notion of state in this context. This in itself is not problematic to the extent one is exploring social behaviour in the 'marketplace', but since regulation is the purported response to market failure, an analysis of the many instances of market failure inevitably solicits the presence of the state. Thus, when the public interest theory of regulation perceives regulation as the coordinated correction of varieties of market failure by simulating outcomes that the market would have configured in the absence of such failure, it is implicitly believed that a selfless state acts to effect such correction. This is problematic because, among other things, such understanding of regulation treats the state as a black box. Since the state is viewed as a black box, there is no space for the isomorphic image of market failure—government failure. To quote a perceptive statement made by Coase (1964), while acting as a discussant for a series of papers on regulation, 'Until we realise that we are choosing between social arrangements which are all more or less failures, we are not likely to make much headway.'

In the first part of this paper, we construct an approach, which attempts to negotiate an understanding of the 'failures' referred to by Coase, allowing us to analyse the pattern of governance of regulation. At the outset, we enter into the social arrangement of the state by schematically representing it as a series of institutions that derive authority from a constitutional structure—in particular developing the doctrine of separation of powers as an analytical device. We follow this by placing regulation in this scheme of constitutional governance. We use the analytical tools developed in 'Separation of Powers and Regulation' to develop some case studies to illustrate the approach. (See the section 'Case Studies' in this paper). While we look specifically at insolvency and competition in India and briefly touch on the issues surrounding the structure of central banks, we believe that our analysis can extend to a number of other regulatory institutions as well.

The Constitution

While the understanding of the state as a social arrangement is the substance of political philosophy, this can be slippery territory for economics. The hazard stems both from the methodology and the evaluative norm of efficiency (wealth maximization) employed by economics. We do not directly engage with any of these issues; instead we move towards employing an instrumental perspective on the state by asking—What is it in practice that defines the modern liberal state? The answer probably lies in its privileging of representative democracy as the fundamental and primary value pursued. Such representative democracy can be constructed in a variety of forms—for instance it could either be a presidential or parliamentary democracy; it could be based on proportional or majoritarian representation.

Whatever the case may be (again, we do not engage with such questions in the interest of focusing on the problem at hand), it is almost invariably true that in a liberal democracy the Constitution is the highest source of law in a nation state.[1] The Constitution creates the state as a social arrangement by specifying offices and the powers and procedures of these offices. To phrase this in the language developed by the literature on constitutional public choice—it can be viewed as the document that specifies the rules of the game within which social arrangements are required to function. This characterization extends both spatially and temporally. In the temporal sense, constitutions play a particularly vital role of mitigating uncertainty—by restricting in period choices, which may be inimical for the long-run social good (Brennan and Hamlin 2000).

[1] This idealization, of course, changes in a globalized setting where at times, reference is made to a higher code governing the conduct of nations.

In addition to specifying the grand rules, constitutions also typically seek to guarantee and promote a set of normative values in society. Thus for instance the Constitution of India sets out the task of justice, liberty, equality and fraternity as the central aim—as do the constitutions of many other nations. One way of interpreting such normative values is to read them as a series of functional concerns that are essentially incorporated into the structure of the Constitution. Thus, liberty, which provides the individual with the freedom to choose, seeks to expand the domain of individual action. The notion of justice similarly has a number of attributes that includes both the concerns of equity and efficiency and equality of status and opportunity similarly have both process and consequentialist dimensions.

To balance these concerns and in particular, the concern of liberty—understood in the 'negative' sense (Berlin 1961), liberal constitutions are typically constituted to include the doctrine of separation of powers, motivated by the elemental Montesquian argument that since the state has three powers —legislative, executive and judicial, concentrating these powers in any one or two bodies would diminish liberty (Montesquieu 1949). Economists have recently addressed this structural argument by showing that the doctrine of separation of powers improves social welfare by reducing the quantum of rent seeking activity in the economic system (for example, see Laffont 2000; Padovano et al. 2003; Perrson et al. 1997).

However the doctrine can also be invoked in a more functional sense that complements the structural explanation emphasized by Montesquieu. We have explored such a functional interpretation of separation of powers in an earlier work where we analysed judicial activism—developing the functional aspect of the doctrine by drawing on the notion of transaction costs[2] to look at the social implications of the doctrine being breached (Anant and Singh 2002). More specifically, it was argued that the endemic presence of transaction costs makes it imperative that when the state exercises a choice, such choice be delegated to the institution best equipped to minimize transaction costs—a breach of this acts to raise transaction costs and therefore results in a misallocation of resources. Thus, one can view the broad divisions engendered by the separation of powers doctrine—the legislature, executive and judiciary, as being justified on the grounds that each branch is equipped to process different categories

[2] We follow Allen's definition of transaction costs as the resources used to establish and maintain property rights (Allen 1999).

of information and therefore, possesses a different mechanism of decision-making.[3] In this scheme, activism comes to be defined as a branch extending its mechanism of decision-making on the grounds of privilege onto problems that are the forte of some other branch. The consequences of such activism can be ambiguous, in the sense that depending on the circumstances, activism can either enhance or diminish social welfare.

While these structural and functional arguments make a persuasive case for a strong or strict separation of powers, there is another dimension to the separation of powers doctrine that needs to be noted. It has recently been pointed out that the doctrine not only separates decisions but also requires interaction across the branches of the state; such interaction can be understood as a bargain, which in turn, implies that interactions between the branches can be quite costly in terms of negotiating costs (Cooter 2000). For instance, if a law passed by the legislature is held to be unacceptable by the judiciary, the response is to either reframe the law or to accept the rejection of the law. The negotiation costs associated with such processes can aid the impulse towards unitary concentration of power that assists the speed and expediency of decision-making, but then costs emerge from the violation of the doctrine of separation of powers. A case in point here is the progressive destruction in India of the

[3] To briefly describe these specializations—the representative legislature captures the aggregated preferences of the voting population and makes laws keeping in mind, the impact of such legislation on distribution. The executive which executes the will of the legislature, often making technical decisions in the face of incomplete information, drawing on scientific, epidemiological and statistical studies, can be viewed as a hierarchical body that makes decisions in the face of incomplete information. The judiciary resolves disputes keeping in mind procedural, statutory and constitutional limits. Since judicial decisions necessarily need to be perceived as being fair, judicial information is gathered from contesting parties in conformity with rules of evidence and procedure, and since evidence comes in from conflicting sources, courts can typically be thought of as processing imperfect information. It can therefore be argued that an allocation problem facing the state would be ideally slotted for resolution in the appropriate branch of the state. Thus, a contest over a jointly-produced surplus should appear before the court because the precise amount contributed by a party is private information, which the court translates into verifiable evidence given by each party and makes an assessment of the apportionment. The executive would process a famine because statistical, scientific and epidemiological data needs to be processed to assuage the uncertain effects of the famine. If it is accepted that the diktat of the law is essential for society to function as a cooperative endeavour, then laws need to be made by an agency of the population at large that is presumably sensitive to the distributional impact of these laws across the population—a role fulfilled by the legislature.

fundamental right to property, consequent to a series of moves by the legislative/executive branches of the Indian state to establish unitary power. This process has, among other things, generated social costs associated with the violation of the doctrine of separation of powers, both in a structural as well as functional sense (Singh 2004).

This suggests the following typology—if the separation of powers doctrine is strongly maintained, social costs associated with the violation of the doctrine are held under check and systems are generated for bargaining across the branches of the state, leading, among other things, to predictable governance, but causing attendant negotiation costs to be borne in terms of resources and speed of decisions. On the other hand, if the separation of powers doctrine is weakly maintained, there is a high likelihood of social costs being generated by rent seeking behaviour and/or activism, but resource use is minimized in the sense that the unitary institution is able to advance with the act of making decisions with haste.

Separation of Powers and Regulation

This typology can be advantageously harnessed to analyse the project of structuring regulation. Regulation, particularly the form that is getting to be quite ubiquitous in India currently, can be understood as being associated with special categories of contracts that require to be governed by special regulatory agencies created by the state. The explicit or implicit presumption behind setting up such bodies is the belief that standard contract law inadequately services certain contracts, such as those associated with public utility provision, because unlike discrete contracts, these contracts on the one hand involve substantial degree of asset specificity and on the other hand, benefit a large number of users—sometimes as large as the voting population. In these instances, the regulator plays the role of administering the contract by achieving a balance between, to use Goldberg's phrases, the producer's 'right to serve' against the consumer's 'right to be served' (Goldberg 1976). If it is accepted that the act of regulation is to administer contracts that cannot be adequately performed under the aegis of contract law, the question clearly arises as to how the 'administrator of contracts' is placed in relation to the constitutional scheme.

Since the administrator or the regulator needs to process a variety of information which includes concerns such as assessment of benefits and costs that accrue to the target population as a result of the regulation, the nature of technology, its distribution and the structure and implementation of contracts between producers, resource owners and final consumers, the act of regulation reflects an amalgam of functional skills we have referred to earlier viz., legislative, executive and judicial, signifying that regulatory activity involves a hybrid conglomeration of the three functions. In principle, there need be no objection to a hybrid institution that combines elements of the three functions of the state as long as it is possible to slot the various dimensions of a regulatory problem in the appropriate functional slot. Further, it follows that the regulator must be empowered with adequate resources and structures in order to process the different kinds of information needed for its decision-making. This is however more likely only if there is a strong doctrine of separation of powers in place. If on the other hand, the doctrine is weakly exercised overall then there is the hazard that the constituent departments of the hybrid body may be over and/or under-delegated. Such over/under-delegation can lead to social costs analogous to the costs imposed by activism—in fact inappropriate delegation is but a variant of activism. We seek to develop this point by looking at a few case studies in the next section of this paper.

Case Studies

Insolvency Tribunals

The reforms initiated in the Indian economy in 1991 as well as the debate on financial systems after the Asian crisis brought forth the need to modernise the law on insolvency, particularly as it relates to corporate insolvency. To deal with this class of issues the Indian government appointed a committee in 1999—referred to widely as the Eradi Committee (chairman Justice B. Eradi) to examine the law relating to insolvency of companies. Independent of this exercise, the Reserve Bank of India constituted a set of advisory groups to examine the status of India's compliance with the international financial standards and codes.[4] As part of this exercise an Advisory Group on Bankruptcy Law[5] comprising lawyers, financial market experts and academics was set up. We do not take up the wider issue of bankruptcy or debt recovery here; instead we confine ourselves to

[4] 'Report of the Standing Committee on International Financial Standards and Codes', Reserve Bank of India, May 2002.

[5] One of the authors was a member of this group.

an analysis of the structure of governance recommended by the two bodies.

Turning first to the Eradi Committee, which recommended:

(Para 7.1) The whole issue of law relating to insolvency of companies should be viewed not only on basis of the existing provisions of Part VII of the Companies Act, 1956 but also other relevant laws having a bearing on the subject, such as Sick Industrial Companies (Special Provisions) Act, 1985, (SICA), Recovery of Debts due to Banks and Financial Institutions Act, 1993, UNCITRAL Model Law on Cross Border Insolvency approved by United Nations (Annexure A) and International Monetary Fund report on 'Orderly and Effective Insolvency Procedures' (Annexure as B) The Committee, therefore, recommends that the provisions of Part VII of the Companies Act, 1956, be amended to include the provisions for setting up of a National Tribunal which will have (a) the jurisdiction and power presently exercised by Company Law Board under the Companies Act, 1956; (b) the power to consider rehabilitation and revival of companies—a mandate presently entrusted to BIFR/AAFIR under SICA; (c) the jurisdiction and power relating to winding up of companies presently vested in the high courts. In view of above recommendations, Article 323B of the Constitution should be amended to set up National Tribunal. SICA should be repealed and the Companies Act, 1956 be amended accordingly.

(Para 7.2) In continuation with the committee's recommendation in Para 7.1, the committee recommends that the *tribunal should be headed by a sitting judge or a former judge of a high court and each of its benches should consist of a judicial member and a technical member*. Tribunal shall have such number of members as may be prescribed by the central government.

(1) *The principal bench of the tribunal should be located at New Delhi and its benches should be located at the principal seats of each high court.* (2) The central government may set up more such benches if so required (emphasis added)

The key point to be noted here is that the committee recommended setting up a tribunal to try cases of insolvency, which would not be subject to the jurisdiction of the high courts and therefore also called for an amendment to the Constitution. (The need for a constitutional amendment is clarified below.) In contrast, the RBI advisory group chose to recommend the installation of a Special Bankruptcy Bench in each high court to deal with insolvency. They reasoned:

In spite of the fact that tribunalisation of justice is now a settled fact especially after L. Chandra Kumar [(1997)3SCC, 261], there is a philosophical debate going on as to the nature, extent, structure and power. Even Justice Eradi Committee commented that in order to make National Tribunal able to quicken the dispute resolution, Article 323A and B of the Constitution is to be amended. This group does not think that such a step, bypassing the judiciary, is necessary or possible: (a) A special bench of the high court as a full time bankruptcy court shall serve all purposes as well as quickening the issue of the procedure recommended; (b) A special bench of the high court will be able to bring multidimensional knowledge necessary for restructuring/reorganisation and bankruptcy proceedings; and (c) A special bench shall add validity of action in all renegotiated proposals and on the failure of restructuring process, quicken the insolvency proceeding.

To appreciate the contrast between the two recommendations, it is essential to look at both the rationale for instituting tribunals and their operation in India. A tribunal is a good example of a hybrid institution that straddles a line between the executive and judicial functions. In India many activities, labour and environment to name a couple, are governed by tribunals usually justified by the need for specialist knowledge and by the call for expediency in a clogged legal system, but their success is by no means clear. An evaluation by the Malimath Committee on the functioning of tribunals has been particularly telling:

Several tribunals are functioning in the country. Not all of them, however, have inspired confidence in the public mind. The reasons are not far to seek. The foremost is the lack of competence, objectivity and judicial approach. The next is their constitution, the power and method of appointment of personnel thereto, the inferior status and the casual method of working. The last is their actual composition; men of calibre are not willing to be appointed as presiding officers in view of the uncertainty of tenure, unsatisfactory conditions of service, executive subordination in matters of administration and political interference in judicial functioning. For these and other reasons, the quality of justice is stated to have suffered and the cause of expedition is not found to have been served by the establishment of such tribunals.[6]

The Malimath Committee also recommended that instead of instituting tribunals, changes be carried out within the high courts, dividing them into separate divisions for different branches of law as is the case in England. It stated that appointing more judges to man the separate divisions while using the existing infrastructure would be a better way of remedying the problem of pending cases in the high courts, rather than creating new bodies. Subsequently an important judgment of the Supreme Court of India, the Chandra Kumar

[6] 'Report of the Arrears Committee' (Malimath Committee) (1989–90) as quoted in L. Chandra Kumar vs Union of India (1997) 3 SCC 261.

judgment,[7] taking a view contrary to the insights of the Malimath Committee, upheld the legal validity of tribunals but insisted that the Constitution required the decisions of the tribunals be subject to the scrutiny of the high courts—hence the call by the Eradi Committee to amend the Constitution. The judgment however did take cognizance of the point that tribunals need to be reformed: 'However, drastic measures may have to be resorted to in order to elevate their standards to ensure that they stand up to constitutional scrutiny in the discharge of the power of judicial review conferred upon them' and suggested certain guidelines to do so.

Turning back to the recommendations of the Eradi Committee and the advisory group, it is important to note that both groups felt that excluding the jurisdiction of the high court would need an amendment to the Constitution. In this context, it may be noted that a subsequent judgment of the Supreme Court[8] recently followed the L. Chandra Kumar case and upheld the creation of debt recovery tribunals and also upheld the requirement for judicial review by the high court under Articles 226 and 227 of the Constitution. The RBI Advisory Group recognized the possibility of constitutional change but felt that apart from other reasons, the political capital to implement such an act would be limited. This suggests an important point that is surprisingly often ignored, that in any enterprise of setting up a regulatory body it is essential to keep in mind the constitutional scheme.

The overall position of the advisory group is similar in spirit to the Malimath Committee recommendation—both feel it is important to preserve the role of the judicial system by improving it and not by creating new bodies, which may be subject to similar if not greater, problems. It also needs to be appreciated that if the rationale for upholding tribunals is to incorporate specialist knowledge, what we have termed earlier as the executive function, this can be done either by a quasi-judicial body (tribunal) or by strengthening the executive capacity of the courts. The advisory group outlined a framework in which a 'trustee' could do this—the idea being that a bankruptcy court needs the expertise that only an effective executive agency can deliver and the trustee could provide this expertise to the court. The Eradi Committee tried to bring in this element of the executive branch of government by asking that remedies to the endemic problems facing tribunals be in tune with the guidelines suggested in the L. Chandra

[7] L. Chandra Kumar vs Union of India (1997) 3 SCC 261.

[8] Union of India and Anr vs The Delhi High Court Bar Association and other, Appeal (civil) 4679 of 1995.

Kumar case. These alternate suggestions point to the fact that the amalgamation of functional attributes, which are important for overall governance, can be done in more than one way.

In spite of this backdrop and experience what has actually materialized does not incorporate the concerns raised by either the Eradi Committee or the advisory group. In December 2002 the Indian Parliament passed the Companies (Second Amendment) Act, 2002 providing for a national tribunal but no amendment was made to the Constitution. The act provides for benches but it is not clear if they will ensure that a bench will be located at the principal seats of each high court. Thus on the one hand, the act seeks to supplant the high courts but on the other, makes no attempt to ensure that the coverage is compatible with the court system or the Constitution. Further the act provides for only a single appellate tribunal. Overall it may be noted that the attempt to restructure the Companies Act has been characterized by a reluctance to pose either the constitutional question or the modified high court solution, not because the coalition governments could not have passed constitutional amendments—over this period at least three[9] constitutional amendments, namely, 84th (electoral delimitation) 85th (Art 16 seniority) and 86th (21A right to education) were in fact, passed. The limitation is rather linked to the inability to negotiate with constitutional entities and an inadequate comprehension of the functional/structural importance of the doctrine of separation of powers.

One of the earlier problems with the old law was its inadequate appellate structure, yet the act provides for appeal only to the Supreme Court—obviously in conflict with the pattern of the court structure and the Constitution. It may be entirely possible that the higher courts may eventually rule this structure to be legitimate as was done with the debt recovery tribunals in 2002[10] but what is certain is that it has led to an extended period of litigation to establish legitimacy. In this context the writ jurisdiction of the high courts has been used to raise issues of the hierarchy of rights and the act continues to be in limbo as a result of a decision of the Madras High Court, which declared it ultra vires of both legislative competence and the Constitution of India.[11] The matter is currently sub judice since the case is under appeal in the Supreme Court. However, the content of the judgment issued by the

[9] In fact there have been nine constitutional amendments in the past four years.

[10] Union of India vs Delhi High Court Bar Association (2002) 4 SCC 275.

[11] Thiru R. Gandhi vs Union of India, Writ Petition No 2198 of 2003, High Court of Madras.

Madras High Court is of great relevance to the argument being made in this paper because it explicitly points out that the act encourages over-delegation of powers in favour of both the executive and legislative branches of the state at the expense of the judicial branch. It is pointed out that such over-delegation is manifested in the act by the executive incidence in the composition, selection and terms of tenure of members comprising the tribunal—furthermore, even the powers of the president of the tribunal are subject to executive control. The following quote from the judgment is representative of the unease of the court with this structure:

> The constitutional guarantee of a free and independent judiciary, and the constitutional scheme of separation of powers can be easily and seriously undermined, if the legislatures were to divest the regular courts of their jurisdiction in all matters, entrust the same to newly created tribunals which can appropriately be labelled, borrowing the language of the US Supreme Court, as 'legislative courts', and assert that such forums not being regular courts and their members not being members of the 'judicial service' of the state, they are not entitled to protection similar to the constitutional protection afforded to the courts.

Consequent to this, the court goes on to conclude:

> If the constitutional scheme and intent are to be preserved, it must be held that the total insulation of the judiciary' referred to in the case of Sampath Kumar is not just for the 'judiciary' comprising of judges appointed to the regular courts. The 'judiciary' in this context must be understood as taking within it's fold, all courts and tribunals and other adjudicatory bodies, whatever be the label assigned to them. The independence and impartiality which are essential for the proper exercise of the judicial power, are to be secured not only for the courts but also for tribunals and their members, who, though they do not belong to the 'judicial service'; are entrusted with judicial powers.

The court then went on to order:

> In the light of foregoing discussions it is declared that until the provisions in parts 1B and 1C of the Companies Act introduced by the Companies (Amendment) Act, 2002, which have been found to be defective inasmuch as they are in breach of the basic constitutional scheme of separation of powers and independence of the judicial function, are duly amended, by removing the defects that have been pointed out, it would be unconstitutional to constitute a tribunal and appellate tribunal to exercise the jurisdiction now exercised by the high courts or the Company Law Board.

This judgment is noteworthy because it does not seek to restrict the powers of the legislature to legislate nor does it seek to limit the creation of tribunals. The argument is in fact more subtle, stating that the constitutional guarantees of an independent judiciary and separation of the judiciary from legislative and executive functions would be negated if Parliament were to create tribunals that substitute for courts under the control of the executive. The point is that substitute forums must also fall within the framework of constitutionally mandated separation of powers. If indeed the doctrine of separation of powers is not upheld in the interest of expediency—real or imagined, the social costs that are generated by violation of the doctrine (both in a functional as well as structural sense) are bound to make new regulatory bodies ineffective.

Competition Commission

The Competition Commission envisioned by the new Competition Act, 2002 poses a similar problem. The expert committee that had proposed the new competition bill had suggested that the composition of the commission be done through a selection committee that includes the chief justice of India. However, when the bill was finally placed before Parliament the government moved an amendment to restrict this and said that 'chairperson and other members shall be selected in the manner as may be prescribed'. Further, the selection committee included the law minister instead of the chief justice, contrary to the assurance given to Parliament. The first chairperson selected was from the bureaucracy. This resulted in a PIL with the Supreme Court asking how a bureaucrat can be asked to 'discharge a judicial function'. The controversy led to the cancellation of the appointment delaying the formation of what is a critical regulatory body.[12]

To appreciate the issue involved it is important to realize that competition law in India, as in other countries, has two elements. The first pertains to the intent of the law, which creates a set of rights relating to the functioning of markets. More specifically it enshrines competition as an entitlement, and agreements and actions that seek to adversely effect competition are sought to be restricted.[13] The second

[12] This PIL has subsequently been disposed of on the assurance by the government that it will make suitable amendments to the law (Writ Petition (civil) 490 of 2003, order dated 20 January 2005). However the Supreme Court has made it clear that the matter can be raised again if the amendments are not satisfactory.

[13] For instance in the Competition Act, 2002 this is performed by stating:

3 (1) No enterprise or association of enterprises or person or association of persons shall enter into any agreement in respect of production, supply, distribution, storage, acquisition or control of goods or provision of services, which causes or is likely to cause an appreciable adverse effect on competition within India.

element of the law pertains to how the law has been structured to perform the intended task. Such structuring needs to be sensitive to the fact that the act of ensuring competition requires both executive and judicial skills. The executive harnesses specialized knowledge of assessing markets, and judicial involvement ensures procedural and substantive objectives are complied with and in particular, asymmetric information is processed in an apt fashion.

The problems raised in the PIL before the Supreme Court relate to this dimension of the law. The question is not a merely the facile issue of whether the head of the commission should be a judge or a bureaucrat. While it can be argued that competition authorities in other parts of the world are headed by non-judicial personnel (as indeed the Union of India is reported to have argued before the Supreme Court in the case mentioned above) it needs to be appreciated that such structures must be consistent with the nature of separation of powers in that society. For instance, in the US, adjudication of competition cases is performed by the courts with an executive element provided by the FTC; in England, by a body headed by specialists, which is embedded in their legal system with appeals to an appellate authority, the high court and the House of Lords; and in Australia by a judge assisted by experts, again with a provision for judicial separation. The point is that in all these instances there is sensitivity to the functional separation of powers,[14] a sense that is clearly lacking in the Indian structuring of the act. Thus in the Indian case while the identity of the person heading the commission—bureaucrat or judge may not in itself be more than a turf war, it is important to emphasize the wider need to include a judicial arm and the functional skills it represents in an amalgamated body that seeks to regulate economic activity.

---

(2) Any agreement entered into in contravention of the provisions contained in subsection (1) shall be void.

4 (1) No enterprise shall abuse its dominant position.

(2) There shall be an abuse of dominant position under subsection (1), if an enterprise.

(a) directly or indirectly, imposes unfair or discriminatory (i) condition in purchase or sale of goods or service; or (ii) price in purchase or sale (including predatory price) of goods or service, (b) limits or restricts (i) production of goods or provision of services or market therefore; or (ii) technical or scientific development relating to goods or services to the prejudice of consumers; or (c) indulges in practice or practices resulting in denial of market access; or (d) makes conclusion of contracts subject to acceptance by other parties of supplementary obligations which, by their nature or according to commercial usage, have no connection with the subject of such contracts; or (e) uses its dominant position in one relevant market to enter into, or protect, other relevant market. More broadly, for an analysis of this aspect of the law, see Bhattacharjea (2003).

[14] OECD (1997), 'Judicial Enforcement of Competition Law', proceedings of a seminar on Judicial Enforcement of Competition Law. OECD/GD (97)200.

Concern with the structure of the law throws up an additional problem related to the geographic separation between the Centre and the states. The provisions of the Competition Act have wide coverage, incorporating all goods and services and all possible markets, thus including in its remit both nationwide markets as well as specific local or regional markets. In this context it needs to be noted that the Constitution clearly provides for separate domains of executive intervention through the vehicle of central, state and concurrent lists in the Seventh Schedule of the Constitution. This raises a number of interesting possibilities; for instance, agricultural markets are covered by the state list, provoking an intriguing question as to whether the commission can institute an inquiry in relation to some practice in these markets. If the commission is understood to be an arm of the executive, then the issue of distribution of powers across the Centre and the states will also clearly arise, possibly bringing up the question as to whether the central executive is interfering in a market that is clearly provided for in the state list. Even if the power of the commission to inquire and adjudicate were upheld, the issue of the ability of the state government to grant a public service exemption will remain as a residual concern, since the act states that the power to issue an exemption lies with the central government.

Autonomy of Central Banks

The broad nature of these concerns with the structure of institutions extends to the final example in this paper—the case of central banks. The independence of the central bank can be viewed from three perspectives based on the three broad roles of the RBI[15] as the formulator of monetary policy, banker to the Centre and the states and as the regulator of banks.

The principal theoretical justification of independence comes from the role of central banks in formulating monetary policy. The economic background for this stance comes from considerations of time inconsistency in government policy, when policy-makers can resort to monetary stimulation to trigger short-term output cycles. This then leads to discussions about the objectives of monetary policy and the need or importance to segregate them from fiscal policy. It may also be that the need for autonomy arises due to the political business cycle, where electoral outcomes may have real effects due to changes in policy

[15] See Chandavarkar (2005) for a detailed discussion of these issues.

preferences.[16] This in turn, becomes the basis for worry about financial market instability and its related consequences. The International Monetary Fund (IMF) with its concerns for financial market stability argues for independence for the authority with clearly defined financial objectives. The problem is that autonomy of monetary policy is closely linked to the degree of autonomy prevalent in the framing of fiscal policy. Thus if the state wishes to be able to maintain the ability to run fiscal deficits it will also be required to run an accommodative monetary policy. It may be noted that the recent advisory group reviewing fiscal and monetary policies emphasized the need for a tight regime of fiscal discipline before one can give autonomy to the monetary authority.[17] Traditionally the fiscal authority of the state has needed to work closely with the legislature since taxation and the provision of public goods are both classically legislative decisions. So the question of separation of the monetary and fiscal authorities is also about what critics like Stiglitz would term as a loss of democratic control.

Other dimensions of independence relate to an assessment of other roles of the RBI, relating to its status as a banker to the central and state governments and a regulator of the banking systems. Thus in a recent article Chandavarkar (2005) argues the need to insulate the banking and regulatory functions of the central bank from political imperatives. At one level one may argue that this is talking about separation between different wings of the executive. However it may be noted that there is another dimension to this as well—relating to the separation of the central bank authority from political (legislative?) interference. Unlike the functional argument on the role of monetary policy this argument is based on an institutional perspective. The resolution of these puzzles, we would suggest, is as much in the realm of theory as in the appreciation of the importance of the doctrine of separation and the constitutional framework of governance.

Conclusion

The three cases presented reflect a certain interplay suggested in the section, 'Case Studies' of the paper.The concern with such interplay is not regarding the substantial intent of these institutions i.e.,

[16] See Kydland and Prescott (1977) 'Rules rather than Discretion: The Inconsistency of Optimal Plans', *Journal of Political Economy,* also Alberto Alesina (1987), 'Macroeconomic Policy in a Two-Party System as a Repeated Game', *Quarterly Journal of Economics.*

[17] 'Report of the Standing Committee on International Financial Standards and Codes' as well as the 'Report of the Advisory Group on Transparency in Monetary and Financial Policies' are available at *www.rbi.org.* Also see Anant (2003).

to adjudicate insolvency cases, to encourage competition and engineer monetary policy, but rather their design, keeping in mind the constitutional schema and the norms such a schema seeks to perpetuate. Thus it was suggested that insolvency tribunals constructed to encourage executive over-delegation could lead to the social costs associated with structural and/or functional violation of the doctrine of separation of powers—too much power with executive and too little ability to provide crucial judicial processing of information in the event of disputes. While this may make for 'speedy' decisions, both the structure and functioning of the tribunals also reflect a breakdown in the process of inter-institutional bargaining. It is again this inability to embed the inter-institutional bargain within the confines of the doctrine of separation powers that causes one to critique the Competition Act, 2002 as an inappropriately structured law. If indeed such a law remains insensitive to the doctrine of separation of powers, it is likely to generate its own social costs. The crucial point of these examples is to highlight the role played by the doctrine of separation of powers and the importance of inter-institutional bargaining. This failure of dialogue across institutions and an incoherent appreciation of the doctrine has become one of the key impediments to reform.

Postscript

It has been mentioned in the text of this chapter that the cited decision of *Thiru R Gandhi vs Union of India, Writ Petition No 2198 of 2003, High Court of Madras*, was repealed to the Supreme Court. Recently the Supreme Court has responded with a judgment [*Union of India v. R. Gandhi, (2007) 4 SCC 341*]. The judgment begins by saying that existing decisions have not adequately addressed the issue as to what extent the powers of the High Court can be transferred to tribunals. The judgment goes on to say 'There is as yet no demarcating line to show that, except for powers exercised under Articles 226 and 227, Parliament has the legislative competence to vest intrinsic judicial functions, traditionally performed by courts in any tribunal or authority, outside the judiciary. The question to be determined is whether such "wholesale transfer of powers" as contemplated by the Companies (Second Amendment) Act, 2002 would offend the constitutional scheme of separation of powers and independence of judiciary, so as to aggrandise one branch over the other.'

Recognizing the importance of the matter the judgment continues by stating, 'Since the issues raised in the appeals are of seminal importance and are likely to have serious impact on the very structure and independence of the judicial system, we are of the view that the issue with regard to the constitution of the tribunals and the areas of their jurisdiction needs to be given a fresh look and, therefore, *the matter deserves to be heard by a Constitution Bench.'* (emphasis added)

References

Allen, Douglas W., 1999, 'Transaction Costs' in Bouedewijn Bouckaert and Gerrit De Geest (eds.), *Encyclopaedia of Law and Economics*, Edward Elgar, Cheltenham and University of Ghent. Also available at *http://encyclo.findlaw.com/0740book.pdf*.

Anant, T. C. A., 2003, 'The View from India' in Benu Schneider (ed.), *The Road to International Financial Stability: Are Key Financial Standards the Answer?*, Palgrave Macmillan in association with ODI.

——— and Jaivir Singh, 2002, 'An Economic Analysis of Judicial Activism', *Economic and Political Weekly*, vol. 37, no. 43, 26 October, pp. 4433–9.

Berlin, Isaiah, 1961, *Two Concepts of Liberty*, Clarendon Press, Oxford.

Brennan, H. Geoffrey and Alan P. Hamlin, 2000, *Democratic Devices and Desires*, Cambridge University Press, Cambridge.

Chandavarkar, Anand, 2005, 'Towards an Independent Federal Reserve Bank of India: A Political Economy Agenda for Reconstitution', *Economic and Political Weekly*, 27 August.

Coase, Ronald H., 1964, 'The Regulated Industries: Discussion', *American Economic Review*, May, pp. 194–7.

Cooter, Robert D., 2000, *The Strategic Constitution*, Princeton University Press, New Jersey.

Goldberg, V., 1976, 'Regulation and Administered Contracts', *Bell Journal of Economics and Management Science*, vol. 7, pp. 426–52.

Laffont, Jean-Jacques, 2000, *Incentives and Political Economy*, Oxford University Press, Oxford.

Montesquieu, Baron de, 1949, *The Spirit of the Laws*, (trs.) Thomas Nugent, Hafner Press, New York.

Padovano, Fabio, Grazia Sgarra and Nadia Fiorino, 2003, 'Judicial Branch, Checks and Balances and Political Accountability', *Constitutional Political Economy*, vol. 14, pp. 47–70.

Perrson, Torsten, Gerard Roland and Guido Tabellini, 1997, 'Separation of Powers and Political Accountability', *The Quarterly Journal of Economics*, vol. 112, issue 4, pp. 1163–202.

Singh, Jaivir, 2004, '(Un)Constituting Property: The Deconstruction of the "Right to Property" in India', Centre for the Study of Law and Governance Working Paper Series, CSLG/WP/04-05, Jawaharlal Nehru University.

3

Potential Problems in the Implementation of the Competition Act, 2002

Aditya Bhattacharjea

Introduction

India's new competition regime has had a long gestation period, which is not yet over. The Competition Bill was first tabled in Parliament in August 2001, discussed by a standing committee for almost a year, and finally the Competition Act was passed with several modifications by both Houses in December 2002. Some of its administrative and enabling clauses were put into effect by notification, and the Competition Commission of India (CCI) was formally constituted with one member and a skeleton staff in October 2003. But further expansion of the CCI for enforcement of the competition-related provisions of the Act was held up by a writ petition filed in the Supreme Court, questioning the exclusion of the judiciary in the appointment of the Chairman of the CCI.

In response to the writ petition, the government filed affidavits indicating that it would propose amendments so that the Chairman and members would be chosen by a selection committee presided over by the Chief Justice of India or his nominee, and that appeals would be heard by an appellate authority headed by a judge. The Court disposed of the writ petition in January 2005, declining to pronounce in a theoretical contexton the questions raised, before

In September 2007, the government withdrew the amending bill referred to in this chapter, and introduced and passed a more comprehensive Competition (Amendment) Act, 2007. However, the various implementation issues I have discussed remain valid concerns (see Postcript).

an actual amendment was passed. It however, indicated that 'it might be appropriate for the respondents i.e., the government to consider the creation of two separate bodies, one with expertise that is advisory and regulatory and the other adjudicatory. This followed up by an appellate body as contemplated by the proposed amendment, can go a long way in meeting the challenge sought to be raised in this writ petition based on the doctrine of separation of powers recognized by the Constitution.'[1]

Although the Government's affidavits in 2004 had indicated that it had already decided on the nature of the amendments required, only in March 2006 did it get around to tabling an amending Bill, which not only addressed the issues raised in the writ petition, but also proposed to amend many other sections of the Act. At the time this chapter was last revised (May 2006), the Bill had been referred to the Parliamentary standing committee on Finance, its ultimate passage was some way off, and even thereafter, the modifications might not have met the approval of the Supreme Court. Even if it does, the rules for selecting the Chairman and members of the CCI and the proposed Appellate Tribunal will have to be drawn up, and the appointments made. As things stand therefore, the substantive provisions of the Competition Act will not be enforced for some time, and the 1969 MRTP Act remains the country's operational competition law.

However, there are several potential problem areas in the Competition Act which could hamper the ability of the CCI to implement it effectively as and when it is allowed to do so, defeating the objective of promoting competition, and possibly undermining the CCI's credibility, depriving it of both public and political support. This chapter spells out some of these problems. The section 'Features of the Competition Act' is an overview of the positive and negative features of the Act, concentrating on the latter in order to point out possible pitfalls. The section, 'Institutional Capacity Building' discusses the problem of technical capacity that will be required for the effective implementation of even the non-controversial sections of the Act and the final section concludes the paper with some suggestions.

Features of the Competition Act

To begin with the positive features, the new Act improves upon the MRTP Act in many ways. It covers the usual three areas of anti-

[1] Brahm Dutt vs Union of India, (2005) 2 SCC 431.

competitive agreements between firms (Section 3), abuses of a dominant position by a single firm (Section 4), and 'combinations' (i.e., mergers and acquisitions, dealt with in Sections 5 and 6) with a much more modern approach. It wisely avoids areas such as monopolistic pricing and 'unfair trade practices', to which the MRTP Act devoted entire chapters. These should not have been part of the competition law in the first place. Unlike the MRTP Act, anti-competitive practices such as cartels and predatory pricing are now defined. Several criteria are laid down for judging whether an agreement is anti-competitive, a market position is dominant, or a merger will have an adverse effect on competition, although there are some inconsistencies in these criteria that I shall point out. Criteria for determining the relevant geographical or product market are also listed. Detailed time-bound steps have been laid down to guide the process of inquiry and adjudication. Firms violating the new law can be fined substantial amounts for non-compliance: ten per cent of their turnover, or one-third of the profits of a cartel, as against the modest fines provided for in the MRTP Act. Various sections of the Act authorize the CCI to hire professional consultants, to engage in competition advocacy, and to give advice to the government and sector regulators on competition-related matters. All these are welcome developments.

The new Act explicitly provides (Section 32) for its application against firms or persons located abroad whose practices have an anti-competitive effect in India. This will remedy the problem caused by the Supreme Court's judgment in the Haridas Exports case, which held that the MRTP Act had no such extra-territorial application.[2] It is good that the Act contains what amounts to a restatement of the 'effects doctrine', which determines jurisdiction for competition laws in most countries of the world. It also provides (Section 18) for the CCI to enter into arrangements with foreign competition agencies. Both sections will help in dealing with anti-competitive practices of foreign firms.

Another provision that was inserted in response to the Haridas Exports judgment was, however, ill-advised: sub-section 33(2) permitted the CCI to issue temporary injunctions to restrain any party from importing goods if the import is likely to contravene the Act's

[2] Haridas Exports vs All India Float Glass Manufacturers' Association (2002) 6 SCC 600. See Bhattacharjea (2003) for a discussion of this and similar cases.

sections on anti-competitive agreements, abuse of dominance, or combinations. Such injunctions could be given without hearing the other party. This as I have argued at length elsewhere, was self-defeating: countering an anti-competitive practice involving imports with a further restriction of competition in the form of an import prohibition amounts to chopping off one's head to cure a headache, and would also be inconsistent with WTO rules (Bhattacharjea 2003). Fortunately, the 2006 Amendment Bill proposes to delete this sub-section.

There are, however, several remaining lacunae, loopholes and inconsistencies in the Act, which will create problems once actual enforcement begins. Four such specific problems are discussed here, incorporating changes proposed by the Amendment Bill. I also comment briefly on the implications of the amendments with which the government proposes to restore the role of the judiciary.

The 'Development' Criterion

The list of objectives prefacing the Act was amended when the Competition Bill was moved in Parliament, to include the phrase 'keeping in view of the [sic] economic development of the country'. Correspondingly, the following new clause 19(4)(l) was inserted into the list of criteria for determining whether a firm enjoys a dominant position: 'relative advantage, by way of the contribution to the economic development, by the enterprise enjoying a dominant position having or likely to have an appreciable adverse effect on competition'. A similar clause 20(4)(m) has been inserted into the list of criteria for determining whether a combination (i.e., a merger or acquisition) would have an adverse effect on competition.

I submit that these clauses are meaningless and potentially dangerous. Unlike the other listed criteria, they in no way, help to determine the effect on competition; instead, they invite the competition authority to condone blatantly anti-competitive activities by large corporations that purport to be promoting development. The relationship between competition and development, and even the meaning of development itself, are controversial, even amongst economists who have been studying them for years. Section 38 of the MRTP Act at least listed specific circumstances (the so-called 'gateways') that could be adduced to rebut the presumption that a particular Restrictive Trade Practice (RTP) was against the public interest. The Competition Act, however, leaves it entirely to the CCI's subjective understanding of 'development'. It will be open to varying interpretations, leading to inconsistent verdicts, unnecessary harassment, and uncertainty, that will adversely affect the investment climate.

Regulating Anti-competitive Agreements

In competition law, there is a standard distinction between practices that are condemned *per se*, and those to which a 'rule of reason' can be applied, with positive and negative outcomes being balanced on a case-by-case basis. Section 3(3) of the Competition Act appears to be a *per se* cartel prohibition, because it decrees that certain agreements (price-fixing, output restricting, market-sharing or bid-rigging, generally known as 'hard-core' cartels) are *presumed* to have an adverse effect on competition, and such agreements are prohibited by section 3(1). However, section 19(3) muddies the waters To understand why, it needs to be quoted in full:

3(3) The Commission shall, while determining whether an agreement has an appreciable adverse effect on competition under section 3, have due regard to all or any of the following factors, namely:—

(a) creation of barriers to new entrants in the market;
(b) driving existing competitors out of the market;
(c) foreclosure of competition by hindering entry into the market;
(d) accrual of benefits to consumers;
(e) improvements in production or distribution of goods or provision of services;
(f) promotion of technical, scientific and economic development by means of production or distribution of goods or provision of services.

Now, criteria (a) to (c) help to determine 'whether an agreement has an appreciable adverse effect on competition', the professed aim of this sub-section.[3] But (d) to (f) do not: instead they provide various arguments that can be used to justify such agreements. (The 'development' criterion is fortunately, missing.) Note that these clauses are applicable to all of Section 3. It is not clear whether they can override the prohibition of hard-core cartels in sub-section 3(3). It would seem that the phrase 'while determining whether an agreement has an appreciable adverse effect on competition' steers the sub-section away from hard-core cartels, which are deemed to be anti-competitive, but other readings might be possible. Criteria (d) to (f) appear to be

[3] I am unable to discern any real difference between clauses (a) and (c): they mean the same thing in different words.

a simplistic adaptation of Article 81(3) of the EU Treaty reproduced almost verbatim as Section 9 of the UK Competition Act of 1998, which permits exemptions for efficiency-enhancing agreements and concerted practices, provided that they allow consumers a fair share of the resulting benefits. The EU and UK provisions however, impose additional conditions: they require that the agreement or practice does not impose restrictions that are unnecessary to attaining the efficiency objective, and does not allow for substantial elimination of competition. All these conditions are mandatory, whereas those in the Indian Competition Act are permissive. The EU, moreover, has given 'block exemptions' to certain kinds of agreements, and has issued detailed guidelines on how efficiencies will be assessed for other agreements. In India, the door has been kept wide open to subjective case-by-case interpretations, in a context in which there is very little comprehension of the economics of such agreements. Legitimate cooperation may be penalized, while blatantly competition-restricting arrangements may be condoned.

The latter possibility is further enhanced by an 'Explanation' attached to section 3(3), which specifically excludes efficiency-enhancing JVs from the cartel prohibition. This again superficially resembles similar provisions elsewhere, but with crucial differences. A 'block exemption' has been available since the mid-1980s in the EU for JVs devoted to research and development, subject to certain conditions. In the US, the 1984 National Cooperative Research Act allowed such ventures to be treated under a 'rule of reason', allowing offsetting efficiency benefits to be considered, unlike other arrangements that restrict competition, which are treated as illegal *per se*. Research JVs have also been allowed more recently to engage in joint production to allow commercial exploitation of the fruits of such efforts. In contrast, the JV exemption in the Indian Competition Act is neither limited to R&D, nor imposes any other conditions. Of course, the exemption applies only to the *per se* prohibition, and JVs may still be investigated and found to be engaging in anti-competitive practices under a rule of reason. But suppose some manufacturers set up a JV in the form of a common sales agency and justify it on the grounds that it permits a reduction in the costs of transportation and distribution, part of which they will pass on to consumers; this justification would be dismissed out of hand in the EU or US as a cloak for a naked cartel, but it may well pass muster under the Competition Act.

All this goes to show that the apparently draconian cartel prohibition in the Competition Act is actually quite mild. But in another respect it is too stringent: it would rule out cartels formed with official authorization for the purpose of rationalization and restructuring of an industry, which played an important role in Japan, Germany and the EU. Ironically, the case for such cartels was strongly advocated by India in its submission to the WTO Working Group on Trade and Competition Policy.[4]

The 'Meeting the Competition' Defence

An 'Explanation' has been inserted into Section 4 (which deals with the abuse of a dominant position) so as to exclude from its purview unfair or discriminatory conditions or pricing if they are adopted to 'meet the competition', i.e., to match rival offers. But the wording of the Explanation explicitly includes *predatory* pricing, which is defined in a subsequent 'Explanation' to the same section as pricing below cost 'with a view to reduce competition or eliminate the competitors'. The 'meet the competition' defence in conjunction with this cost test will allow firms who have the financial resources to incur temporary losses, or what economists call 'deep pockets' to engage in predatory pricing, to drive out more efficient rivals. This defeats the objective of prohibiting predatory pricing.

Furthermore, a publicly-announced *commitment* by a firm that it will meet the competition is actually anti-competitive. A dominant firm making this commitment can deter small potential entrants since it can offer consumers a low matching price only on its marginal sales, while the entrants must offer it on their entire sales. The European Commission imposed a fine of 20 million Euros on the chemical giant Solvay for engaging in this exclusionary practice in its sales of soda ash, even though it acknowledged that Solvay had undertaken this and other restrictive measures under pressure from import competition.[5]

The Leniency Programme

The 2006 Amendment Bill goes some way to improving Section 46, which allows for imposition of a reduced penalty on a participant in a cartel who makes full disclosure of having violated the Act, provided

[4] WTO document WT/WGTCP/W/216 (2002), available at *www.wto.org*.

[5] See Commission decision COMP/33.133-c: Soda Ash-Solvay, *Official Journal of the European Communities*, 2003 L10, pp. 1–50, especially paragraphs 24–35, 49, and 63–6.

that such disclosure is vital. The Act originally provided that such reduction would be available only to the first participant who came forward, and would not be granted after commencement of any proceedings or even an investigation. This would be akin to expecting a criminal to confess his crime before the police even got to know of it. I had pointed out in Bhattacharjea (2003) that the leniency programmes adopted in the USA in 1978 and in the EU in 1996 remained largely ineffective for many years mainly because they were discretionary and did not apply after an investigation had begun.

The proposed amendment to the Competition Act allows for a reduced penalty to any firm (not just the first) that provides vital information up to such time that the Director General submits his report to the CCI. However, it does not lay down the extent of reduction, nor what kind of information will be considered 'vital'. What the drafters of the amendment do not seem to appreciate is that such leniency programmes are not meant to be like the 'voluntary disclosure' or 'regularization' schemes with which India's central and state governments have repeatedly condoned massive illegalities, whether in tax evasion or unauthorized construction. In dealing with cartels, the appropriate analogy is not with such schemes, but with the provisions for getting an accused to 'turn approver' in criminal cases. For the leniency programme is meant to take the form of the famous 'Prisoner's Dilemma', in which the incentives should be structured in such a way as to make confessing a dominant strategy for each cartel member. The idea is not to let offenders off with a slap on the wrist and a promise of good behaviour, but to induce each one to provide sufficient evidence to convict the other cartel members, knowing that the latter have the same incentives. Each cartel member should be in a hurry to be the first to come forward with the necessary evidence before others do so; even better, firms will be dissuaded from forming a cartel in the first place. (In game-theoretic terms, the non-collusive outcome is the subgame-perfect equilibrium, and collusion remains 'off the path of play'.) That is why such programmes are known as 'whistleblower' clauses. It is also why in the EU and US, leniency programmes were revised (in 1993 and 2002, respectively) so as to *guarantee* complete amnesty to the first firm to provide evidence to commence an investigation, and successively lower reductions in penalty for those that provide useful evidence subsequently. This led to a substantial increase in the number of firms willing to provide information. But if there is no certainty of the payoff to any firm, as in the proposed amendment to Section 46 of the Indian Competition

Act, the very purpose of the provision is defeated, and firms will not be induced to provide information. On the other hand, as the clause stands, complete amnesty can be granted or a token fine can be levied on *all* firms that provide information about their role in the cartel, again defeating the purpose of the provision, but certainly bringing it more in line with the 'soft' Indian state's attitude to law enforcement.

Restoring the Role of the Judiciary

T.C.A. Anant and Jaivir Singh have dealt with the issue of the separation of powers elsewhere in this volume, with the controversy over the CCI as an example, and I do not propose to comment on it here. But the extensive changes with which the 2006 Amendment Bill proposes to get around the Supreme Court's strictures will have several negative consequences for the implementation of the Act, even if they meet with the Court's approval. In order to restore the role of the judiciary, the Bill creates a Competition Appellate Tribunal (CAT) which must be headed by a current or former Judge of the Supreme Court or Chief Justice of a High Court. It also provides that the Chief Justice of India or his nominee will chair the selection committee for appointments to both the CCI and the CAT. A judge need not head the CCI, but it has been deprived of the power to award compensation or imprisonment. Its orders on monetary penalties can be executed through the income tax authorities, and penalties for contravention of other orders will be imposed by civil courts.

The problem is that the Tribunal has been created by abolishing four of the ten posts that had earlier been provided for the CCI, and the latter will now take decisions collectively as a collegium of up to seven members, rather than in benches of at least two members as originally intended. Consequently, the provisions for regional benches and at least one specialized merger bench in the original Act are to be deleted by the amending Bill, which is unfortunate. A body sitting only in Delhi is inaccessible to parties elsewhere in such a vast country, and mergers do require specialized expertise. Moreover, the collegial approach in the CCI, and the interposition of the Appellate Tribunal and civil courts will inevitably slow down the rate of disposal of cases.

Institutional Capacity Building

Another range of problems concerns the ability of the CCI to implement the many technical provisions in the new Act, which were not there in the MRTP Act. The multifarious criteria for determining dominance in Section 19(4) and the anti-competitiveness of mergers in Section 20(4) require proficiency in modern industrial economics as well as statistical analyses of the economic conditions of the industry under consideration. These criteria will be of little help to a body that lacks institutional memory or theoretical understanding of their significance. Although the 2006 Amendment Bill provides for the staff of the MRTP Commission (MRTPC) to be transferred to the CCI, their expertise will be of little use, because the MRTP Act used very different criteria, and the Commission often side-stepped them by resorting to the overarching concepts of 'public interest' and 'manipulation of prices' which proved decisive in many cases.[6] The Director General's office has (unsuccessfully) initiated enquiries against firms for normal business behaviour such as reducing capacity utilization or increasing prices more than costs. This perhaps represents a concern for establishing a 'just' price, which is not the function of a competition agency. Further, the Commission's limited resources were diverted to dealing with the large number of cases of individual consumer dissatisfaction relating to deficiency in service (often non-delivery of flats or cars booked with dealers), or adjudicating allegations of false advertising or misleading prize schemes, under the rubric of Unfair Trade Practices (UTP), included in the Act by the 1984 amendment. For various reasons, consumers have found the MRTP route far more effective than resorting to the Consumer Protection Act (CPA), which had similar provisions. With its energies devoted to such issues, the investigative, prosecutorial, and adjudicatory wings of the MRTPC were unable to develop an understanding of the important economic arguments required for the enforcement of a modern competition law like the Competition Act.

Lack of expertise is likely to create special problems for merger review, which was deleted along with most of Chapter III of the MRTPA (dealing with concentration of economic power) by the 1991 amendment, has been reintroduced in the Competition Act. Pre-merger notification is voluntary, with a proviso that approval would be deemed to have been granted if no decision is reached in 90 days. But Section 31 of the Act allows the CCI to look post-facto into a merger for which approval was not sought in advance, and to undo or modify it if it sees fit. (Section 28 also allows the CCI to divide an enterprise enjoying a dominant position.) This unscrambling of firms'

[6] On these issues, see Bhattacharjea (2003), and the earlier papers cited therein.

assets is likely to be a hugely costly operation, for which there is no official expertise thanks to the non-enforcement of Section 27 of the MRTPA. This allowed the government, after a reference to the MRTPC, to order the division of firms or severance of interconnections between them, and was the only section retained in Chapter III after the 1991 amendment. But it was not used.

Expertise is lacking even for prior evaluation of mergers, which has not been possible since 1991. Even before that, it was focussed more on preventing the concentration of industrial ownership rather than market power, and mergers were usually sanctioned or denied by the government without reference to the MRTPC. This was part of the discredited 'licence-permit raj'. Modern merger review requires a careful balancing of the anti-competitive effects of greater concentration against several possible efficiency gains. While the merging firms would no doubt be keen to exaggerate the latter, there is no denying that Indian industry is in the process of restructuring in the face of intensifying foreign competition. It is also trying to overcome the legacy of a decade of excess entry that followed the abolition of domestic investment licensing, which had encouraged installation of excess capacities in a range of industries, fragmented amongst too many firms.[7]

Mergers may also be required because the existing policy towards 'sick industries' simply keeps resources unemployed for the duration of extremely protracted winding-up proceedings. Section 20(4)(k) of the Competition Act does provide that the 'possibility of a failing business' may be considered as a criterion while assessing whether a combination is anti-competitive. However, this 'failing firm defence', often used in the US, is supposed to be applied from the perspective of *competition*: if the firm that is the target of the merger was likely to close down, the merger will not reduce competition more than it would have been reduced anyway. The 'failing firm' argument is generally not invoked to maintain utilization of resources or to save jobs. If a broader social objective is intended, the Act should specify it explicitly.

For all these reasons, there is an urgent need to build up the capacities of the CCI and its staff. Multiple skill-sets would be required. First, proper understanding of the technical criteria in the Competition

[7] Goldar and Kumari (2003) give evidence of growing excess capacity due to the investment boom in the early 1990s, and show that it had a depressing effect on total factor productivity growth. For empirical evidence that the growing number of mergers in India over the last two decades is a response to regulatory changes such as industry delicensing and amendments of the merger-related sections of the MRTP Act, see Agarwal and Bhattacharjea (2006).

Act, especially those listed explicitly in Sections 19 and 20, presupposing fairly advanced training in a modern branch of industrial economics that is taught at the post-graduate level in only a handful of Indian universities. Second, many of these criteria also require advanced statistical and econometric techniques, and familiarity with statistical sources pertaining to industry and trade. Third, knowledge of corporate accounting practices would be essential to produce the kind of evidence required by some of the criteria. Fourth, investigation of cartels will involve police skills, as cartels are similar to other types of criminal conspiracy, and (as frequent news reports about 'tender mafias' and 'contractor mafias' show) they are often part of organized crime networks. With inadequate investigative resources, the MRTP Commission could not successfully prosecute a single covert cartel in recent years. Finally, as in other countries, prosecution should be entrusted to specialized antitrust lawyers who understand the underlying economic reasoning, rather than general counsel who argue a variety of cases for the government.

The CCI should therefore be staffed with multi-disciplinary professionals with a firm grounding in the environment of Indian business. While the 2006 Amendment Bill requires the chairman of the CAT to be a judge, no such background is required for the chairman of the CCI, and given the government's track record with respect to all other regulatory agencies, it is almost certain that the post will be filled by a civil servant. Given the background of India's senior civil servants, such a person can certainly provide effective leadership and coordination for a multi-disciplinary team (as in the UK), and would perhaps be better qualified in this respect, than a judge (or an academic!). Senior staff positions, too, are likely to go to bureaucrats, who are no doubt capable people. But the prospect of being transferred after a few years will inhibit their incentive to acquire the relevant skills themselves. Whatever skills they acquire will be lost to the CCI when they move out. To ensure continuity and retention of experience, a permanent cadre should be considered, drawn from officers with suitable background and aptitude, supplemented by direct recruitment through the UPSC. Outside professionals should be brought in at senior levels, if necessary on consultancy contracts, as in Securities and Exchange Board of India (SEBI) and Telecom Regulatory Authority of India (TRAI). The CCI must also have a library of books and journals on antitrust law, economics and practice, as well as electronic databases on industrial statistics, and computing facilities with statistical packages. A well-staffed and well-equipped in-house research division will be necessary to counter the arguments of experts who will undoubtedly be hired by private parties to appear before the Commission and to advise their lawyers.

Members of the CCI and CAT who will sit in judgment, whether they come from the judiciary or bureaucracy, will also need to be sensitized to the techniques of modern competition analysis, in order to prevent judicial activism unrelated to the purpose of the Act. According to the preamble and Section 18, its purpose is the promotion of competition and protection of consumer interest. The MRTP Commission sometimes interpreted its mandate to promote the 'public interest' in a way that protected *competitors* and producer interests rather than competition, in the name of protecting investors' funds and workers' jobs (see Bhattacharjea 2003). In the Competition Act, such public interest issues can be dealt with by *exempting* certain categories of enterprises from provisions of the Act, for example cartels to promote small enterprises, or to save jobs in a declining industry. But under Section 54 of the Act, authority for granting exemptions has been given to the central government, not the CCI. It is important that these exemptions should be granted on the basis of sound criteria, rather than political favouritism, and here the CCI staff can play an important role after they gain experience and expertise. In many countries, the statute itself lists exempted sectors, or the power to grant certain types of exemption is delegated to the antitrust agency. If amendments along these lines are not feasible in the Indian context, then at least the CCI's mandate under Section 49 to give advice on reference from the government should be strengthened, to encourage advice even without a specific reference. And the government's power to issue binding policy directives to the CCI (Section 55) should not be abused, although the fate of the supposedly independent telecom regulator TRAI leaves one with little confidence that this will in fact be the way things turn out.

Conclusion

The 2006 Amendment Bill does correct some of the flaws in the 2002 Competition Act. However, several flaws remain, which were discussed in this paper. They arise out of conceptual confusion between criteria related to competition and those related to other objectives, and lack of understanding of some basic economic principles governing the 'meet the competition defence' for dominant firms and leniency schemes for cartel participants. Combined with the problems resulting from inadequate professional resources in the CCI discussed in the section, 'Features of the Competition Act', these flaws are likely to lead to inconsistent and arbitrary decisions, which will undermine its credibility and possibly invite a political backlash. The CCI, as and when it is fully constituted, and also the government, should wake up to these problems before serious enforcement begins, so as to avoid more serious ones in future.

It is almost certain that corporate lawyers will be prepared to exploit the loopholes in the Act on behalf of their clients. In particular, large multinational firms, with far greater experience in competition cases in their global operations, and with the resources to hire better lawyers, will benefit disproportionately. Indian firms, without comparable experience, will have to incur huge costs in hiring expensive lawyers, consultants and expert witnesses, which is the norm in antitrust cases in developed countries. As shown above, some provisions of the Act are already biased in favour of multinationals. For example, the 'meet the competition' defence for predatory pricing is tilted in favour of firms with deep pockets, while in the case of efficiency-enhancing joint ventures, the Act does not require the kind of conditions that would be imposed in Europe and the US. Thus, if the Act is implemented at all seriously, those sections of Indian business that are unable to bring to bear the necessary legal firepower or political influence are likely to feel the heat of an unfamiliar regime.

The Competition Act should therefore be thoroughly re-examined, perhaps in the course of the discussion of the 2006 Amendment Bill. Although the government has the power, under Section 65, to remove difficulties in giving effect to the provisions of the Act without parliamentary approval, the changes required to deal with the problems discussed above are probably too significant to bypass Parliament. They will need to be resolved by making further amendments to the Act.

Even thereafter, the Act should be implemented in a phased manner. The government's original intention, although not spelt out in the Act, was to use the first year after its commencement solely for advocacy and capacity building, the second for implementing the sections dealing with anti-competitive agreements and abuse of dominance, and to commence merger review only in the third year. It is not clear whether 'commencement' means 2003 when some administrative sections were notified and the skeleton CCI began functioning, or some future date when the full CCI is in place. If it is the former, enforcement of all sections of the Act can commence almost immediately, but it would be advisable to adopt the latter interpretation. The CCI can devote itself mainly to building up its technical capacity and educating industry and trade on the need to modify their behaviour. Merger review, in particular, should be deferred. Otherwise the CCI will be swamped with cases, and will be unable to do justice to them in view of the unrealistic deadlines for approval laid down in the Act, the complexity of merger review, the lack of technical expertise, the abolition of merger benches, and the need for all cases to be considered collegially by the full Commission.

Postscript

In September 2007, the government withdrew the amending bill referred to in this paper, and introduced a more comprehensive one, the Competition (Amendment) Bill, 2007. This was passed by both houses of Parliament without debate. The decks have thus been cleared for appointing members of the CCI and appellate tribunal, and enforcement of the Competition Act is expected to begin by mid-2008. The new amending bill substantially increased penalties, made merger notification mandatory and extended the time limits for CCI decision from 90 to 210 days. However, it did not address any of the conceptual problems I have mentioned here, even though some of them had been raised in the report of the Parliamentary Committee that reviewed the 2006 bill: Compare Lok Sabha Secretariat, Standing Committee on Finance (2006–07), Fourteenth Lok Sabha, Ministry of Company Affairs: 44th Report (December 2006), para 64, and my suggestions in 'Amending India's Competition Act', *Economic and Political Weekly*, 41(41), 14 October 2006. And of course, the capacity-building issues I have raised remain valid, more so as most of the officials who have served in the CCI since it was set up in 2003–04 have either left or will be coming to the end of their terms by the time implementation begins in 2008.

References

Agarwal, Manish and Aditya Bhattacharjea, 2006, 'Mergers in India: A Response to Regulatory Shocks', *Emerging Markets Finance and Trade*, 42, pp. 47–66.

Bhattacharjea, Aditya, 2003, 'India's Competition Policy: An Assessment', *Economic and Political Weekly*, vol. 38, pp. 3561–74, 23 August.

Goldar, B.N. and Anita Kumari, 2003, 'Import Liberalization and Productivity Growth in Indian Manufacturing Industries in the 1990s', *The Developing Economies*, vol. 41, pp. 436–60.

4

Compacts, Conventions and Codes

Initiatives for Higher International Labor Standards

KAUSHIK BASU

Introduction

The International Labor Standards (ILS) movement is meant to be an initiative to promote better working conditions and higher living standards for workers in the Third World. It therefore seems baffling that the most vociferous opposition to ILS comes from the Third World, and not just from elite groups and government, but from workers and grass-roots activists. This opinion from the South, encountered all over developing countries, however, gets little representation in international forums and global meets. Is the dissent from the South based on a misperception of the South of its own interests? Or is it founded on a realistic perception of global politics and power? The purpose of this essay is to argue the latter—that the Southern apprehension is understandable; and to ignore this while drafting policy for the well-being of the workers will not only be an injustice, but will give rise to global tensions and instability.

The contemporary world has seen a bewildering number of initiatives for ILS, the latest being the UN's Global Compact, which attempts to make big firms and corporations join hands in a voluntary contract to adhere to certain minimal labor standards. This stands in contrast to the International Labor Organization (ILO)'s effort to

This paper was first published in *Cornell International Law Journal* (*CILJ*), Vol. 34, No. 3, 2001.

make *nations* ratify 'conventions', which then requires them to enforce minimal labor standards within their national boundaries; and in even sharper contrast to the proposed plan to introduce a 'social clause' in the WTO agreements, which would then allow the international community to place trade sanctions on countries that violated minimal labor standards.

It will be argued in this paper that, while global opinion has become more sophisticated and nuanced in recent years, and some of the more recent proposals, such as the UN Global Compact, are better than some of the earlier plans, on the whole the existing ILS initiatives are ill-conceived and are likely to have undesirable fall-outs. For any ILS effort to succeed and to actually help those that it is meant to help, it is imperative to take account of the opinions of developing nations. Accordingly, the paper ends with a discussion of global democracy.

In summary, it is argued here that at this stage ILS is best left to individual nations and only a minimal global coordination, and, further, that this global coordination is best done through the ILO and the UN. The WTO, *the way it currently functions*, is not the appropriate body for enforcing labor standards. In the long run, there must be an effort to democratize global organizations and institutions, such as the WTO, and when that is done, or at least when the process is reasonably underway, can global organizations be seriously entrusted with the task of promoting higher international labor standards.

The Issues and the Historical Background

Most people, when they think of labor standards, think of the law as its natural hand-maiden. If workers are to be better off, avoid excessively hazardous work, keep their children out of the workplace, and so on, our natural tendency is to think of the law as the natural instrument for achieving these. Thus we may think of direct laws, such as minimum wage legislation and the legal prohibition of child labor, and indirect laws which enhance worker power, such as the right to bargain collectively, as the essential instrument for raising worker welfare.

A large part of mainstream economics is a warning that this kind of reasoning is faulty. It reminds us that the absence of government action does not necessarily mean that labor standards will remain low. As productivity and the demand for labor rise, workers *can* achieve higher living standards, through the forces of the market. The mere threat that a worker may quit his or her job could ensure that he or she will be paid well and not be exposed to excessive risks, be made to work excessive hours and so on. Of course, some economists go overboard and argue that the well-being of the worker can be left entirely to market forces.

In reality, there are two broad reasons why interventions may be called for. First, markets often fail because of externalities or asymmetric information or the difficulties of monitoring, and we may need laws to correct for these failures; and even when markets do not fail the market outcome may be more inequitable than what we are willing to tolerate. Second, even when each nation prefers a higher labor standard, this may be impossible to achieve unless several nations coordinate their behavior. When this happens, not only do governments immediately come into play, but the need arises for an internationally coordinated effort. The subject of International Labor Standards pertains to this second kind of intervention.[1]

The historical roots of the labor standards movement go far back into history, with the English Factory Act of 1802, introduced by Sir Robert Peel, being treated as a landmark. The problem of inter-country coordination in the context of labor standards dates back to 1818 and in particular to the writings of Robert Owen, followed soon thereafter by the advocacy of numerous French intellectuals and activists.[2] Awareness of the inter-regional nature of the labor standards problem increased through the nineteenth century and early twentieth century as the federal government of the United States battled to curb inter-state competition and adopt common labor standards. The US historical experience nicely mirrors the current global problems.

In the US, the first legislation was enacted by the state of Massachusetts in 1837. Thereafter different states brought in different legislation, often backing down for fear that firms and capital would leave and go to states where labor laws were more lax. Some of this history is nicely recounted by Florence Kelly.[3] The openness of this inter-government competition is transparent from the following account in her book (p. 91): 'For lack of uniformity progress has been hindered in many states, notably in the glass industry which, during 1904, successfully represented to the legislature of New Jersey that, if

[1] This view of ILS is explicit in Basu (1999). Also Chau et al. (2000).

[2] See Engerman (2001). See also Charnovitz (1987).

[3] See Kelly (1905). See also Moehling (1999).

deprived of the privilege of employing boys under the age of 16 at night, it would migrate to Delaware and West Virginia, where no such restrictions yet await it.'

The inter-state competition came to an end as recently as 1938 with the passing of the first nationwide law in the US to monitor labor standards—the Fair Labor Standards Act.

After the Second World War and especially in the last one or two decades, as the process of globalization gathered momentum, and labor and, especially capital, began to move more freely across nations, the labor standards concern spilled beyond national and regional boundaries and became properly an international matter. Ever since the formation of the ILO in 1919 there was a forum for these international concerns. But for a long time the ILO was an ineffective body, with some doubts about its survival. Initially it had only 44 member nations. Membership initially grew slowly; but after 1946, once the ILO became an agency of the United Nations, membership grew rapidly, and by 1969 it had 174 members.

With the globalization of these concerns the idea of labor standards began to get codified. They were classified under four kinds of 'rights': *Basic Rights*, which included the right against involuntary servitude, injunctions against exploitative child labor and discrimination; *Civic Rights*, which gave workers the freedom of association and collective bargaining rights; *Survival Rights*, which ensured a minimum wage, accident compensation, and the right not to be exposed to excessive hazards; and *Security Rights*, which placed restrictions on employers from firing workers and gave workers the right to retirement benefits.[4]

Resisting the tendency for proliferating labor standards and recognizing that if the same standards are to be imposed on all regions, from sub-Saharan Africa to Western Europe, the requirements have to be fairly minimal, there has now emerged what is often referred to as the list of 'core labor standards'.[5] These consist of (1) prohibition of forced labor, (2) prohibition of discrimination in employment, (3) right to freedom of association, (4) right to bargain collectively, and (5) prohibition of exploitative child labor.

While the core labor standards are much more reasonable and realistic, the crux of the matter is not the agreement, in the abstract, of the importance of these minimal standards—most reasonable people will accept these—but the practical interpretation of these precepts and the methods used to implement them.

[4] See Portes (1990); Maskus (1997); Singh (2001).

[5] For discussion, see Swinnerton (1997).

Existing Initiatives and Their Shortcomings

There are two broad classes of global actions that have been used thus far to promote higher ILS. Following my earlier usage[6] I shall call these *extra-national* and *supra-national* actions. Extra-national action is action taken by a nation within its own territory, which creates incentives in other countries to improve ILS. An example of an extra-national action is the so-called Harkin's bill or more formally, the Child Labor Deterrence Act, which has, fortunately, remained a bill. The aim of this bill was to enable the US to put a ban on any import, which has a child labor input. The law works within the US but creates incentives in other nations to keep children out of the labor force, because otherwise they will not be able to export to the US.

The weakness of the bill is its failure to recognize that (1) parents do not typically send their children to work out of sloth but they do so out of desperation and (2) there are worse things that can happen to a child than labor, such as starvation. In the poorest nations an abrupt halt to child labor is likely to cause children to suffer acute poverty and hunger. Clearly, we must not be so single-minded in eradicating child labor that we are prepared to do so by making children starve. Secondly, this kind of extra-national action is likely to drive children away from the export sector to other sectors, which may be worse for the children's welfare. There is now mounting evidence from Nepal's carpet industry and Bangladesh's garment industry that the anticipation of legislative and other punitive actions by industrialized nations have driven children away to prostitution.[7] The trouble with such bills is that even if they are inspired by a genuine concern for workers in the South, as they often are, they enable protectionism in the North. Interestingly, while the current versions of the Harkin's bill appeal only to the welfare of the child in motivating the legislation, the early versions of the bill had open reference to the fact that child labor in the Third World may cause unemployment in the North.[8]

What the above observation suggests is that child labor has to be attacked at a nationwide level and must not be confined to the exports sector.[9]

[6] Basu (1999).

[7] See UNICEF (1995) and Brown et al. (1999).

[8] A superior extra national legal action is the Sander's Amendment of the Tariff Act of 1930. This seeks to ban imports of goods that use *forced* child labor. This move towards distinguishing between different forms of child labor is a move in the right direction.

[9] See Basu and Van (1998).

A supra-national action is an action undertaken by a *collectivity* of nations to sanction against the violation of minimal labor standards. Two prominent examples of supra national action are the UN Global Compact and the various ILO conventions. In the case of the Global Compact, companies voluntarily agree to abjure certain practices and in the case of the ILO conventions, countries commit to adhere to certain standards. The important difference between these two voluntary schemes is that they place the primary responsibility of ILS on different agencies. The Global Compact places the responsibility on the multinationals and big corporations and the ILO conventions place the responsibility on the nations, and primarily the Third World nations, since these are the potential violators of the standards.

Perhaps the most potent form of supra-national action that is being contemplated is to have a social clause in the WTO provisions, which would then allow the WTO to impose trade sanctions on an erring country. The risk of empowering the WTO thus is that this will become a powerful instrument of protectionism in the North.[10] There is already some evidence of how well-meaning legislation can be misused by lobbies that have power enough to do so. An interesting case in point is the use of the Sander's Amendment against the Brazilian company, Sucocitrico Cutrale. The charge was that the company was using children to pluck oranges. However, as the *Wall Street Journal* pointed out this was probably an act of reprisal headed by the Teamsters Union against Cutrale for downsizing some minute Maid plants it had bought from Coca Cola Co. in Florida.

It has to be kept in mind that the problem is not just that the power of the WTO will be misused, but that, as things stand, it is likely to be used disproportionately by industrialized nations against developing countries, simply because the latter do not have the resources—money or the expertise—to fight out cases in Geneva. Hence, the across-the-board negative reaction of developing countries to the idea of empowering the WTO seems to be not without basis.

Faced with these criticisms, there is a groundswell of opinion in the industrialized nations, at least among the intelligentsia, to use more informal, and therefore flexible, arrangements to raise labor standards.[11] What has caught a lot of the liberal attention is the idea

[10] Much has been written about the dangers of giving WTO the power to uphold ILS; see Bhagwati (1995); see also Srinivasan (1996).

[11] For a very interesting suggestion of how to organize a flexible system see Fung et al. (2001). Their scheme shares the spirit of the UN Global Compact in one respect—

of 'product labeling', that is, to have stickers on 'suspect' goods, such as carpets, soccer balls, and processed foods, which declare that these goods are 'child labor free' or, more generally, produced under circumstances that meet a minimal ILS.[12] Hence, the ultimate decision whether to boycott such a product or not is left as a decision of individual consumers. In fact the UN Global Compact is likely to have a very similar effect. By publicizing the list of companies that are signatories to this compact it can create a sense among consumers about which companies meet with minimal labor standards and they can then boycott the others or buy from them only when there is a substantial price advantage.

I would however like to argue that such informal schemes are likely to be deeply unfair. There is, first of all, the large question as to whether moral judgements ought to be dispensed through the markets. At first sight, this may appear to be an instance of the consumer's sovereignty. But a preference against a carpet which uses child labor, is not quite the same thing as one's preference for red apples or against green apples. The former is intimately tied to the urge to sanction a certain kind of behavior. It is a moral preference of a particular kind, which may be called a 'sanctioning preference'. While social sanctions do play important roles in civic life, it is not obvious that that is always the right method for dispensing justice. And there is good reason for this. When we express an interest in one good over another as a form of our sanctioning preference, our aim is not just to gratify a personal hedonism, such as when a person buys a red apple, but to punish or reward some people, for instance, those involved in the production of a certain good and in the process violate or adhere to certain standards. But in that case what we really want is that those who violate certain standards should be punished to a certain degree, for instance, by losing a certain percentage of their business—say 40 per cent. But there is no way for a *single* consumer to express this preference in the market. If he boycotts the good in an effort to hurt the producer and all those involved in the manufacture of a certain product, how does he know that all other consumers will not do the

---

they both place the primary responsibility for upholding standards on the corporations. However, the scheme does have important flaws; see the comments in the same issue of *Boston Review* by Pranab Bardhan, Robin Broad, Mark Levison, David Moberg, Guy Standing, Heather White and myself.

[12] For analyses of product labeling see Brown (1999); Basu et al. (1999); Bachman (2000)

same and so end up drying up 100 per cent of the business, instead of exactly 40 per cent. Likewise when you decide to buy a particular brand name to reward the manufacturer a certain amount, there is no way to ensure that the right number of consumers will do the same and that the reward will be commensurate with the good act. In brief, there is a huge coordination problem in the dispensing of justice that cannot be solved by the atomistic decisions of thousands of individual consumers. Not surprisingly, punishments dispensed through informal social sanctions often turn out to be witch-hunts causing disproportionate pain to some and too little pain to others. Not surprisingly, when it comes to justice, most societies prefer to use a centralized, non-democratic system, namely, that of the courts and the judiciary. The free market is not the right instrument for passing moral judgements.

More specifically, the method of product labeling has the disadvantage of being too blunt an instrument. It treats all countries on par. Take for instance, child labor. Some sub-Saharan African countries, such as Ethiopia, have a huge dependence on child labor, with close to 45 per cent of all children in the age group 10 to 14 years working. On the other hand, in most Asian countries, including China and India, the participation rates are much lower (respectively 11 per cent and 14 per cent).[13] If consumers in industrialized nations begin to totally boycott goods with a child-labor input, it is arguable that some of these countries, where the participation rates are low will suffer, but be able to withstand the boycott. On the other hand, for several African countries and even some Asian and Latin American countries—the poorer ones—there may be a major adverse impact on the economy, causing a disproportionate suffering for all, including the children, who were meant to be protected by this action.

Secondly, this action is likely to be biased in favor of large manufacturers. Consider a small producer of soccer balls in Pakistan. For him the production unit is likely to double up as factory shed and bedroom. For such a producer to persuade a labeling agency that it does not use child labor and so should get a label, will be very hard, since the children are never far away from the areas of production. On the other hand, a large producer can centralize its production and prevent children from even entering the factory. This is in fact exactly what Reebok International has done in Sialkot, Pakistan.

[13] These and other statistics were compiled by the *ILO: Economically Active Populations: Estimates and Projections, 1950–2010*, Geneva, ILO (1996).

Finally, these informal methods of product boycott share the problem of extra-national action discussed above, which drive bad practices, such as the use of child labor from the export sector of developing countries to the indigenous sectors, where conditions are often worse.[14]

What then are we to do to improve labor standards?

Recommendations

One general recommendation for upholding labor standards that economists make and is worth repeating, is the importance of keeping trade channels from the Third World open. It is the greater demand for goods from the Third World that translates into a higher demand for labor and through that raises the bargaining power of workers. This argument has been made so many times[15] that there is no reason for me to dwell on it beyond endorsement.

A related and more specific recommendation, in the context of child labor, is for policies that improve conditions in the adult labor market. While some of the early work held parents responsible for child labor, it was argued in Basu and Van[16] that a child's non-work is likely to be a luxury good in a household's decision-making. In other words, parents do not like to send their children to work if they can help it; it is only when they are driven by acute economic hardship that they send their children to work.[17] This does not deny that there are exceptions in the form of abusive parents who buy their own leisure by making their children work and that other factors, such as the availability of decent schooling have a large influence on the incidence of child labor. But in general, when child labor is a mass phenomenon as in contemporary developing countries, it is wrong to equate child labor with child abuse. It follows from this, that a policy for eradicating child labor should treat the parent as an accomplice

[14] For an interesting study in the context of Bangladesh, of how global monitoring can backfire, see Kabeer(2000).

[15] See, for instance, Dixit (2000); Jafarey et al. (1999)

[16] See References at the end of the paper. See also Swinnerton et al.(1999). Very different kinds of problems arise with street children, but unfortunately there are as yet few studies on this, an exception being William Myers, *Alternative Services for Street Children* (1988).

[17] There is ample evidence for the luxury axiom. For empirical studies that shed light on this axiom see, for instance, Ray (2000); Bhalotra (2000); Emerson et al. (2000); Freije et al. (2000).

in this task rather than adversary. Hence, if we can intervene to reduce adult unemployment and raise adult incomes, parents on their own will withdraw children from the labor market. There will be no need to use the stick to achieve this. So, somewhat paradoxically, the one policy always worth using to combat *child* labor is to improve the conditions of *adult* labor.

All these policy interventions through the market are desirable but they will clearly take a lot of time to implement. So even if in the long run we use them, we have to think of more direct interventions in the short run. What should these be? We have seen above how it is likely to be better to rely on conventions such as the ones adopted by the ILO or compacts such as that of the UN, rather than the use of the social clause by the WTO. Yet, even these are not good enough. Nor is it a good idea to leave sanctions to the consumers.

As things stand the main agency for labor standards policy has to be with the national governments, which can tailor the policy to each nation's specific needs and context. Yet this alone is not enough, since labor standards have an important inter-country dimension to it. The tension is not between the North and the South but between the South and the South, as argued in Basu (1999) and Kanbur and Chau (2000). With globalization it is now easier for capital to move from one country to another. So it is only natural that when one developing country contemplates raising a particular standard it worries that it will drive capital to another developing country. This was borne out quite strikingly when, because of political reasons the US stopped importing carpets from Iran. It was like a controlled experiment. With one developing country's exports cut off, another developing country took over the business. In this case India became the largest exporter to the US. It is this very fear that exports will shift to another developing nation that ties the hands of individual governments of developing countries from taking more action. On the other hand, the chances of an export activity shifting from a developing nation to an industrialized nation because of the raising of a labor standard are negligible because they have such widely differing comparative advantages. There is therefore, need for multi-country coordinated action, but the coordination has to be among the developing countries in their own collective interest.

Hence, we need a global organization to do the coordination. The difficulty stems from the fact that there is no organization that adequately represents the opinion and interests of developing nations. A pre-requisite for handing over labor standards policy to an international organization is the democratization of the organization. Indeed, the WTO, in principle, could be an enforcer of ILS, *if* developing countries felt it represented their interest adequately.

So, though for now we do not have too many options, other than relying on market-oriented policies, such as bolstering the demand for adult labor in developing nations and keeping open trade channels, and for some effort by national governments, there has to be a major effort to democratize international organizations, such as the WTO, so that they can then be entrusted with the important task of crafting and implementing policies for better labor standards.

The democratization of international organizations is a large topic. The concluding section of this essay is a brief incursion into this complicated subject.

Restructuring International Organizations

One concomitant of globalization and technological progress, that has either gone unnoticed or been hushed up by those who did notice it, is that it has a natural corrosive effect on global democracy. As a consequence of this phenomenon, even if individual countries become democratic, the aggregate of global democracy may well be on the wane. Democracy entails many things—the existence of a variety of political and legislative institutions, avenues for citizens to participate in the formation of economic policies that affect their lives and, in the ultimate analysis, a certain mind-set. Yet at the core of it and in its simplest form, democracy requires that (1) people should have the right to choose those who rule them and (2) the principle that the vote of each person should count as much as another person's.

Next, note that globalization, almost by definition, means that nations and people can exert a greater influence on other nations and the lives of citizens in other nations. Moreover, what is not true by definition but is a fact is that this power of one nation to influence another is by no means symmetric. The US, for instance, can cut off virtually all the trade lines of Cuba. It can do so not only by curtailing its own trade with Cuba but by threatening punitive action against those who trade with or invest in Cuba. This is not just a hypothetical possibility but the Helms-Burton Act in the US is testimony to how this can actually happen. Cuba, on the other hand, can do little to hurt the American economy or polity. Likewise, China can do things to Taiwan, which Taiwan can in no way, reciprocate.

As the world shrinks and powerful governments develop a variety of instruments and ways to influence the lives of citizens in other nations, it is no longer enough for people to be able to choose the leaders of their own nations. Since transnational voting does not happen (and even its hypothetical suggestion sounds absurd to us), globalization is bound to cause a diminution of global democracy.

Thanks to globalization there is a variety of instruments that nations can use to influence outcomes elsewhere. For the purposes of the current essay the most important is the cessation of international trade, such as would happen if the WTO were empowered to enforce ILS. International trade (after a slow-down in the years between the two World Wars) has risen steadily. These global linkages have fuelled unprecedented growth rates of national incomes (during the 1990s China grew at around 8 per cent per annum and India at 6.5 per cent) but they have also created new vulnerabilities. Governments and international organizations can now use the threat of disrupting these flows (or the lure of releasing greater flows of money or goods) to enforce conformity to certain kinds of behavior. And such threats have been used. International organizations have given money while insisting that the developing countries fulfil certain conditions, many of which have had nothing to do with ensuring repayment. These conditionalities have, at times, even been contradictory, such as requiring the debtor nation to practice democracy and for it to privatize certain key sectors, unmindful of the fact that this may be against the collective wishes of the people. Some of these conditions have been blatantly in the interest of the donor nation. In 1998, during the Asian crisis, the rescue package put together with money from several industrialized nations, most prominently Japan and the US, had clauses that required Korea to lift bans on imports of certain Japanese products (which Japan had for long, been trying to sell to Korea) and to open up its banking sector to foreign banks (an item that had long been on America's bilateral agenda with Korea). Some of these demands may well be good for the borrower, but that is not the issue here. From the point of view of assessing global democracy what is relevant is that people of the weaker nation have very little say in the imposition of these policies.

Given that the benefits of democracy are ample, as academic research has shown and non-academics always knew, this erosion of global democracy must have negative fall-outs. Indeed, it is arguable, that the rise in global unrest and instabilities are a manifestation of this retreat of democracy. And the inchoate demands of the protestors in the streets of Seattle and Washington may be founded in an intuitive but ill-articulated perception of this erosion of democracy.

What can be done about the erosion of global democracy? Utopian schemes such as a global government or a global bank that is answerable to all nations in the world are a distant dream. The process of globalization will course on, and inter-country democracy will continue to get bruised. It will be some time before this can bring us to discussing global governance and banking. In the meantime what is open to us are small measures, namely that of strengthening the democratic structure of global institutions, such as the World Bank, the IMF and the WTO. These are small measures, but extremely important.

The lesson therefore is, ironically, quite different from what the protestors in Seattle and Washington, and also some arch conservative groups in industrialized nations, want, to wit, the dismantling of these organizations. On the contrary, we need to restructure these organizations and recognize that they have an especially important role to play today. Of course, there will be need for vigilance. There is enough evidence that powerful politicians in powerful nations like to think of international institutions as valuable only to the extent that they can use them to their own advantage.

On 20 January 2000, Senator Jesse Helms, arguably the most important congressional voice in the US told the council members of the UN: 'If the United Nations respects the rights of the American people, *and serves them as an effective tool of diplomacy, it will earn and deserve their respect and support.* But a United Nations that seeks to impose its presumed authority on the American people, without their consent begs for confrontation and—I want to be candid with you—eventual US withdrawal.' (My italics—but also my hunch that those would be Helms' italics). Helms had gone on to express distaste for 'supranational institutions', including the international criminal court which was created last year. What is most damaging about this kind of remark is that any organization that meets with Jesse Helms' approval, immediately becomes suspect from the point of view of the world as a whole. The last thing that a credible international organization will now want is Jesse Helms' blessing. A WTO or a UN that has Helms' blessing and is entrusted with enforcing international labor and environmental standards will immediately be unacceptable to other nations, especially the developing countries, whose interests are often orthogonal to that of industrialized nations.

What we need to work on is to give nations, rich and poor, equal say, at least in international organizations that are supposed to play a mediating role in world economics or international relations. This horizontal equity is violated in most organizations through at least one of two routes. First, there is the open channel, which gives a larger share of votes to the nations contributing more to these organizations. This is certainly true of the IMF and the World Bank. The second route is through the lack of transparency of decision-making. One can see the importance of this for democracy by looking at policy-making within a country. If the process of decision-making is visible to all, it becomes difficult for any group or lobby to hijack the agenda. The same holds true for international organizations. Big and powerful nations, by virtue of contributing senior personnel and money to these organizations have much greater access to them. So if decisions occur behind opaque walls they are much more able to divert the agenda to suit their own interests. Take the case of the WTO. While it does follow the important principle of one-country one-vote, it is widely perceived as a preserve of powerful and rich nations. This is because of what some analysts call the 'green room' effect, that is, what goes on behind the scenes.[18] It is the green room where the agenda gets set on what is to appear on the table for all member nations to discuss and vote on, and a lot of the end results get determined at that stage. If the WTO is to become a more democratic institution, it must not allow its green room to be hijacked by a few.

This problem is nowhere more obvious than in the drafting of international labor standards. These are ostensibly being designed in the interests of the workers of developing countries. But, the form that these standards are tending to take—and the increasing talk of using trade sanctions to impose these standards—is close to what protectionist lobbies in industrial nations seek. This is not surprising given the greater access that the lobbies of rich countries have in the corridors of power in international organizations.

Most sound surprised by this criticism of global institutions. The fact that *the questioning* of the practice of richer nations (who contribute more funds) exercising more voting power in these organizations sounds outrageous, simply shows how far away we still are from *global* democracy. It does not at all seem outrageous that Bill Gates does not have multiple votes in the US elections on the ground that he contributes more to government coffers. In fact, the suggestion that he could have more votes sounds outrageous. This is because democracy within a nation is a much more settled idea.

[18] See Schott, J. et al. (2000).

But fortunately, opinions change. Multi-nationals nowadays talk in terms of environmental responsibility and the importance of respecting labor standards, even when that implies having to take a cut in profits. This seems to violate age-old beliefs and also the textbook description of multinational corporations. When the one-person one-vote idea first came about, the rich feudal landlords must have been shocked and cried foul at this blatant injustice and the chaos in the process of decision-making that this would cause. But no longer does this democratic principle *within a nation* seem strange.

Now with the call for restructuring international organizations ringing out from the streets of Seattle and Washington and also congressional committees, such as the recent one headed by Allan Meltzer,[19] this is a good time for us to think through some of these issues not just from the point of view of economic efficiency and greater cost effectiveness but from the point of view of representation of the poor. It is only when we manage to make these changes in the structure of international organization will we be able to entrust them with important tasks such as monitoring labor and environmental standards across the globe.

References

Bachman, Sarah, 2000, 'The Political Economy of Child Labor and its Impact on International Business', *Business Economics*, July.

Basu, Arnab, Nancy Chau and Ulrike Grote, 1999, 'Guaranteed Manufactured without Child Labor', mimeo: College of William and Mary.

Basu, Kaushik, 1999, 'International Labor Standards and Child Labor', *Challenge*, vol. 42, pp. 80–92.

_____, 1999, 'Child Labor: Cause, Consequence and Cure with Remarks on International Labor Standards', *Journal of Economic Literature*, vol. 37, pp. 1083–119.

_____, and Pham Hoang Van, 1998, 'The Economics of Child Labor', *American Economic Review*, vol. 88, pp. 412–27.

Bhagwati, Jagdish, 1995, 'Trade Liberalization and Fair Trade Demands: Addressing the Environment and Labor Standards Issue', *World Economy*, vol. 18, pp. 745–59.

Bhalotra, Sonia, 2000, 'Is Child Work Necessary?' mimeo: Cambridge University.

Brown, D., A. Deardorff and R. Stern, 1999, 'U.S. Trade and Other Policy Options and Programs to Deter Foreign Exploitation of Child Labor', Discussion Paper No. 433, Research Seminar in International Economics,

[19] *Report of the International Financial Institution Advisory Commission* (2000).

School of Public Policy, The University of Michigan. Also available at: *http://www.spp.umich.edu/rsie/workingpapers/wp.html.*

Brown, Drusila, 1999, 'A Transactions Cost Politics Analysis of International Child Labor Standards', in Alan Deardorff and Robert Stern (eds.), *Social Dimensions of U.S. Trade Policies*, University of Michigan Press, Michigan.

Charnovitz, Steve, 1987, 'The Influence of International Labor Standards on the World Trading Regime: A Historical Review', *International Labor Review*, no. 126, pp. 565–84.

Chau, Nancy and Ravi Kanbur, 2000, 'Race to the Bottom, From the Bottom', CEPR working paper 2687, Cornell University.

Dixit, Avinash, 2000, 'Discussion of 'A Transactions Cost Politics Analysis of International Child labor Standards', in Alan Deardorff and Robert Stern (eds.), *Social Dimensions of U.S. Trade Policies*, University of Michigan Press, Michigan.

Emerson, Patrick and Andre Souza Portela, 2000, 'Is there a Child Labor Trap? Inter-generational Persistence of Child Labor in Brazil', mimeo: Cornell University.

Engerman, Stanley, 2001, 'The History and Political Economy of International Labor Standards', mimeo: Rochester University.

Freije, Samuel and Luis-Felipe Lopez-Calva, 2000, 'Child Labor, School Attendance and Poverty in Mexico and Venezuela', mimeo: Cornell University.

Fung, Archon, Dara O'Rourke and Charles Sabel, 2001, 'Realizing Labor Standards: How Tranparency, Competition and Sanctions could improve Working Conditions Worldwide', *Boston Review*, vol. 26, February/March.

Jafarey, Saqib and Sajal Lahiri, 1999, 'Will Trade Sanctions Reduce Child Labor? The Role of Credit Markets', mimeo: University of Essex.

Kabeer, Naila, 2000, *Power to Choose: Bangladeshi Women and Labor Market Decisions in London and Dhaka*, Verso, London.

Kelly, Florence, 1905, *Some Ethical Gains through Legislation*, Macmillan, London.

Maskus, Keith, 1997, 'Should Core Labor Standards be Imposed through International Trade Policy', mimeo: World Bank, International Trade Division.

Moehling, Carolyn, 1999, 'State Child Labor Laws and the Decline of Child Labor', *Explorations in Economic History*, vol. 36, pp. 72–106.

Myers, William, 1988, 'Alternative Services for Street Children: The Brazilian Approach', in Assefa Bequele and Jo Boyden (eds.), *Combatting Child Labor*, ILO, Geneva.

Portes, A., 1990, 'Where More Can be Less: Labor Standards, Development and the Informal Economy', *Labor Standards and Development in the Global Economy*, US Department of Labor, Washington, D.C.

Ray, Ranjan, 2000, 'Child Labor, Child Schooling, and Their Interaction with Adult Labor: Empirical Evidence for Peru and Pakistan', *World Bank Economic Review*, vol. 14, pp. 347–67.

Schott, Jeffrey and Jayashee Watal, 2000, 'Decision-making in the WTO', in Jeffrey Schott (ed.), *WTO After Seattle,* Institute for International Economics, Washington, D.C.

Singh, Nirvikar, 2001, 'The Impact of International Labor Standards: A Survey of Economic Theory', mimeo: University of California, Santa Cruz.

Srinivasan, T. N., 1996, 'International Trade and Labor Standards from an Economic Perspective', in Pitou van Dijck and Gerrit Faber (eds.), *Challenges to the New World Trade Organization,* Elsevier, Amsterdam.

Swinnerton, Ken, 1997, 'An Essay on Economic Efficiency and Core Labor Standards', *World Economy,* vol. 20, pp. 73–86.

_____, Rogers and Carol Ann Rogers, 1999, 'The Economics of Child Labor: Comment', *American Economic Review,* vol. 89.

UNICEF, 1995, *Girls in Especially Difficult Circumstances: An Action Report,* Kathmandu:UNICEF.

5

Globalization and the Politics of International Corporate Taxation

A View From India

RAHUL MUKHERJI

Introduction

Information and communications technology (ICT) has enabled corporations to use offshore facilities for outsourcing commercial activities. This has expanded the service trade significantly but poses challenges for tax authorities. India's service trade has benefited enormously from the information communications technology revolution. Yet, digitization-driven global economic integration raises questions about a poor country's ability to tax this growing commerce in the context of the political economy of rules governing international taxation.

There is no international organization governing international corporate taxation. To address this problem of global governance, the World Bank, the IMF, and the Organization for Economic Cooperation and Development (OECD) have initiated an International Dialogue on Taxation to lend policy coherence at the global level.[1] The international taxation of business profits has received some attention among economists and tax experts, but students of international political economy have shown little engagement with this issue area. A few political scientists have pointed out that digitization-driven

This paper was first published in *India Review*, Vol. 3, No. 2, April 2004, pp. 89–113.

[1] See 'Developing the International Dialogue on Taxation,' which can be downloaded from *www.itdweb.org/documents/BG3.html*. The Dialogue was initiated in March 2002.

globalization made it tough for sovereign states to tax corporations, since commerce became increasingly transnationalized. Such transnational problems, they argued, merited transnational solutions.[2]

This paper stresses the transnational nature of the problem, and suggests a typology of state interests, which will shape the political economy of rules governing international corporate taxation. These interests can be understood in terms of capital abundance and capital scarcity within different countries. It will argue that residence-based rules will favour capital-abundant countries while source-based rules may be good for capital-scarce exporting countries like India, without necessarily hurting the interests of capital-abundant countries.[3] The problem arises because information technology makes it easy to carry out value addition in different parts of the world.

Trade and commerce should yield revenues that need to be invested in human and physical capital in a poor country like India. If states that created value were unable to tax their corporations, their ability to serve their societies could be jeopardized. This paper explains the reasons why capital-scarce producer countries like India have an interest in a specific set of rules that give due emphasis to the source of value creation. The content of the emerging rules on taxation will have an impact on India's ability to raise revenues from corporate taxation. India's interests are similar to those of other capital-scarce countries that can provide services via the electronic route but are not major market countries. These countries include Russia, China, Philippines, Australia, South Africa and Ireland.

International corporate taxation can provide resources for public goods and human welfare. Will globalization hurt the revenue collecting power of the state? Some argue that the drive towards competitiveness in trade will increase taxes for labour in relation to taxes for corporations, thereby hurting the interests of workers. Moreover, foreign direct investment and portfolio investment can exit to low-tax locations. Taxes for corporations could be replaced by indirect taxes, which are regressive, as they do not discriminate between the rich and the poor. Corporate taxation can be replaced by the taxation of income but it is not easy to raise revenue through income taxation in poor countries.

[2] The political scientists who have drawn attention to the issue of globalization and international corporate taxation are Ethan Kapstien and Roland Paris. See Kapstein (2001) and Paris (2003).

[3] I will discuss source- and residence-based taxation at some length in the two sections devoted to these topics.

Moreover, progressive income taxation may be tough in countries where there are no powerful institutions to protect the interests of the poor. Scholars like Phil Cerny and Susan Strange have pointed out that the state has become a dependent variable whose institutions need to be explained in terms of the needs of comparative advantage. The postwar consensus about the welfare state has thus been eroded.[4]

Geoffrey Garret and Duane Swank have argued persuasively that the 'compensation state' is still alive in an era of competitiveness. Their rigorous statistical work showed that taxes on capital and consequent social spending were not affected in the industrialized countries of the West. They reasoned that high spending on labour was justified in an era of globalization because it provided the political and economic stability necessary for comparative advantage in a particular sector. Corporatist institutions that allowed cooperation between trade unions and the state mitigated the 'race to the bottom' among tax authorities. Scandinavian countries characterized by such labour-friendly institutions were highly trade dependent and spent a great deal on their citizens. Government spending could be essential to guard against the social disruption associated with high levels of trade dependence.[5]

The 'compensation thesis' notwithstanding, there is an emerging consensus that while taxes on corporations are not collapsing, tax on labour has increased in relation to the tax on capital.[6] Even Geoffrey Garret's masterly thesis in defence of the 'compensation state' noted that corporate taxation in the 1990s was affected by globalization. In his own words: 'The erosion of the relationship between social democratic corporatism and higher rates of corporate taxation is the only piece of evidence ... that is consistent with the view globalization constraints on redistributive big government began to bite in the 1990s.'[7] Swank found that budget deficits with capital mobility led to a decline of the welfare state in Sweden, Finland, Denmark, and Germany.[8]

Recent studies show that social spending in developing countries was negatively affected by globalization to a much greater extent than in developed countries. Developing countries, which were generally characterized by low levels of labour power, were unable to

[4] See Cerny (1990) and Strange (1996).

[5] See Garret (1998); Swank (2002); Swank et al. (2002) and Steinmo (2002).

[6] See Schulze et al. (1999) and Tanzi (2001).

[7] Garret (1998), p. 138. See also pp. 17–18, 137–9.

[8] Swank (2002), pp. 277–9.

keep up their social spending, unlike many countries in the developed world that formed a part of Garret's and Swank's studies.[9] There was reason to be worried about the proliferation of tax havens as a result of the 'commercialization of sovereignty'. Small states with little or no economic infrastructure were able to attract finance capital due to their low rates of taxation.[10]

The outsourcing of service activities to India poses concerns for India's revenue department. This is the trade activity where India's service sector has comparative advantage. Aided by ICT, its corporations are increasingly becoming dependent on corporation-to-corporation trade, an area of international taxation that is getting tough to administer. Furthermore, the significance of outsourcing for India increased after the US restricted the number of foreigners who could travel to the US to provide services. In November 2001, Republican Congressman Tom Tancredo introduced the HR 3222 Act, titled 'The Hi-Tech Work Fairness and Economic Stimulus Act of 2001'. The Act was aimed at reducing the annual number of US H-1B visas from the current 195,000 to 65,000.[11] In 2000, Indian workers secured about 64.9 per cent of H-1B visas followed by the Chinese, who secured approximately 8.08 per cent of work visas.[12] In 2003, Indiana's Lieutenant Governor Kathy Davis overturned a $15.1 million deal between the state government and the Tata America International Group, the American subsidiary of Tata Consultancy Services, which would have saved the Indiana taxpayer about $8 million, on the grounds that enough was not being done for Indiana workers.[13] The American opposition to Indian service providers traveling to the US has increased India's dependence on the offshore model for exporting its services via the electronic route.

The offshore business picked up very well for Indian service providers. Taking advantage of the Internet and more exclusive corporate networks such as Intranets, global corporations found it easy to find their service providers in India. Kolkata-based Pricewaterhouse Coopers, which was taken over by IBM, provided

[9] Rudra (2002).

[10] Palan (2002).

[11] Mahalingam (2003).

[12] Murthy.com, 'Interesting H1B Statistics for 2000—India, Land of Techies', *www.murthy.com/UDtechie.html*. The website suggests that the data was procured from the US's Immigration and Naturalization Service.

[13] rediff.com, 'BPO Backlash! US State Nixes TCS Deal', *www.rediff.com/money/money/2003/nov/22bpo.html*.

software for constructing virtual markets. Indian software firms were customizing the customer relationship management software products of Oracle and Seibel for transnational firms.[14] Much of India's software work demanded converting the old systems of corporations written in Cobol and Fortran into new programming languages such as C+ and Java. This work earned India $2.1 billion out of a total export basket of $5.7 billion. A BCG (Boston Consulting Group)–NASSCOM (National Association of Software and Service Companies, New Delhi) study in 2001 had predicted the role of e-solutions in India's information technology export basket. It was evident that outsourcing would drive this business.[15] This $180 billion business in 2000 included activities such as customer relationship management, supply chain management, enterprise resource planning, information management, Internet services, and application service provision.[16] India's software and services exports are poised to grow at a rate between 26 per cent and 28 per cent from $12 billion in 2003 to $15.5 billion in 2004.[17]

Indian corporations excelled in taking advantage of offshore facilities to a greater extent than the BCG–NASSCOM study had predicted. A Gartner study predicted that it would be tough to beat India with respect to the scale of operations in the short run. In most other countries the labour pool was smaller and it would be tough to get large scale work done. India possessed strengths with respect to the quality and quantity of qualified English speaking manpower with requisite infrastructure. In the information technology enabled services (ITES), business process outsourcing (BPO) segment, human resource services involved payroll management; customer care involved call centres, remote maintenance, and support centres; payment services pertained to back-office support for credit and check processing; digital content development included animation, engineering design, and website design; administration involved data processing, medical transcription, and insurance claims processing; and finance dealt with revenue accounting. According to the Gartner

[14] Customer relationship management involves using the Internet to collect customer data, which can be processed and used to target customers.

[15] For the success of the global offshore model due to information technology see Cairncross (2001), chapter 6. For an understanding of how Indian firms exploited the global offshore model see Mukherji (2002).

[16] The Boston Consulting Group (BCG) and NASSCOM (2001), pp. 16–17.

[17] NASSCOM, 'NASSCOM Estimates $12 Billion Exports this Year', downloaded from NASSCOM's virtual media room, *www.nasscom.org/artdisplay.asp?Art_id = 2359.*

Group, offshore IT services and offshore business process outsourcing services in India would register a compound annual growth rate of 29 per cent and 68 per cent respectively between 2002 and 2007.[18] According to NASSCOM, the information technology-enabled services-aided business process outsourcing grew by 59.1 per cent in 2002–03, and was likely to grow by 54 per cent to about $3.6 billion in 2003–04. Customer care and payments and billing services recorded the highest growth rates in this ITES-BPO segment.[19]

To give just one example, Wipro, one of India's top three IT companies, announced a 19 per cent increase in net profit (Rs 2.74 billion or approximately $6.08 million) in the third quarter ending 31 December 2003. Vivek Paul, its US-based vice president, was bullish about the prospects of the offshore model despite labour resentment in the US.[20]

India turned global after 1991. After years of import substitution that could be reversed neither by a severe balance of payments crisis in 1966 nor by the oil shocks, India's political economy had become resistant to increased trade orientation.[21] Rajiv Gandhi tried hard to change course in the 1990s and provided some support to the information technology sector.[22] It was left for Dr Manmohan Singh under the prime ministership of P. V. N. Rao to change course by making a virtue of necessity during India's second severe balance of payments crisis in 1991.[23] Trade orientation was introduced by substantial reforms in industrial and trade policy, the financial sector, and by allowing foreign investment with greater ease.[24] The National

[18] Dataquest, 'Gartner Study Projects Outsourcing to be the Fastest Growing Segment in IT Industry', *www.dqindia.com/content/gartner/103071805.asp*. See also SearchCIO.com, 'Gartner: Offshore Outsourcing Horse Has Left the Barn', *searchcio.techtarget.com/qna/0,289202, sid19_gc913695,00.html*. See also MVIRDC World Trade Centre and Rajiv Gandhi Institute for Contemporary Studies, 2003, *Digitized Trade Rules and India's Service Sector*, Mumbai and New Delhi.

[19] NASSCOM, 'ITES-BPO Industry to Grow 54% by FY04,' *www.nasscom.org/artdisplay.asp?Art_id = 2361*.

[20] *Business Standard* (2004). For an interesting story about a much smaller firm iGATE, which recently won a contract probably worth $20 million see *Asiatimes.com*, 'iGATE with' 5 Year Deal with US Firm': *www/atimes.com/atimes/South-Asia/FA22Df01.html*.

[21] For the political economy of the 1966 balance of payments crisis see Mukherji (2000). For an analysis of the two oil shocks see Ahluwalia (1986).

[22] For the half-hearted reforms of the mid- to late-1980s, see Kohli (1990).

[23] Mukherji (2004).

[24] Ahluwalia (2002).

Democratic Alliance Government sustained the momentum and pursued privatization with some vigour.[25]

The reforms helped India's service sector by making imports cheaper and by improving the information technology infrastructure.[26] When the global offshore model worked without the need for the work visa, there was political resistance in the US to US service sector jobs deserting to India. In March 2004, the Senate passed the Defending American Jobs Act of 2004, which received 70 votes in favor and 26 votes against it. The Act would discourage outsourcing in privatized federal work, federal procurements and state government procurement of federal work. The Act was supported by the trade unions AFL-CIO and the Communication Workers of America.[27] States have been more proactive than the Federal Government in this regard. States that either have legislation or bills introduced to curb outsourcing included New Jersey, Indiana, Michigan, North Carolina, South Carolina, California, Colorado, Connecticut, Kansas, Maryland, Michigan, Missouri, Mississippi, South Dakota, Washington, and Tennessee.[28] In addition, the city of Philadelphia in Pennsylvania is also in the process of introducing legislation.[29]

The success of the offshore model raises puzzling questions for the taxation of business profits when value addition from different parts of the globe becomes much easier to aggregate into a single product. Will digitization-driven globalization lead to an erosion of precious revenue for developing countries like India? This paper situates India's interests with respect to the taxation of business profits primarily in the context of the preferences expressed by the US and Australia. It will deal with two explicitly trade-related issues concerning international corporate taxation, namely source-based taxation and permanent establishment. How can poor countries like India protect their tax base to ensure sustainable economic growth?

This paper argues that digitization-propelled international trade may erode the fiscal authority of states. If that happened, the gains for India's revenue department from the taxation of service sector profits

[25] Nayar (2002); Thakurta (2002); Kapur et al. (2004).

[26] Saxenian (2003).

[27] See Gross Grant, 'Lawmakers Push Offshore Outsourcing Legislation', *www.info-world.com/article/04/03/05/HNoffshoregovt_1.html* (5 March 2004).

[28] American Electronics Association, 'Outsourcing Legislation in the States', *www.aeanet.org/GovernmentAffairs/gamb_StateOutsorceSummary.asp* (updated 17 February 2004).

[29] Press Trust of India, 'US Cannot Run Away From Outsourcing', *www.expressindia.com/fullstory.php?nwesid = 29464* (19 March 2004).

for value creation in India would not be realized. Globalization should aid social spending in a poor country. Unilateral attempts to fix this problem will lead either to tax erosion or to double taxation. Digitized trade, or the trade in goods and services aided by the Internet and related channels, made it easy to penetrate foreign markets without the need for physical presence in a foreign country. This generated significant debates in international taxation, on the salience of source- versus residence-based taxation, and the definition of what should constitute permanent establishment.

The case for global standards is made in two stages. The following two sections review the debates on source-based versus residence-based taxation and permanent establishment respectively. The section, 'Governing International Corporate Taxation' concludes by making the case that the problem of international taxation in the digitized world has no unilateral answers. Rather the problem is one of creating global standards that will check both double taxation and tax evasion, and will facilitate compliance. If some countries impose source-based rules and others, residence-based rules, this may lead to double taxation. Unilateral adoption of residence-based rules may empower tax havens and lead to massive tax evasion. Servers as permanent establishment would either enrich tax havens or server-rich countries in the short run. This paper suggests a view sympathetic to the interests of capital-scarce countries like India, which have the potential for exports. It also pays due regard to the interests of capital-abundant countries like the US, the EU states, and Japan.

Source-based versus Residence-based Taxation

The debate regarding residence- versus source-based taxation concerns the extent of the ties between people who own, control and manage an enterprise, versus the location where most business employees, property and activities are situated. It concerns the location where business profits may be taxed. The primacy of source-based taxation owes its origin to four economists from the US, The Netherlands, the UK and Italy, who were commissioned by the League of Nations in 1921 to evolve general principles in order to solve the problem of double taxation. Their work provided the foundation for source-based taxation, which is the basis for double taxation treaties between countries.[30]

[30] 'Report on Double Taxation', League of Nations, Doc. No. EFS 73 F. 19 (1923). My knowledge about this report is from Frost (1997), pp. 1459–62.

The economists disentangled the idea of situs from the idea of origin. Situs is a physical location where property is situated, or where the business transaction takes place. Origin is the specific place where income is produced. They explained that origin is:

> the place where wealth is produced, that is, the community of economic life which makes possible the yield of the acquisition of the wealth. This yield or acquisition is due, however, not only to a particular thing but to the human relations which may help in creating them.[31]

The economists opined that wealth originates through people who reside in a community, and it would be a mistake not to look at the people who create that wealth. In colonial times, the situs (residence) of a corporation trading in tea could be England but the human agencies (source) that help to create the wealth from tea plantations could be in a multitude of countries. The human agencies involved could be the superintendent of the plantation (in the country of the plantation), transport agencies that bring tea to the market (in the plantation country and market countries), the residence of the chief executive responsible for policy (which could be where the situs is or anywhere else), and the place where the sales agents and markets are located. All these factors would have to be taken into account and assigned weights to establish the source of income.

For the purpose of digitized trade, it is important to note that the economists divided business income into three categories: (1) business profits closely related to immovable property (e.g., mining income), (2) business profits derived from factories, and (3) business profits derived from commercial establishments with a fixed head office. The economists were mindful of the fact that control was more easily possible from a distance with the advance of transportation and communication technology. They concluded that the country of source had the preponderant right to tax such business income. Income from stocks and bonds, however, could be taxed in the country of domicile (residence).

This is the basis of the present system of international taxation. Taxing rights related to business profits reside in the country of source, and taxing rights related to more passive types of income like dividends and interest are predominantly assigned to the country of residence. Double taxation is avoided, and an unnecessary burden on commerce is removed.

[31] Frost (1997), p. 1460.

Courts in the US have upheld the principle of source-based taxation, evident in *Piedras Negras Broadcasting Co. v. United States* (1941). The issue was whether a Mexican radio station that had US source should thereby have been subject to US tax? The operator of the radio station executed all the contracts with advertisers in Mexico and performed all the services required of the contracts in Mexico. All the broadcasts originated in Mexico as the station's only studio was in Mexico. The taxpayer maintained a US address in a hotel room where it counted and allocated the funds it received each day. The majority of the listeners and 95 per cent of the broadcasting station's income were in the US. In concluding that the source of the taxpayer's income was located outside the US, the Fifth Court looked to the location of the taxpayer's physical and human capital in deciding what dominated the characterization of source.[32]

Why did the US court decide not to tax the firm in the US, even though most of the revenues came from the US? Source-based taxation emphasizes the salience, for the purposes of international taxation of business profits, of the place where value creation takes place rather than the location where the service is consumed. Since value creation was taking place entirely in Mexico the revenue collecting operation in the US was not considered significant enough for the purposes of taxation in the US.

The US has contemplated implementing residence-based taxation. The US Treasury's White Paper in 1996, which was meant for discussion and critical appraisal only, made the case that e-commerce leads to such complications that ultimately source-based taxation may become obsolete, and, the time had come for *shifting to residence-based taxation*.[33] This is a significant development because it challenges a 75-year-old system supported by over 1,000 bilateral treaties. The Treasury's paper was not contradicted by the White House's Report on Global Electronic Commerce in July 1997.[34] Joseph Guttentag, the senior advisor to the assistant secretary (tax policy), Department of Treasury in 1996, has upheld the same principle in an article published in November 2001.[35] The OECD's Model Tax Treaty is guided by residence-based principles.

[32] Frost (1997), pp. 1463–4.

[33] Department of Treasury, *Selected Tax Policy Implications of Global Electronic Commerce* (Washington: Office of Tax Policy, 1996), sections 7.1.1–7.1.5, *www.treas.gov/taxpolicy/library/internet/txt*.

[34] Frost (1997), p. 1458; Hellerstein (2002).

[35] Guttentag (2001).

The Treasury's view suggested that it might be tough to link an item of income to a specific geographical source in an age of digitization. A transnational firm providing services such as consulting could easily use the Internet to exploit value addition taking place in its subsidiaries in a number of countries. Finding the source of each component of the income could be a cumbersome process. Second, residence-based taxation by reducing the importance of the distinctions between business profits, royalties and income from services would make it easier to implement it. The US Congress's Tax Reform Act (1986) adopted residence-based rules for the sale of certain non-inventory property, and in the case of certain ocean and space activities. Moreover, all taxpayers according to the Treasury's view are resident somewhere. It would therefore be easy to tax US residents.[36]

The problems with this view are manifold. First, public finance experts and tax lawyers have argued that the question of residence is not settled easily either. The US uses the place of incorporation test, while many other countries rely on the 'place of effective management', as a test for residence.[37] According to two eminent legal authorities, Doernberg and Hinnekens, 'If the definition of residence is artificial and easily manipulated, granting exclusive authority to residence countries is not a good solution.'[38]

Second, even if residence found a universally acceptable definition, it (residence) could be shifted with greater ease for tax planning purposes than the source of value creation. While it might be tough to locate where a transaction took place, it is not easy to obliterate the human endeavor that led to these transactions.[39] It is not easy to take Bangalore or Silicon Valley to Monte Carlo. But digitization makes it easy to incorporate a firm in Monte Carlo and outsource work to Hyderabad. The EU is promoting the Portuguese island of Madeira in the Atlantic, several hundred miles off the west coast of North Africa, as an e-commerce hub for tax planning purposes.[40]

[36] Department of Treasury, *Selected Tax Policy Implications of Global Electronic Commerce*, section 7.1.5.

[37] The place of incorporation test concerns where a firm is legally incorporated. The 'place of effective management' takes into account a number of factors that decide where the firm is managed. A firm may be incorporated in one place but be effectively managed from another. For guidance on the 'place of effective management' for the purposes of e-commerce see OECD((2001).

[38] Quoted in McLure (2001). McLure elaborates on this problem in the same article.

[39] Frost (1997), p. 1471.

[40] Hardesty (2002).

Tax havens or low-tax locations could negatively affect the fiscal sovereignty of producer countries if taxation was based on residence. Tax havens have benefited due to the sovereign control of governments over fiscal policy in an age of information technology, when corporations and individuals can easily shift resources to realize the gains from low-tax locations. According to one estimate, 20 per cent of total private wealth and 22 per cent of the external assets of all banks were invested offshore.[41] Despite the movement of finance capital to offshore locations, source-based rules have ensured that the richest countries of the world are still the ones where wealth creation is taking place. The OECD has sought to curb tax havens.[42]

The digitized route aids corporate entities to incorporate themselves in tax havens, and to outsource their work anytime, anywhere. If taxation were based on residence rather than on source, then large corporations would have the incentive to incorporate themselves in low-tax locations; they could outsource work to regions where value could be created at low cost. Value creation resulting from outsourcing could occur in India, but the firm which outsourced its activities, would be taxed only where it was headquartered. This would contradict the benefit principle of taxation.[43] Countries that provide benefits in the form of the physical and human capital essential for value creation, should be able to raise the revenue which aided the creation of an environment of productivity in the first place.

Two further benefits accrue to capital-abundant countries from an application of the residence principle. First, transnational corporations headquartered in capital-abundant countries would not have to worry about the tax rules of the host country. This capital export neutrality would make investment decisions at the headquarters relatively easy. Second, all capital-abundant countries with their multinationals headquartered in their respective territories would be able to tax global profits. Thus, EU-headquartered transnational corporations would be able to tax profits generated in the US, and American multinationals would be able to do the same with profits generated in the EU. Since capital-abundant countries have

[41] On the emergence of tax havens see Palan (2002), pp. 151–76. On the relationship between the proposed residence-based taxation of e-commerce and the facilitation of tax havens see McLure (2001), p. 336; Li (1999).

[42] See OECD, *Harmful Tax Competition* (Paris: OECD, 1998). It can be downloaded from *www.oecd.org/dataoecd/33/0/1904176.pdf.*

[43] On the benefit principle in relation to e-commerce taxation see Li (1999), p. 1456; McLure (2000).

multinationals with operations in each other's territories, the benefits to such countries would be mutual. Rich countries within the OECD, which are able to tax the global revenue of their transnational corporations, have favoured this approach.

For poorer countries like India, China, Philippines, Russia, South Africa, and even Australia, which depended more on the taxation of value creation within their territory than on revenues from the global profits of their transnational firms, the incentives were just the opposite. If the residence principle were followed, then value creation in these countries in aid of transnational firms headquartered within rich countries would be taxed where the transnational firm was headquartered. Countries with few corporations with global operations would lose revenue to those with more such corporations. This could lead to a redistribution of revenues in favour of capital-abundant countries. The developing-country view represented within the UN and some recent work within the OECD, which consulted representatives from India and Australia, brings out this conflict of interest rather well.[44]

The residence principle is not easy to administer. Vito Tanzi has suggested that US transnational firms have been underreporting their profits by using certain transfer pricing methods. For example, a global corporation can finance capital investment in a subsidiary from a loan from a low-tax country rather than from equity capital. Instead of receiving dividends it will receive interest payments. The company will show lower profits because of the limited use of equity capital and will pay lower taxes. Another easy way to show lower profit in the subsidiary is to show research and development charges, and high charges for the use of brand names or patents. Such manoeuvres are reducing the tax from capital incomes in capital-abundant countries.[45] Apart from these problems, the exchange of information among tax authorities is not an easy process. Sometimes the data may not be available or may be stored in formats that are not easily retrievable. Tax havens that have commercialized their sovereign rights may view data sharing as an infringement of their sovereignty.[46]

Source-based principles, on the other hand, allow for taxation where value was created. Firms incorporated in the US subcontract their

[44] Tanzi (1995). See also OECD (2003). This was a public discussion draft that could be downloaded from *www.oecd.org/dataoecd/2/38/20655083.pdf*.

[45] Tanzi (1995), pp. 99–101.

[46] Tanzi (1995), pp. 86–9.

work to firms in other countries. If non-US firms were able to work for US customers without the need for significant presence in the US, they would be able to avoid taxation in the US according to source-based principles, and, would be taxed in countries where value was created. Residence-based principles, on the other hand, would lead to the taxation of the same business in the US, and to loss of revenue for source countries. Countries like India and Australia are likely to collect most of their revenues through source-based taxation rather than via residence-based taxation.[47]

Indian business interests lay predominantly in the work outsourced to them in the area of software services for legacy application, supply chain management, customer relationship management, enterprise resource planning, information management, and banking and financial services. Outsourcing of business processes such as call centres, billing and payments operations, and customer care were a high growth area. Similarly, most Australian businesses facilitated by the NET involved work sourced in Australia rather than work sourced elsewhere but coordinated by companies incorporated in Australia. This included travel, books, consulting, and ICT services. If Indian and Australian companies were treated in the way Piedras Negras Broadcasting Company was treated by the US (based on source), this would benefit Indian and Australian business and revenue authorities.

Australia, India, and South Africa have argued for the continuing vitality of source-based taxation. *The Australian White Paper* (December 1999) was a significant statement in favour of source-based taxation. It asserted that Australian jurisprudence begins with the comment by Isaacs J in *Nathan v FC of T* (1918): 'The legislature in using the word 'source' meant, not a legal concept, but something which a practical man would regard as the real source of income.'[48] If, in the case of services involving highly specialized knowledge, the result of the performance of a service became more important than the location at which the service was really performed, by giving undue emphasis to the place of contract, the place of payment, or even where the services were utilised, then there could be increased scope for locating such activities for tax planning purposes. The assumption here was that such activities (more easily identified with residence rather than

[47] On the matter of equity considerations arising out of residence-based taxation, see Frost (1997), p. 1472; Hellerstein (2002), pp. 17–18; and Li (1999), p. 1457.

[48] Australian Taxation Office, *Tax and the Internet: Second Report December 1999* (Canberra: Australian Government Publishing Service, December 1999), p. 79.

source) could be more easily relocated to tax havens rather than the relocation of the actual performance of a highly-skilled service.[49] One may conduct deals related to the supply of high-end embedded software in tax havens, but such software may only be produced in the Silicon Valley. To quote the position of Australian law: 'Unless income is derived from property used in Australia or from acts done in Australia there would seem little likelihood that an Australian court would find that the source of the income was in Australia.'[50]

The Indian Finance Ministry's Report (July 2001) expressed concern regarding the distributional issue involved with the shift from source- to residence-based taxation even more explicitly. Especially worrying for India's tax authority was the fact that equilibrium in revenue sharing between countries of source and countries of residence was not even one of the stated objectives of the OECD or the US at the time when the report came out. It made arguments similar to the ones above about the problems of determining residence. It opined that there was no substitute to the 'place of effective management test'. When the 'place of effective management' was difficult to determine after giving due consideration to a variety of factors, source-based taxation should prevail.[51]

Table 5.1 summarizes the arguments made above. The source principle is favorable to all countries that create value, including the capital-abundant ones. The residence principle is favourable for capital-abundant countries with global operations. The source principle gives autonomy to the host state to decide which sectors it wishes to invite investments in. Both source-based rules and residence-based rules are tough to administer. Source principles discourage tax planning. Residence would be a new standard, which will involve negotiating costs. Countries like India, Australia, and South Africa which need to tax value creation within their territory, enjoy autonomy with regard to directing foreign investment and discourage tax havens from benefiting from precious revenue, have understandably argued in favour of the time-tested source principle.

[49] Australian Taxation Office, *Tax and the Internet: Second Report December 1999*, p. 91.

[50] Australian Taxation Office, *Tax and the Internet: Second Report December 1999*.

[51] Central Board of Direct Taxes, 'Report of the High Powered Committee on Electronic Commerce and Taxation' (New Delhi: Ministry of Finance, Government of India, 2001), pp. 60–5.

TABLE 5.1: COMPARISON OF TYPES OF CORPORATE TAXATION

Source-based	*Residence-based*
1. Revenue collection for all countries creating value. Favourable for capital-scarce countries.	More favourable for countries with many firms that operate globally.
2. Capital import neutrality. All firms operating from abroad face similar tax conditions in host country. Greater autonomy for host country taxpolicy for deciding investment.	Capital export neutrality. Investors need not take account of domestic tax conditions in the host country. Simpler world for the investor.
3. Tough to administer without international cooperation.	Tough to administer without international cooperation.
4. Tax havens discouraged.	Tax havens encouraged.
5. Established norm.	New standard with negotiating costs involved.

Permanent Establishment

The mainstay of the double taxation convention is the concept of permanent establishment (PE), that constitutes the threshold of commercial activity in a foreign country beyond which a firm can be taxed in that country. In other words, it indicates the amount of financial and human investment required in a foreign country by a firm so that it could be said to have established residence in that country for the purposes of taxation. Consistent with the logic of the League's economists, the OECD Model Treaty sets three conditions: 'a fixed place of business through which the business of the enterprise is wholly or partly carried out.'[52] PE has three key elements: (1) the existence of a place of business; (2) the fixed nature of this place of business; and (3) conducting the business of the enterprise through this fixed place (i.e., agents who are dependent on the enterprise conduct its business through this fixed place). Economic allegiance must involve having people working for the enterprise in another country through a fixed place of business. The case of PE would not arise if people dependent on the enterprise simply went to set up

[52] OECD model Treaty, article 5(1).

machines in another country. If an enterprise merely leases industrial, commercial or scientific equipment, buildings or intangible property to an enterprise of another state, this does not constitute a PE of the lessee. Generally, PE does not include the use of facilities merely for the purposes of storage, delivery or display of goods.[53]

Digitization enables corporations to engage in commercial activities abroad without the need for them to operate through a fixed place of business with dependent agents at work. Since the threshold of economic activity in the age of digitization has less to do with the physical corporate presence through PE, states have begun to worry about their ability to tax businesses that may penetrate foreign markets without the need for human involvement in the foreign country. The likelihood of uncertain tax revenues in the age of digitization has led to considerable thinking within the OECD regarding how to adjust the concept of PE to take account of the special circumstances created by digitization.

The OECD has taken the following position on Article 5 of the OECD Model Tax Convention. The majority view within the OECD is that a website hosting arrangement does not constitute PE as it does not constitute a tangible personal property.[54]

Second, the majority view is that human intervention is not required at the place of permanent establishment.[55] This view is backed by a case in German law, where the German Supreme Tax Court held that a German stretch of an automated underground pipeline owned by a Dutch company that supplied oil to German customers constituted German PE.[56] If automation performed all the functions of human agency, then human agency would not be central to PE.

Third, if a website used a server hosted by an Internet service provider (ISP) these contracts do not result in PE. Merely using scientific, commercial and industrial equipment that is the property of another company is not enough to establish PE.

Consistent with the precedent in German law, if a firm using a website has a server at its own disposal (i.e. if it owns the server), then this could lead to PE. For PE, the server would have to be fixed in a certain place for a sufficient amount of time. The business operation

[53] For a brilliant discussion on this topic, see Frost (1997), p. 1467.

[54] Spain and Portugal have taken the opposite view. See OECD, *Taxation and Electronic Commerce*, p. 80.

[55] OECD, *Taxation and Electronic Commerce*, p. 81.

[56] Frost (1997), pp. 1469–70.

needs to be wholly or partly carried out at the location where the server is present. Merely auxiliary functions performed by the server such as providing a communications link, advertising goods and services, relaying information through a mirror server for security and efficiency purposes, gathering market data for the enterprise or supplying information, is not sufficient for PE.[57]

The core functions of the enterprise have to be determined on a case-by-case basis. For example, for ISPs hosting websites or other applications, servers are an essential part of their commercial activity and could not be treated as preparatory or auxiliary. Automated servers for ISPs could constitute permanent establishment even without the involvement of human agency. On the other hand, if an e-retailer is using its own server at a given location, this is not enough to conclude that the activities being carried out by the server satisfy the threshold of preparatory or auxiliary activities.[58]

Finally, an ISP does not constitute an agent of the enterprise for the purposes of PE. This is due to the fact that they do not have the authority to conclude contracts, nor could they do so on a regular basis.[59]

There is a technological problem behind the notion that automated company-owned servers could constitute PE if they perform the core functions of the firm. The geographical location of a server in a particular country is not central to locating the business activity in that country. Servers would therefore migrate to low-tax locations, enriching tax havens. Soon it might be possible to put these devices in satellites that orbit the earth.[60]

Servers as PE could erode the tax base of market countries. This might encourage firms to evade taxes by locating their servers in low-tax locations. There may be a need to look at the source of income rather than put undue weight on the server for locating the place where taxation should occur, especially because the source of income cannot migrate to low-tax locations as easily as the servers can. Second, servers as permanent establishment would benefit the US most, as the majority of the world's servers are located in the US.

[57] OECD, *Taxation and Electronic Commerce*, pp. 82–5.

[58] OECD, *Taxation and Electronic Commerce*, pp. 84–5.

[59] OECD, *Taxation and Electronic Commerce*.

[60] Lodin (2001); Kobrin(2001). New Jersey-based Internet companies were discouraged when they learned that if a company put its server for hosting its data in New Jersey, this would constitute business presence in the state; see Hellerstein (2002), p. 12.

The US Treasury's paper in 1996 had made general remarks about the possibility of extending the concept of PE to e-commerce. The Treasury was satisfied with the OECD's work on PE.[61] The UK had opposed the possibility that servers may constitute PE.[62]

The *Australian White Paper* reflected on this issue. It deemed at least six months as being time enough for a server to be considered fixed. While movement within a building might constitute no deviation from the fixed place, it worried about the OECD's ambiguity about the movement of portable servers from one building to another, or from one city to another.[63]

It noted the problem of tax havens. It found that some types of business require PE while other types do not. In an earlier age, source rules were applicable to a foreign firm until the firm got engaged in sufficient economic activity in a foreign country to require a fixed place of work involving sufficient human intervention (i.e. PE). This led to a fairly equitable sharing of revenue between countries of source and countries of residence, and avoided double taxation. In the world of digitized trade, the residence of servers has little to do with the location of business. The Australian Taxation Office held that the way to deal with this problem could be to define taxation in a resident country based on a threshold of economic activity rather than on physical presence, or to develop specific provisions about treating business profits under electronic commerce.[64]

The Indian Finance Ministry's Report criticized the definition of servers as PE for the following reasons. It pointed out that there is no necessary correlation between the location of the server and the country of business, thus creating the possibility that relocation of servers could enrich tax havens due to such regulation. This would create uncertainty with regard to the collection of tax revenues. It suggested the need for an alternative to the concept of PE within the OECD or the UN. It was concerned that the server as a PE might

[61] Department of Treasury, *Selected Tax Policy Implications of Global Electronic Commerce*, section 7.2. That the treasury is satisfied is evident from Guttentag (2001, 552).

[62] OECD, *Taxation and Electronic Commerce*, p. 82.

[63] Australian Taxation Office, *Tax and the Internet: Second Report December 1999*, pp. 98–9.

[64] Australian Taxation Office, *Tax and the Internet: Second Report December 1999*, pp. 107–10.

threaten the existing equilibrium between countries of residence and countries of source. To avoid this problem, the Finance Ministry opined that when the 'place of effective management' is tough to determine, source-based rules should apply.[65]

The debate regarding whether or not a server should constitute PE is a debate among countries concerned with the distribution of revenue in a digitized world. All countries worry about an erosion of their tax base if electronic commerce goes untaxed. However, the geographical distribution of revenue in a world where servers could constitute PE, will redound to the advantage of countries with a high density of servers. The US is the undisputed leader in the area and will benefit in the short run if servers are defined as PE. Server-scarce countries like India, which may have benefited from source-based taxation, would lose out on revenues with this definition. This explains the opposition of UK and India to this definition, as well as the Australian concern with the distributional consequences of servers as PE.

In the long run, however, both countries of source and countries of residence have something to fear from the possibility that servers as PE will enrich low-tax locations, as the geographical location of servers is not systematically related to the geographical location of business activities.

Governing International Corporate Taxation

There is no international body to coordinate corporate taxation in the digitized age. The League of Nations had done pioneering work on the taxation of business profits, which is incorporated in bilateral double taxation treaties among countries. This work has now been taken over by the OECD. Digitized trade is forcing countries to evolve standards or norms that will govern international taxation. This section draws on the insights of the previous section to cull out the reasons why policy coordination is essential for maintaining fiscal sovereignty.

The paper has highlighted the relationship between the rise of digitized trade and the uncertain future of corporate taxation. The standards proposed for digitized trade taxation for ensuring fiscal

[65] Central Board of Direct Taxes, GOI, 'Report of The High Powered Committee on Electronic Commerce and Taxation', pp. 64–75.

sovereignty in two vital areas of international corporate taxation, namely source—versus residence-based taxation and PE, will have consequences for the global distribution of revenue. Can the conflict of interest be overtaken by the common interest in preserving fiscal sovereignty for revenue collection and trade promotion?

Standards or rules are very important for any kind of governance. Sometimes a rule is uncontroversial. It benefits everyone equally. For example, 'drive to the left' of the road could be a rule. If everybody followed this rule, all would benefit equally from this rule. If some followed the 'drive to the left' rule and others followed the 'drive to the right' rule, there would be more accidents.

At other times, some rules benefit some people more than others. For example, free trade may benefit exporters and consumers but not domestic producers who cannot compete in the international market. The government will have to weigh the concerns of the winners and losers before it can decide how open its economy must be to exports from foreign countries. Similarly, states need to come together and discuss their concerns regarding rules pertaining to corporate taxation in the digitized trade (Table 5.2). The above discussion highlighted who the winners and losers might be if a particular rule comes into operation. There is a need for the international community to deliberate the concerns of different countries before arriving at a compromise that minimizes costs and maximizes gains.[66]

The Internet makes it easy for countries where valuable ICT services are being produced to penetrate markets without the need of a permanent establishment in these countries. The Treasury's suggestion to shift from source-based taxation to residence-based taxation seems to be motivated by the US's perceived uncertainty regarding revenue collection via the source-based route in the Internet age. The argument that the administration of source-based tax collection is tougher than residence-based collection is problematic due to the absence of a widely accepted standard governing the definition of residence and the administrative reasons mentioned above.

Defining residence as the principle of taxation will lead to a shift in revenue collection in favor of capital-abundant countries like the US and other rich OECD countries. India is predominantly a capital-scarce country where value creation is being sourced. It will continue to plead for the continuing vitality of source-based taxation.

[66] Kaul et al. (1999).

TABLE 5.2: STANDARDS FOR TAXING DIGITIZED TRADE

Recommendations	*Pros*	*Cons*
Source-based Taxation	(1A) Benefits all source countries—consistent with benefit principle *Good for India*.	(1A*) Monitor possible erosion of tax base in market countries. Need for a moderately costly 'escape clause.'
	(1B) Avoids enriching tax havens.	
	(1C) Current equilibrium in revenue distribution between source and market countries unaltered.	
Server not PE	(2A) Consistent with traditional source-based principles. *Good for India*.	
	(2B) Will check disparity of revenue-sharing between server-scarce and server-abundant countries.	(2B*) Monitor possible revenue erosion in market countries. Need for a moderately costly 'escape clause.'
	(2C) Tax havens discouraged.	

There are three benefits from this approach. First, while the US is the major market it is also a significant creator of value in ICT services. There is reason to believe that value creation sourced in the US and propelled by corporations like Intel, Microsoft, Dell, Amazon, and Cisco, among others, will protect US revenues if source remains the principle for taxation. The Information Technology Association of America has opposed the Defending American Jobs Act of 2004 on the grounds that the US's ICT sector exports much more than it imports. It is necessary to keep the US economy open so that others do the same, realizing the benefits of global economic interdependence. The American Electronic Association also seems to have a similar view.[67]

Second, maintaining an old standard (source) is much cheaper than negotiating numerous bilateral treaties based on a new one

[67] Grant Gross, 'Lawmakers Push Offshore Outsourcing Legislation', *www.infoworld.com/article/04/03/05/Hnoffshoregovt_1.html* (5 March 2004). American Electronics Association, 'Outsourcing Legislation in the States,' *www.aeanet.org/GovernmentAffairs/gamb_StateOutsourceSummary.asp* (last updated 17 February 2004).

(residence) all over again. Third, residence-based taxation is likely to empower tax havens. This will erode the fiscal sovereignty of all source countries, which produce goods and services that benefit due to digitization. Since the US is a major source of value creation in the ICT sector, its tax authorities, in conjunction with other major source countries, should thwart the ability of havens to exploit residence-based taxation.

Revenue authorities in market countries should continue to monitor their revenues. The perceived uncertainty for fiscal authorities in market countries can be guarded through an 'escape clause', in the case of drastic shortfall in revenues as a result of source-based taxation in the digital age. Escape clauses need to be moderately priced, so that the cost of escape avoids both defection and easy escape. If the conditions for opting out of the source-based principle are tough to comply with, countries facing a fiscal crisis will defect unilaterally and enact residence-based principles. On the other hand, if it is too easy to adopt the residence standard, then countries which have not suffered significant fiscal injury will adopt the residence standard if that fetches them more revenues at the cost of others. For source-based taxation to be the standard there must be sanctions against the easy use of the residence principle.[68]

The OECD has defined automated servers using a fixed location for a certain period, and performing certain core functions of the firm, to be a candidate worthy of PE. A fixed place of business, involving considerable human and financial intervention, where commercial activity takes place over a period of time, is the conventional norm of PE. The current definition rules out the need for human intervention. The US, as the most server-abundant country, would benefit. Automated fixed servers performing the core functions of a firm, as PE, will help to tilt the distribution of revenue derived from ICT services in favor of the US.

Server-scarce countries have understandably opposed this move. Servers as PE will redistribute revenues away from server-scarce to server-abundant countries. India and the UK have opposed this move. Australia, while cautious in its judgment, has noted the lack of connection between the physical presence of servers and the magnitude of revenues.

Server-rich countries will not gain in the long run as a server could migrate to tax havens or even to outer space in the not so distant

[68] Rosendorff et al. (2001).

future. Like residence, PE via an automated server is easier to relocate than a particular skill dependent on human capital and attendant externalities necessary for service production. It is cheap to produce a certain kind of software in the Silicon Valley and another kind in Bangalore because of a combination of wages, skill sets and externalities present in these two locations. These will not easily migrate to tax havens. *The migration of source to tax havens,* being less likely than the migration of servers to tax havens, source-based taxation should remain the mainstay of taxation. Source-based taxation, with the possibility of escape from it in case of serious injury *to a country's revenue, seems to be a viable standard.*

In sum, India and other countries which create value but do not have many global corporations of their own will negotiate in favor of source-based taxation and against the OECD view that automated servers performing the core functions of a firm be defined as permanent establishment. These include China, Russia, Philippines, Australia and South Africa. This view merits attention.

The need for standards on the basis of a global consensus is acute. Without standards legitimated by sovereign governments, tax collection will not be easy in a digitized world. These standards could be based on source. They need to guard against tax havens and evolve 'escape' rules for countries hurt by the altered distribution of revenue as a result of digitized trade. Such rules may be moderately costly, so that with 'escape' it is neither too expensive to stay within the fold, nor too cheap to free-ride on the global consensus. There is the need for an organization based on sovereign equality for checking unilateralism and promoting coordination. The crucial question is, when will states learn that benefits from cooperation outweigh the losses from unilateralism.[69]

References

Ahluwalia, Montek S., 2002, 'Economic Reforms in India Since 1991: Has Gradualism Worked?', *Journal of Economic Perspectives,* vol. 16, no. 3, Summer, pp. 67–88.

——. 1986, 'Balance-of-Payments Adjustments in India, 1970–71 to 1983–84', *World Development,* vol. 14, no. 8, July, pp. 937–48.

[69] On how the WTO brought an end to US unilateralism, see Bhagwati (2002). The US promoted the WTO because the gains from multilateral trade cooperation outweighed the gains from unilateralism. For arguments in favour of a World Tax Organization, see McLure (2001), p. 340; Tanzi (2001).

Australian Taxation Office, 1999, *Tax and the Internet: Second Report December 1999*, Australian Government Publishing Service, Canberra, December.

Bhagwati, Jagdish, 2002, *Free Trade Today*, Princeton University Press, New Jersey, pp. 95–8.

Business Standard, 2004, 'Wipro Net Up 19% at Rs. 274 cr', 22 January, New Delhi, pp. 1, 10.

Cairncross, Frances, 2001, *The Death of Distance*, Harvard Business School Press, Boston, MA.

Cerny, Philip G., 1990, *The Changing Architecture of Politics: Structure, Agency, and the Future of the State*, Sage, Newbury Park, CA.

Frost, David L., 1997, 'The Continuing Vitality of Source-Based Taxation in the Electronic Age', *Tax Notes International*, vol. 15, no. 8, 3 November.

Garret, Geoffrey, 1998, *Partisan Politics in the Global Economy*, Cambridge University Press, Cambridge, UK.

Guttentag, Joseph H., 2001, 'Key Issues and Options in International Taxation: Taxation in an Interdependent World', *Bulletin for International Fiscal Documentation*, vol. 55, no. 11, November, pp. 551–2.

Hardesty, David, 2002, 'E-Commerce Taxation Around the World', *E-Commerce Tax News*, 24 November, *www.ecommercetax.com/doc/112402.html*.

Hellerstein, Walter, 2002, 'Electronic Commerce and the Challenge for Tax Administration', Seminar on Revenue Implications of E-commerce for Development, World Trade Organization—Committee on Trade and Development, Geneva, 22 April.

Kapstein, Ethan, 2001, 'The Third Way and International Order', in Anthony Giddens (ed.), *The Global Third Way Debate*, Polity Press, Oxford, pp. 378–9.

Kapur, Devesh and Ravi Ramamurthi, 2004, 'Privatization in India', Rahul Mukherji (ed.), *Economic Reforms: Political Economy of India*, Oxford University Press, New Delhi.

Kaul, Inge, Isabelle Grunberg and Marc A. Stern, 1999, 'Defining Global Public Goods', Inge Kaul, Isabelle Grunberg, and Marc A. Stern (eds.), *Global Public Goods*, Oxford University Press, New York and Oxford, pp. 2–19.

Kobrin, Stephen J., 2001, 'Territoriality and the Governance of Cyberspace', *Journal of International Business Studies*, vol. 32, no. 4, Fourth Quarter, p. 694.

Kohli, Atul, 1990, *Democracy and Discontent*, Cambridge University Press, Cambridge and New York, chapter 11.

Li, Jinyan, 1999, 'Rethinking Canada's Source Rules in the Age of Electronic Commerce: Part 2', *Canadian Tax Journal*, vol. 47, no. 6.

Lodin, Sven O., 2001, 'International Tax Issues in a Rapidly Changing World', *Bulletin for International Fiscal Documentation*, vol. 55, no. 1, January, p. 5.

Mahalingam, T. V., 2003, 'The Great Indian Job Threat', *DataQuest*, 15 January, New Delhi, pp. 66–71.

McLure, Charles, 2001, 'Globalization, Tax Rules and National Sovereignty', *Bulletin for International Fiscal Documentation*, vol. 55, no. 8, August.

——, 2000, 'Implementing State Income Taxes in the Digital Age', *National Tax Journal*, vol. 53, no. 4, December, pp. 1287–305.

Mukherji, Rahul, 2004, 'Economic Transition in a Plural Polity—India', Rahul Mukherji (ed.), *Economic Reforms: Political Economy of India*, Oxford University Press, Delhi.

——, 2002, 'The Governance of Digitized Trade Taxation', Rajiv Gandhi Institute for Contemporary Studies Working Paper Series 36, Rajiv Gandhi Foundation, New Delhi, pp. 2–12.

——, 2000, 'India Aborted Liberalization—1966', *Pacific Affairs*, vol. 73, no. 3 Fall, pp. 375–92.

MVIRDC World Trade Centre and Rajiv Gandhi Institute for Contemporary Studies, 2003, *Digitized Trade Rules and India's Service Sector*, Mumbai and New Delhi, pp. 13–19.

Nayar, Baldev R., 2002, 'The Limits of Economic Nationalism in India: Economic Reforms Under the BJP Led Government, 1998–1999', *Asian Survey*, vol. 40, no. 5, September/October, pp. 792–815.

OECD, 2001, *Taxation and Electronic Commerce*, OECD, Paris, pp. 145–57.

——, 2003, *Are The Current Treaty Rules For Taxing Business Profits Appropriate For E-Commerce?* OECD, Paris, November.

Palan, Ronen, 2002, 'Tax Havens and the Commercialization of State Sovereignty', *International Organization*, vol. 56, no. 1, Winter, pp. 151–76.

Paris, Roland, 2003, 'The Globalization of Taxation? Electronic Commerce and the Transformation of the State', *International Studies Quarterly*, vol 47, no. 2, June, pp. 153–82.

Rosendorff B. Peter and Helen V. Milner, 2001, 'The Optimal Design of International Trade Institutions: Uncertainty and Escape', *International Organization*, vol. 55, no. 4, Autumn, pp. 829–57.

Rudra, Nita, 2002, 'Globalization and the Decline of the Welfare State in Less Developed Countries', *International Organization*, vol. 56, no. 2, Spring, pp. 411–45.

Saxenian, AnnaLee, 2003, 'Bangalore: The Silicon Valley of Asia', Anne O. Krueger (ed.), *Economic Policy Reform and the Indian Economy*, Oxford University Press, New Delhi, pp. 169–92.

Schulze, Gunther G. and Heinrich W. Urspring, 1999, 'Globalization of the Economy and the Nation State', *The World Economy*, vol. 22, no. 3, May, pp. 320–2.

Steinmo, Sven, 2002, 'Globalization and Taxation: Challenges to the Swedish Welfare State', *Comparative Political Studies*, vol. 35, no. 7, September, pp. 839–62.

——, 2002, 'The New Political Economy of Taxation in Advanced Capitalist Democracies', *American Journal of Political Science*, vol. 46, no. 3, July, pp. 642–55.

Strange, Susan, 1996, *Retreat of the State,* Cambridge University Press, Cambridge.

Swank, Duane, 2002, *Global Capital: Political Institutions and Policy Change in Developed Welfare States,* Cambridge University Press, New York

Tanzi, Vito, 2001, 'Taxation and the Future of Social Protection', in Anthony Giddens (ed.), *The Global Third Way Debate,* Polity Press, Cambridge, pp. 188–97.

_____, 2001, 'Globalization and the Work of Fiscal Termites', *Finance and Development,* vol. 38, no. 1, March, pp. 34–7.

_____, 1995, *Taxation in an Integrating World,* The Brookings Institution, Washington, DC.

Thakurta, Paranjoy G., 2002, 'Ideological Contradictions in an Era of Coalitions', *Global Business Review,* vol. 3, no. 2, July–December, pp. 201–23.

The Boston Consulting Group (BCG) and NASSCOM, 2001, *E-commerce Opportunities for India Incorporated,* New Delhi.

6

Investigating Social Norms

Towards an Understanding of 'Embeddedness' in Regulation

SHAILAJA FENNEL

Introduction

In the last two decades there has been a rapid increase in new technologies and opportunities in economies, both in developed and developing countries. The narrow view of dealing with the economic externalities that might emerge from these new technologically-induced opportunities is that of 'internalizing' externalities (Demsetz 1968). There are also broader approaches that view the economic activities that emerge from grasping these opportunities as needing a wider notion of legislation through regulation to ensure efficiency and equity (Prosser 1999). The role of the law is not merely to privatize economic production but also to provide regulation of economic activity, and is now regarded as an illustration of the larger ongoing relationship between government and industry rather than a simple-minded attempt to restrict the private sector (Vogel 1998). The notion that regulation provides a set of rules by which a specially designated authority ensures a sustained and directed control of private activity to ensure benefits to the wider community, has been at the heart of the new thinking on regulation.

The idea that deregulation and re-regulation are opposing phenomena that indicate a market-friendly and centralizing government policy respectively has given way to an understanding that these might operate sequentially in a sector, and there could be differing directives across sectors (Ayres and Braithwaite 1992). There is a greater willingness to work with the historical and technological pathways adopted within an industry in evaluating the impact of a particular regulatory structure (Cole 1999). There is also a readiness to examine a wide range of institutional designs with which to direct the behaviour of economic agents that draws on the literature on common property rights (Ostrom et al. 1993, Ostrom 2005). The role played by social norms in regulating economic actors is consequently, gaining importance as an alternative or a complement to the legal rules brought in by a regulatory framework.

The experience of slow growth arising out of state-regulation in the 1990s in the developing world and the problems of de-regulation in the developed world have resulted in a joining of hands in a quest for new and better forms of regulation in recent years. The impacts of political and administrative structures on the regulatory regime introduced into an industrial sector imply that poor governance could be a serious stumbling block to influencing economic behaviour (Levy and Spiller 1994). The singular focus on government-directed regulatory regimes using formal rules has consequently, given way to examination of the influence of informal rules and social norms on the economic behaviour of producers (Etzioni 2000). The role played by internalized social norms and those imposed externally in regulating human behaviour has been widely recognized in sociology but less readily brought into mainstream economic analysis (Elster 1989). The possibility of drawing on social norms to regulate the behaviour of economic agents has emerged as a new area in law and economics since the 1990s (Posner 1997).

The section, 'Role of Social Norms' will examine the centrality of social norms in the quest for new ways to regulate economic behaviour. The section, 'Regulation, Evolution and History' reviews the current thinking on the relationship between law and regulation with particular attention to the emergence of concepts of reflexive law that form the theoretical basis for the emergence of alternatives to state regulation, such as self-regulation and co-regulation. 'State, Socity and Changing Regulatory Regimes' revisits the current understanding of mutuality and embeddedness to suggest the need for a more interdisciplinary approach to regulation. The section 'Exploring the Need for Regulation in the Provision of Services' draws on examples in service delivery to illustrate potential problems with the current phase of deregulation arising from a lack of recognition of the role played by social norms.

Role of Social Norms

Social norms are regarded as an important pre-condition to ensure that individuals behave in a cooperative manner even when they might prefer not to. The various types of norms prevalent in society and the reasons for their observance have become a matter of considerable interest in the literature on law and economics.

Distinction has been made between social norms that are external to the individual and community and those that have been internalized by individuals to form a preference structure. The external view of a social norm regards it as being akin to a tax or sanction that affects the cost of a particular (prohibited) action while the consideration of a social norm as internal to an individual's decision-making process is that it affects the way he regards himself. These views differ with respect to the location of the trigger that sets compliance to the social norm into operation, with the external view implying that an individual works to a social norm enforced externally by a non-governmental entity based on a cost/benefit calculation of compliance while the internal view locates the trigger within the individual obliging him to obey the norm. The external view has been further broadened to include the presence of reciprocity and reputation as the main reasons that people engage in norms (Ellickson 1991). Norms would consequently work well in close-knit groups or when reputations are monitored and where the rules 'governing an individual's behavior that third parties other than state agents diffusely enforce by means of social sanctions' are in place. The costs that underlie the external view emphasize the possibility that individuals would default where the costs are deemed to be low or there is a low level of monitoring. Where norms serve as a means of signaling to others, one's low discount rate reflecting the positive benefits of undertaking joint activity, it is possible to regard social norms as 'behavioral regularities that occur in equilibrium when people use signals to show that they belong to the good type. Social norms are thus endogenous: they do not cause behaviour, but are the labels we attach that result from other factors.'[1]

The internalization position posits that people obey and enforce a norm because they internalize its normative element and consequently feel a sense of guilt when they do not concur (Cooter

[1] See Posner (1997), p. 23

2000). A slightly different stance is noted in the view that people's primary motivation for following norms stems from their need for others' approval which serves to maintain their self-esteem while being linked to their sense of diminution when this esteem is not accorded (McAdams 1997). The process of internalization is also linked to the ability to learn to live with 'a different reason' (Cooter 2000). The ability of social norms to change behaviour by affecting the manner in which people regard their economic actions by reworking their beliefs, provides a stronger sense of social change.

When norms are regarded as a function of people's beliefs it allows for the possibility of a 'norm entrepreneur', an individual who can change norms through persuasion (Sunstein 1995).[2] The power of persuasion in changing the manner in which individuals think, arises from a socio-economic understanding of behaviour where individuals change their preferences on account of the introduction of new norms (Etzioni 2000). The possibility that behavioural changes can occur without formal change and that they arise from changes in contracts, standards and conduct, provides an opportunity to move from the realm of regulation by legal rules to regulation from within (Scott 2003).

The distinction between the external and internal impact of social norms might be suggestive rather than exact (Basu 1998) yet the discussion permits the exploration of the various routes through which social norms change behaviour. This might occur through the revaluation of behavioural outcomes or through changing individual beliefs or might in fact, move from one to the other (McAdams 1997). What it does suggest is that internal and external impacts of social norms allow us a handle on changing individual behaviour.

If social norms do operate to change cultural values then it identifies an important binding element in society which ensures strictures on unacceptable behaviour, such as cheating or lying (Etzioni 2000). The ability of social norms to regulate economic behaviour through drawing on the cultural matrix, raises the possibility that each society with its own particular historical past and cultural sub-stratum would develop its own regulatory regime (Scott 2003). There is an emergent understanding that the corpus of norms in the cultural sphere may be likened to the building blocks of a socio-genetic code for that society. Societies share many of these building blocks but differ in the relative weight they give to each one, somewhat like species

[2] See Sunstein(1995).

that share many genes in common but differ in the makeup of their genetic codes.[3] The cultural profile of each society is seen to be represented by a set of memes or cultural coding that is similar to that of the biological coding of the gene and consequently, has the ability to design the setting in which more concrete norms evolve.

The role of social norms that emerges from these sociological and culturally sensitive readings of regulation is that of a self-regulating corpus of rules that can be taken as a possible alternative to that of state regulation. Notions of responsive regulation, co-regulation and self-regulation have come to be regarded as the 'soft' and possibly more effective ways of regulating economic behaviour (Black 1997). These alternative forms of regulation have been increasingly explored in Anglo-American analyses of the law since the 1980s with a growing concern about the state's ability to provide effective regulatory regimes.

Regulation, Evolution and History

There has been a considerable interest in the evolutionary development of law in Europe that stems from a sociologically informed notion of the legal system. The intellectual stimulus for this research is found in the writings of European theorists, Jurgen Habermas and Niklas Luhmann. These theorists have contributed to a theory of law that sees the role of law as emerging from existing social, political and economic systems. In the work of Habermas the relationship between the legal, political, economic and cultural spheres is examined through the 'materialization' of law as a response to the demands of the German welfare state for a more finely-tuned legal system to meet the growing requirements for welfare and social regulation (Habermas 1996). In Luhmann's work the starting point is the functional differentiation of political, economic and social sub-systems with the law being regarded as an instrumental variable that is subservient to other sub-systems but cannot be sustained. These external and internal impositions on the legal system reduce the effectiveness of state-led regulation and push for an exploration of nonstate-based regulation. The driving force for alternative forms of regulation is the understanding that state-led regulation is consistent with the modernizing moment (Tuebner 1983) and that post-industrial society requires a different regulatory form (Scott 2003).

The inability of formal laws of the state to regulate or coordinate

[3] Licht (2001).

economic activity has led to an exploration of other forms of regulation. If societies do emerge from different historical and cultural substrata then it would follow that these different structures will generate an evolutionary process yielding distinct forms of regulation. Among the 'softer' forms of regulation that emerge from the interaction between historical and cultural dimensions in a post-industrial society is that of 'reflexive' regulation. This regulatory form is seen to respond to the demands of industrial structure and replaces the earlier form of repressive laws that constrained economic activity within industry. The generation of 'reflexive' or 'procedural' regulation aims to achieve its intended effects by encouraging self-regulation at the level of the parties and the processes operated by the parties themselves. Consequently it is thought that reflexive law can be used to 'steer' self-regulation so as to induce certain desired ends through second-order effects. The implication is that the new legal framework of 'reflexive law' allows us to build on constructivist insights into regulation that are free from the liberal and welfarist paradigms that usually structure our legal thought (Cohen 2004).

There has been substantial work undertaken within this new paradigm with regard to analysing the regulation of utilities in Europe (Prosser 1999) and further afield (Franco-Montoya 2002). There is however, some concern whether substantive principles can really be fitted into the model of reflexive law and the need to provide for a strong protection of substantive values of public service. Reflexive law may lead to greater regulation and the ability to introduce regulation to previously non-marketized areas rather than a de-regulation of society (Blankenberg 1984). It is felt that the reflexive law approach may reflect the liberal market-based arguments of the 1990s and needs therefore, to be grounded more thoroughly in the politics of modern societies (Prosser 2001).[4]

The notion of responsive regulation has been further developed to identify forms such as self-regulation and co-regulation. Co-regulation is the process whereby associations of firms or professionals at the level of industry concerned promulgate generalized standards for the conduct of trade. The rules in question are arrived at through a process of negotiation and deliberation within the industry. The government oversees or exercises loose supervision in the sense of intervening through competition or antitrust law to curb rules which

[4] I am grateful to Tony Prosser for this insight. My thinking has benefited from an exchange with him during the summer of 2002 regarding the need to bring Habermasian notions into regulatory frameworks.

plainly have an anti-competitive effect or purpose. On the other hand, enforced self-regulation is a form of self-regulation in which regulatory functions are sub-contracted by the state to private firms themselves or industry-level associations. The ability to ensure successfully enforced self-regulation requires the presence of a 'pyramid of regulatory compliance'. Sanctions are structured in such a way as to combine persuasion for the majority at the bottom of the pyramid, reserving direct intervention, for a few at the top. An essential aspect of self-regulation is the retention of a legal sanction which can be deployed as the last resort. The key difference between self-regulation and co-regulation is that the state is ready to intervene, with more stringent and less firm-specific or 'tailored' standards if firms do not agree with their requirements and needs in the case of self-regulation. The success of self-regulation depends on the existence of shared norms among firms within an industry. In the case of co-regulation it requires that consensus building should be possible among member firms (Jorgenson 2002). It has been argued that where self-enforcing norms of this nature are found, the costs of regulatory intervention can be substantially reduced in a number of ways. In particular, where there are 'interpretive communities' of actors, the risk of opportunistic or 'creative' compliance with rules may be reduced (Licht 2001). There is a distinct emphasis on the organizing, if not energizing, role of social norms in ensuring that individual firms move in the required direction in a responsible manner.

The notion that firms can be directed without recourse to state intervention, at least in the first instance, has generated considerable research interest in the possibility of self-generating impulses or norm entrepreneurs that might facilitate this process. The former process has been of particular interest in Europe and the latter is highly commended in the United States. The need for consensus and the important role of communities in ensuring non-state forms of regulation require an understanding of how legal, social, political and economic spheres interact and generate particular regulatory regimes. Whether persuasion at the bottom of the pyramid of regulation will work or there will be a need for economic coercion at the top would depend on the nature of interaction between the state and industry through exploring notions of embeddedness.

State, Society and Changing Regulatory Regimes

Karl Polanyi's work is an established starting point for understanding the role of exchange and markets in a framework of social embeddness

(Svedberg 2001). Polanyi (1957) chronicled the rise and demise of nineteenth century economic liberalism as a 'utopian project' to establish a self-regulated market in *The Great Transformation* (Jessop 2000). The work of Granovetter, on the other hand, broke new ground in the discussion of embeddedness as it refers to buyer-seller relations being integrated in durable interpersonal networks. Unlike Polanyi, Granovetter's approach is micro-oriented, and the 'embeddedness' of economic relations in personal networks is viewed as a general feature of all economic systems. Notwithstanding the micro-orientation, there is considerable emphasis in this work, on durable networks between formally independent business enterprises. This aspect of the concept of embeddedness can also be applied to government-business relations (Evans 2001). Embeddedness would then refer to close personal or organizational and institutionalized relations between government and financial institutions. Embedded autonomy is regarded as the key to the effectiveness of the developmental state, which allows the state to be insulated from the bureaucracy and particularistic interests, while at the same time, maintaining strong links with these sectors. Although the concept of embedded autonomy took a beating in the wake of the Asian financial crisis of the late 1990s it still provides a useful tool for understanding the political and economic linkages between the state and the industrial sector in the developing world. It points to the need for efficient state regulation to ensure the structural transformation of the economy.

The ability of the state to provide regulation in the industrial epoch would appear to sit at one end of the regulatory spectrum and time-line, while at the other is located the post-industrial non-state form of reflexive regulation. Does the state necessarily provide a less effective form of regulation? As the foundation of non-state regulation rests on the historical specificity of economies and societies, it is plausible that the embedded autonomy that characterizes the East Asian state provides a different array of regulatory regimes to those produced in Western Europe.

It has been posited that the move to non-state forms of soft regulation is a part of a neo-liberal agenda which regards society as a collection of competitive individuals connected through market-like contracts (Jessop 2002). At the same time, there are communitarian visions of a self-governing society, in which the social contract is expressed and enhanced through policies using individual contracts to promote social inclusion. These two visions have very different political underpinnings but have increasingly been conjoined in policy prescriptions that view non-state regulatory frameworks as a way forward for providing services to the underprivileged (World Bank 2002).

In the world of development economics there have also been concerns about the poor performance of state-led regulation. The New Institutional Economics (NIE) has provided a new set of tools to analyse the political economy of regulation and de-regulation through measuring the transaction costs associated with exchange in each regime (Levy and Spiller 1994). The attempt to regard regulation and de-regulation in a contractual framework does create difficulty in voicing social concerns regarding consumer welfare. It has been argued that the focus on the economics of de-regulation has resulted in general disregard for the institutional and social basis of regulatory processes (Vogel 1996). Although the NIE emphasizes the central role of transaction costs in directing the development process it has considerable difficulties incorporating the political sphere (Khan 1995). The paradigm is particularly poor in its explanatory power with regard to the 'political settlement', the nature and extent to which nation-states in the developing world have to make payments to a variety of lobbyists and potential rivals prior to any major political and or economic shift in policy.

The notion that non-state regulatory approaches may be more effective, produces difficulties in analysing the way forward for latecomers to development. As the state is a major player in industrializing societies, deregulation has been advocated as a way forward to ensure more market-friendly production processes. If one considers the findings in experimental economics on the endowment effect, this creates serious obstacles to deregulation or even to a transition to different and softer systems of regulation.

Endowment effects are predicted for property rights acquired by historic accidents or fortuitous circumstances, such as government licenses, landing rights or transferable pollution permits. Owing to endowment effects, firms will be reluctant to divest themselves of divisions, plants and product lines even though they may never consider buying these same assets.[5]

In a situation where an existing regulatory regime is manifestly failing and needs to be dismantled to reduce inefficiency and to further production, what would be the consequences of moving from

[5] Kahneman(1996), p. 227.

a state-regulated to a nonstate-regulated regime? If the regime were to be dislodged there would be withdrawal of rights of production under the previous system. This would create a set of losers, with considerable economic and political leverage. The ability of an economy to ride such a change would depend on the ability of these losers to subvert the process (Khan 1995). In the case where there was a pre-existing right awarded to and highly valued by an economic agent and was to be withdrawn under a deregulatory process, there could be a serious obstacle to planned regulatory change. If the operation of an endowment effect were to be considered with regard to regulatory regimes currently in operation it would not be unreasonable to argue that dismantling regulatory rules that removed or altered payments/particular standards could generate a very negative response for regulatees and regulators.

The result of this endowment effect in the regulatory sphere would be a sharp fall in trust on the part of regulatees with respect to the regulator.[6] It would not be unthinkable that such a regulatory change would result in intransigence to the proposed change in regulatory regime, on the part of the regulatees. A successful transition to the proposed regulatory regime would therefore, require payments to the existing regulatees. The emergence of a 'political settlement' as a necessary pre-condition for ensuring change in the regulatory regime highlights the centrality of the political sphere in institutional change (Khan 1995).

The obstacles to changing the regulatory regime in industrializing countries could result in a serious political backlash with a creation of asymmetries between the buyer and the seller in the area of exchange, generating a lower than expected level of trade in a variety of commodities in the near future. The difficulty of disentangling new regulatory regimes from strong endowment effects also casts some doubt on the ability of a single 'norm entrepreneur' located outside the political coalition to facilitate the adoption of a set of social norms in favour of the new regulated system. If on the other hand, we imagined a scenario of regulatory change through the model of reflexive law which encouraged participants to self-regulate, this would require a mechanism of ensuring the participating firms'

[6] The lack of trust between regulatee and regulator on account of changes in regulatory standards and time periods has been discussed by Helm (1995). The point about endowment effect on account of changes in rights was not discussed in that context.

compliance with codes and standards, whether through internal agreement by firms or by external decree.

In the context of India, where the economic liberalization of the last two decades has produced many technological and economic opportunities there has been a considerable interest in the state's attempts to regulate economic activity. Serious doubts have been raised with regard to the ability of the state to provide adequate regulatory frameworks in new areas of economic activity as well as its concern for access and social justice. The poor record of state-led regulation raises important questions about whether the replacement of state regulation by non-state regulation either through an external norm entrepreneur, or through processes of self-regulation and co-regulation which promote the observance of codes and standards, may assist an improved provision of social infrastructure in India. The next section will examine how the provision of social infrastructure, particularly education and housing, can be analysed through this debate on regulation.

Exploring the Need for Regulation in the Provision of Services

There has been a radical shift in mainstream economic thinking on the provision of services in the last quarter of a century. The centrality of the welfare state which regarded education and housing as salient parts of the public sector has given way to privatized provision in these key areas of social and physical infrastructure (World Bank 2005). The new thinking in international policy arenas is that the way forward in educational provision would be to ensure that there is increased decentralization in service delivery. The importance of the local context in ensuring that educational delivery is effective, has creating a growing role for non-governmental organizations (NGOs). The large number of NGOs emerging in the local educational sphere has resulted in considerable diversity in the nature of provision, as well as manner of delivery.

Educational reforms have opened the door to a large number of non-state players, both profit and non-profit oriented. The British education sector has been the subject of managerial reforms which were meant to provide greater independence at the school level. The results of these reforms are seen to have subverted and damaged public service institutions built up on relations of mutuality and a commonality of public interest (Inglis 2000). In India the poor capacity of the state as a service provider makes it necessary to provide a different and more workable provision of education both within and outside the state sector (The PROBE Team 1999). Consequently a wide variety of organizational styles and management practices have arisen among the burgeoning number of NGOs in the field of education provision in India in the two last decades. The opening up of the educational sector has been heralded as a way of providing education to the most underprivileged sections of society (World Bank 2005). There is no doubt that considerable achievements have been made by such initiatives but there is need to be circumspect about the potential regulatory problems that such liberalization may have thrown up.

An indication of potential problems began to emerge from the results of my preliminary research on the emerging models of governance in the delivery of education by the NGO sector. The international goals of 'Education for All' with universal education by 2015[7] and the focus on educational access and inclusion in the Millennium Development Goals appeared to be encountering difficulties in Delhi and Mumbai. My research findings indicated the problem of institutional exclusion that was noticeable in the provision of education to the most underprivileged sectors in the urban environment. One of my research sites was in the newer slums and resettlement colonies in Delhi and my 'gatekeepers' to these communities were the NGOs that worked in these areas.[8] The feature of exclusion was an aspect that was addressed by most NGOs. T. K. Matthew of Deepalaya pointed out that the children who came to his school were from families that were among the poorest urban communities and that the inability of their families to generate adequate income to support them had not prevented the government schools they had previously attended, from charging hidden fees. He was particularly irate about these 'fees of the government schools' that were levied as costs of uniforms, books and other sundries and added up to some Rs 300–400, which he regarded as unsustainable by families in these impoverished areas.

Alternative schools, such as that of Deepalaya are not recognized and as non-government private schools, have an uphill and losing battle with the state authorities, to obtain any additional resources.

[7] *Education For All Global Monitoring Report 2003–05. http://portal.unesco.org/en/ev.php@URL_ID=15006&URL_DO=DO_TOPIC&URL_SECTION=201.html*

[8] Deepalaya is one outstanding example of such an organization providing schools for the poorer sections in Delhi's slums. My thanks to T. K Matthew for taking the time to speak to me and showing me the school I refer to.

These schools are caught in a vicious circle with the state authorities demanding that they make additional provisions, such as upgrading teachers' salaries, better teacher-student ratios and the like. These 'statutory requirements' are cited as pre-conditions for recognition by the government. The absence of any consistent regulatory framework to monitor the performance of these schools is a serious hole in the educational system.

These schools face difficulties as they believe that the families sending children to their schools are too poor to pay school fees. If the schools were to raise their fees to cover the costs of additional staffing, they fear it would push out the very families they work for. They are therefore, in a Catch-22 situation as they are also unable to get subsidies from the state because they have not got formal recognition. The exclusionary consequences of this impasse emerge from the fact that the children attending these alternate schools have already been forced out of the state system as they were unable to pay the hidden fees demanded there and/or because they failed two or more times in the state examinations and were therefore, expelled from the government school system. The inability to regulate new non-state providers of education could result in the emergence of an unregulated provision of education with little monitoring and even less evaluation of the quality of such educational provision.

As the large-scale provision of educational services by the non-governmental sector is a relatively new phenomenon it is not surprising that there are few if any, governance mechanisms in place. However, the regulation of the provision of educational services will need to be addressed beyond the current provision of a common syllabus and examination system. The system of codes and standards that is commonplace in countries like the United Kingdom comes with a warning note regarding the destruction brought about by these rules with regard to mutuality and trust. On the other hand, an unregulated education market is unlikely to provide consumer satisfaction. It is indeed true that many of the families from economically deprived areas of large metropolises are deeply dissatisfied by the level of provision of educational services. What is less often heard is their frustration at not being able to convert educational achievement into gainful employment, and these concerns are unlikely to be met without suitable and appropriate regulation.[9]

[9] Interviews with residents of Gandhi Nagar slum in Colaba, Mumbai showed that parents were unwilling to send their children, especially sons, to local NGO or

The question whether such regulation should be based on a state-regulation model or a self-regulation model needs to be discussed and debated in the near future, if not at present, so that the achievements in this sector do not get subsumed in the debris of some unpredicted regulatory implosion. It would seem worthwhile to look elsewhere at the success in the delivery of the social infrastructure to identify the kind of regulatory structures that may be considered. The benefits of creating a negotiatary framework between the state and major stakeholders so as to ensure a degree of embeddedness through setting up a responsive regulatory regime might be best suited to the sector's needs. The benefits of such negotiatary frameworks have been applauded elsewhere, as in housing provision in Mumbai. The interactions of the municipal officials, the private developers and the NGO alliance were embedded in a transparent and accountable structure that is the consequence of in-depth and detailed exchanges between the individual actors.[10] The principal actors established a series of meetings to provide a channel for familiarizing the different sectors with the various ideologies and practices in the provision of housing for the poor (Appadurai 2002). There was no formal attempt at bringing in a regulatory approach to this set of negotiations of the provision of affordable housing for the urban poor in Mumbai but there was concerted effort over a decade or more, to create trust between stakeholders and work towards an internalization of social norms with regard to the needs of the urban poor.

The creation of such a negotiatary framework prior to any move to developing specific regulatory regimes would facilitate the ready recognition of particular skills and core competencies among stakeholders. Such a framework is particularly conducive to creating local embeddedness between the state and industry. The move towards an embedded approach places the emphasis on the body of social norms that operate among the various stakeholders. It is these social norms that become the key to decisions regarding the choice of a regulatory framework. In particular, the decision of whether co-regulation by within-industry setting of codes and standards or self-regulation should be adopted, would be based on an initial evaluation of the level of mutuality and trust between stakeholders.

government schools due to the poor content of education and the very low correlation between school curriculum and current job opportunities for their sons.

[10] Framework set out in a personal interview with V. S. Dhumal, Mumbai, 29 December 2000.

The advantage of using the existing institutional linkages and norms would be to work with the current structures so as to avoid triggering off an endowment effect of a considerable magnitude. As the regulatory endowment effect arises on account of sudden changes in regulatory regime it might be more useful to build from current norms towards appropriate regimes rather than an imposition of a new regime from without.

The relationship between governance and regulation is complex with critics warning that governance is a neo-liberal formulation of the need for regulation. On the other hand, the possibility of bringing in the state as a stakeholder rather than as a hierarchical top-down mediator in the provision of social structure does change the nature of individual sub-systems in an economy. There is a clear need to understand that regulation in India cannot be regarded as restrictive but the need for responsive regulation raises important questions about the manner in which social norms can be changed to generate consensus and whether the internalization of these norms can be facilitated by bolstering the local embedding of an agreed set of social norms by state and industry in the area of social infrastructure.

Conclusion

The role of social norms in creating reciprocity and mutuality has come under intense scrutiny in the current move-away from state regulation to more open forms of regulation such as co-regulation and self-regulation. The examination of the literature on the new forms of regulation shows that there is a lack of recognition of the ideological and intellectual conflicts that are inherent in our current understanding of these forms. The pathways provided by social theorists and development studies to bring about a more interdisciplinary understanding of regulation by bringing together the economic, political, legal and cultural spheres show that fostering more open regulatory forms might not address barriers to social equity adequately. The implications of these new regimes for universal access, substantive values and codes and standards have been flagged using illustrations of the provision of social infrastructure. These examples indicate the need for a more detailed analysis of the delivery processes and core competencies in the relevant sector prior to any ready adoption of a particular form of regulation. The way forward in regulation in social provision in India requires an innovative approach to working with new technologies and economic opportunities.

Top-down approaches and state-led regulation are unlikely to provide a sustained basis for ensuring growth or increased access for the underprivileged. The possibility of non-state provision provides a valuable opportunity for bringing in more responsive forms of regulation through bringing in codes and standards of conduct rather than imposing economic costs on new providers.

References

Appadurai, A., 2002, 'Deep Democracy: Urban Governmentality and the Horizon of Politics', *Public Culture*, vol. 14, no. 1, Winter, pp. 21–47

Ayres, I., and J. Braithwaite, 1992, *Responsive Regulation: Transcending the Regulation Debate*, Oxford University Press, New York.

Barzel, Y., 1989, *Economic Analysis of Property Rights*, Cambridge University Press, Cambridge.

Basu, K., 1998, 'Social Norms and the Law', in Peter Newman (ed.), *The New Palgrave Dictionary of Economics and the Law*, Macmillan, Hampshire; available at SSRN: *http://ssrn.com/abstract=42840* or DOI: *10.2139/ssrn.42840*.

Black, J., 1997, *Rules and Regulators*, Clarendon Press, Oxford.

Blankenburg, E., 1984, 'The Poverty of Evolutionism: A Critique of Teubner's Case for "Reflexive Law"', *Law & Society Review*, vol. 18, no. 2, pp. 273–90.

Cohen, J. L. 2004, Regulating Intimacy: A New Legal Paradigm, Princeton University Press, Princeton, NJ.

Cole, D., H. Daniel and P. Grossman, Z. Peter, 1999, 'When is Command-and-Control Efficient? Institutions, Technology and the Comparative Efficiency of Alternative Regulatory Regimes for Environmental Protection', *Wisconsin Law Review*, 1999, pp. 887–938.

Cooter, R. D., 2000, 'Do Good Laws Make Good Citizens? An Economic Analysis of Internalized Norms', *Virginia Law Review*, vol. 86, no. 8, pp. 1577–601.

Deakin, S., and J. Cook, 2001, 'Regulation and the Boundaries of Law', *http://www/dti.gov.uk/cld/esrc9.pdf*.

Demsetz, H., 1968, 'Why Regulate Utilities', *Journal of Law and Economics*, vol. 1, no. 1, pp. 55–65.

Edgeworth, B., 2003, *Law, Modernity and Post Modernity: Legal Change in the Contracting State*, Ashgate, Aldershot, UK.

Ellickson, R. C., 1991, *Order Without Law: How Neighbours Settle Disputes*, Harvard University Press, Cambridge, MA.

_____, 1998, 'Law and Economics Discover Social Norms', *Journal of Legal Studies*, 27, pp. 537–52.

Elster, J., 1989, 'Social Norms and Economic Theory', *Journal of Economic Perspectives*, vol. 27, no. 2, pp. 553–65.

Etzioni, A., 2000, 'Social Norms: Internalization, Persuasion, and History', *Law & Society Review*, vol. 34, pp. 157–78.

Evans, P., 2001, *Embedded Autonomy: States and Industrial Transformation*, Princeton University Press, Princeton.

Franco-Montoya, D., 2002, 'The Regulatory Framework of the Newly Privatised Electricity Companies—A Comparative Study of the Chilean and British Cases', unpublished Ph.D. thesis, University of Cambridge, Cambridge.

Granovetter, M., 1985, 'Economic Action and Social Structure: The Problem of Embeddedness', *The American Journal of Sociology*, vol. 91, no. 3, 481–510.

Habermas, J., 1996, *Between Facts and Norms: Contributions to a Discourse Theory of Law and Democracy*, The MIT Press, Cambridge, MA.

Inglis, F., 2000, 'A Malediction upon Management', *Journal of Education Policy*, vol. 15, no. 4, pp. 417–29.

Jessop, R., 2001, 'Regulationist and Autopoieticist Reflections on Polanyi's Account of Market Economies and Market Society', *New Political Economy*, 6(2), pp. 213–32. Also available at *http://www.comp.lancs.ac.uk/sociology/soc130rj.pdf*.

Jorgensen, B.S., 2002. 'Perceived Justice and the Economic Valuation of the Environment: A Role for Fair Decisionmaking Procedures', in A. Winnett (ed.), *Towards a Collaborative Environmental Research Agenda*, Macmillan, London.

Kahneman, D., J. L. Knetsch and H. Thaler, 2000, 'Experimental Tests of the Endowment Effect and the Coase Theorem' in Cass Sunstein (ed.), *Behavioral Law and Economics*, Cambridge University Press, New York.

Khan, M.H., 1995, 'State Failure in Weak States: A Critique of the New Institutional Explanations' in John Harriss, Janet Hunter and Colin M. Lewis (eds.), *New Institutional Economics and Third World Development*, Routledge, London, New York.

Knight, J., 1992, *Institutions and Social Conflict*, Cambridge University Press, Cambridge.

Levy, B and P. Spiller, 1994, 'The Institutional Foundations of Regulatory Commitment: A Comparative Analysis of Telecommunications Regulation', *Journal of Law, Economics, & Organization*, vol. 10, no. 2, pp. 201–46.

_____, 1996 (eds.), *Regulations, Institutions and Commitment*, Cambridge University Press, Cambridge.

Licht, Amir N., 2001, 'The Pyramid of Social Norms: A New Perspective', Available at SSRN: *http://ssrn.com/abstract=264970* or DOI: *10.2139/ssrn.264970*.

Mayo, E., and H. Moore (eds.), 2001, *The Mutual State: How Local Communities can Run Public Services*, New Economics Foundation, U.K.

McAdams, R. H., 1997, 'The Origins, Development and Regulation of Norms', *Michigan Law Review*, vol. 97, no. 2.

Meagher, P., 2002, 'Microfinance Regulation in Developing Countries: A Comparative Review of Current Projects', IRIS working paper.

Ostrom, E., 2005, *Understanding Institutional Diversity*, Princeton University Press, Princeton, New Jersey.

_____, L. Schroeder and S. Wynee, 1993, *Institutional Incentives and Sustainable Development*, Westview Press, Boulder, Colorado.

Polanyi, K., 1957, *The Great Transformation*, Beacon Press, Boston.

Posner, E., 1997, 'Social Norms and the Law: An Economic Approach', *The American Economic Review*, vol. 87, no. 2, pp. 365–9.

_____, 2000, *Law and Social Norms*, Harvard University Press, Cambridge, MA.

Prosser, A., 1999, *The Law and the Regulators*, Clarendon Press, Oxford.

Scott, Colin (ed.), 2004, 'Regulation in the Age of Governance: The Rise of the Post-regulatory State', in J. Jordana, and D. Levi-Faur (eds.), *The Politics of Regulation: Institutions and Regulatory Reforms for the Age of Governance*, Edward Elgar, U.K., pp. 145–74.

Smelser, J. and Svedberg, 1995, *The Handbook of Economic Sociology*, Princeton University Press, Princeton.

Sunstein, C., 1995, 'Social Norms and Social Rules', Chicago Law & Economics Working Paper No. 36, University of Chicago Law School, Chicago.

Svedberg, L., 2001, 'Spelar ideella och informella insatser någon roll för svensk välfärd?' [Do voluntary and informal efforts have any impact on Swedish welfare?], in M. Szebehely (ed.), *Välfärdstjänster i omvandling*. Forskarantologi från Kommittén Välfärdsbokslut. SOU, 2001:52/Swedish Official Government Report Series 2001:52.

The PROBE Team,1999, *Public Report on Basic Education in India*, OUP, New Delhi.

Tuebner, G., 1983, 'Substantive and Reflexive Elements in Modern Law', *Law & Society Review*, vol. 17, no. 2, pp. 239–86.

Vogel, S., 1998, *Freer Markets, More Rules: Regulatory Reform in Advanced Industrial Countries*, Cornell University Press, Ithaca.

World Bank, 2002,World Development Report, *Building Institutions for Markets*.

_____, 2005, World Development Report, *A Better Investment Climate for Everyone*.

7

Electricity Market Regulation in Germany

Response to Common Norms and Specific Interests

ENRICO SCHÖBEL

Introduction

According to the European Union (EU) internal market principle and EU regulation in 1996,[1] the German government has opened former regional monopolistic electricity markets for EU-wide private competition.[2] The national implementation of EU regulation has its basis in the so-called subsidiarity principle, and allows for response to citizens' individual preferences in the member states. The following analysis of German electricity market regulation focuses on national peculiarities in implementing EU electricity regulation.[3]

Due to the natural monopoly character of electricity networks, and for other normative reasons, for example security and diversity

[1] Directive 96/92/EC of the European Parliament and of the Council of 19 December 1996 concerning common rules for the internal market in electricity (Common Position (EC) adopted by the Council on 25 July 1996). For more details of this and later European regulations see for example Boltz 2005, 113 ff. For progress in implementation see the 2005 benchmarking report: European Commission 2005, 2 ff.

[2] Albers 2005, 9 ff., and Büdenbender 2003, 4 ff.

[3] EU regulation is not externally given to the member state, but the result of a complicated decision making process, in which EU institutions, national governments of the member states, as well as lobbying pressure groups, are involved. Due to relatively low transparency and as a result of specific public choice phenomena, political decision making on the EU level has frequently been criticised. For an analysis of democratic legitimization see Tiedtke 2005.

of supply, the creation of market access conditions requires a well-designed regulatory policy. Whereas other member states under the same EU regulation established regulatory agencies very soon, the German government urged influential national industry associations to negotiate market access conditions among themselves.[4] However, this institution of negotiated network access conditions was short-lived. It was replaced very soon when a single network industries regulatory agency was established. The German Telecommunications and Post Regulatory Agency (RegTP) became responsible for electricity and other network industries as well, henceforth taking on the name of Federal Network Agency.[5]

Another German peculiarity is the response to strong individual preferences for environmental protection and ecological sustainability. In accordance with EU regulation,[6] the German government has legislated support for renewable energies. The national policy instruments pursued for promotion of green energy, differ from member state to member state. This allows for a government response to citizens' subjective ecological preferences and specific group interests. Obviously, the German government has responded to particular identifiable interests, when green preferences and interests have been institutionalized in the national electricity market regulation. For example, regenerative wind and solar energy supply has prioritized network access, and is also subsidized.

The German implementation of EU electricity regulation can not only be argued through normative principles of regulation, but also reflects specific interests of groups in the member state. In following Stigler's and Becker's positive theory of why economic regulation occurs,[7] both German peculiarities of regulatory policy, the short-lived institution of negotiated network access conditions and the ecologically oriented electricity network regulation, are analysed as being the government's response to specific interests.

[4] Brunekreeft 2002, 203 ff., and Brunekreeft 2004, 285 ff.

[5] For detailed information about the German Federal Network Agency see the Internet Homepage in English at: *http://www.bundesnetzagentur.de/enid/6c4fa8a2fc9166e545688716a65d3c36,0/xn.html*, 20 May 2006.

[6] Directive 2001/77/EC of the European Parliament and of the Council of 27 September 2001 on the promotion of electricity produced from renewable energy sources in the internal electricity market.

[7] Stigler 1971, 3 ff., and Becker 1983, 371 ff.

Electricity Network Regulation due to Normative Principles

Normative theory of economic regulation asks for intervention by the state, such as establishing a public enterprise or regulating private enterprises, only in cases of market failure.[8] Prominent types of market failure are natural monopolies, public goods, asymmetric information and negative externalities. Networks industries, such as telecommunications, electricity, gas and railways, have a natural monopoly character, which means very high sunk costs, continuously falling average costs, and profitability in the very long run. Therefore economic regulation is necessary.

Traditionally, in many European countries electricity power was provided by public utilities, which were in a monopoly or regional monopoly position. Electricity power was not only publicly provided for the reason that a single non-regulated private enterprise would skim monopoly rent, while the state would be oriented to maximizing social welfare, but also because public utilities were a major income source of many states.[9] Moreover, high sunk costs could be a reason for the non-existence of a market, because a private enterprise would seek profitability in the short run.

On the other hand, public enterprises are classically marked by lower allocative efficiency and x-inefficiencies. Due to efficiency losses, former state monopolies were opened to enable competition among regulated private enterprises. Effective price and entry regulation should enhance allocative and productive efficiency.[10] The opening of electricity markets for private competition requires non-discriminatory access of new entrants to the network.

Besides this, further normative principles can be raised, for instance electricity market liquidity, security of supply, stable power networks, diversity of electricity suppliers, plurality of technologies, openness for technological and product substitutes, technological innovation, desired development of energy prices, ecological sustainability and so on. Hence, positive economic theories are required to answer the question of why regulation actually occurs.

[8] Stiglitz 2000, 89.

[9] Backhaus 1980, 58, and Blankart 1980, 14.

[10] Viscusi/Vernon/Harrington 2005, 377 and 556 ff.

Electricity Network Regulation in Response to Specific Identifiable Interest

A case has been made for economic regulation rooted in normative theories of market failure, for instance natural monopoly and externalities, but such reasoning is rather idealistic, because citizens and particular interest groups may force economic regulation while competing for political influence. Consequently, normative theories have to be linked with positive theories of why economic regulation actually occurs.[11] Positive theories of regulation should consider the behaviour of the concerned politicians, bureaucrats, voters and interest groups.

In the 1960s and 1970s a positive theory of regulatory capture was developed on the basis of some empirical studies.[12] For example, Stigler and Friedland studied electric utility regulation in the US in the 1920s and 1930s,[13] and came to the conclusion that the examined regulations had no or only tiny price effects. Regulatory policy failed to enable competition among firms.

In another empirical study Posner summarized 'that regulation is not positively correlated with the presence of external economies or diseconomies or with monopolistic market structure'.[14] Contrary to normative theories of economic regulation, in many cases firms supported or even lobbied for regulation. Firms or industries were interested in becoming regulated, and influenced the regulator to provide their specific interests, for example stable price level.[15] In terms of information economics, the firms (agent) were better informed than the regulator (principal).[16]

On the basis of selected case studies, Stigler sourced economic regulation to the impact of interest groups.[17] Firms invest in regulation to utilise the state's power to coerce, especially control over market entry of new firms, and thereby manage larger influence than they would have, if they were unregulated. Subsequently, regulation emerges as being the governments' response to economic interests brought forward in competition to lobbying activities of others, also others'

[11] Blankart 1980, 19.
[12] Viscusi/Vernon/Harrington 2005, 379 ff.
[13] Stigler/Friedland 1962, 1 ff.
[14] Posner 1974, 335 ff.
[15] Viscusi/Vernon/Harrington 2005, 379 ff.
[16] Laffont/Tirole 2000, 56.
[17] Stigler 1971, 3 ff.

activities of defence. Peltzman pointed out that the legislator acts to maximize political support to remain in office, a position that is offered by competing interest groups.[18]

Firms or industries are not the only ones lobbying for regulation. Capture theory has been criticized on the grounds that other interest groups, not necessarily firms or industries also lobby and thereby impact on political decision making. For example, social and environmental regulations often don't rely on firms' interest in becoming regulated.[19] Normally, several interest groups are affected, and preferences can be mixed or overlapping. Lobbying on ecologically-oriented green taxation is a very prominent example of overlapping and mixed preferences.

The competition among interest groups for political influence was examined by Becker to unify normative views of market failure and private interest theories. Becker states that groups exert pressure to lower their tax payments or to raise subsidies, where they can benefit from.[20] Cooperation of lobbying interest groups can be efficiency enhancing when taxpayers are both taxed and subsidized, because taxation and subsidization could be equally reduced and wasteful expenditures on pressure could be saved.[21] Besides this, cooperation is a helpful strategy for small groups to become politically recognized,[22] for instance in news publications, parliamentary committees' debates, and so on.

In Germany, associations of industries and other societal groups traditionally have great importance and impact on political decision-making. There are associations of the power industries. This institutionalizing of interests is a dynamic process in democratic systems, such as the German federal system, for example eco-protest has been institutionalized during the last decades.[23]

The German government responded to particular identifiable interests, when establishing the institution of negotiated network access conditions, and ecological-oriented regulations. Citizens' distinct ecological preferences were institutionalized in the national electricity market regulation, e.g. electricity supply from regenerative energy sources gains guaranteed network access.

[18] Peltzman 1976, 211 ff.

[19] Viscusi/Vernon/Harrington 2005, 380.

[20] Becker 1983, 380, and Becker 1988, 87 ff.

[21] Becker 1983, 389, and Becker 1988, 92.

[22] Becker 1988, 99.

[23] Rucht/Rose 2001, 269 ff.

Specific German Institution of Negotiated Network Access Conditions

The European Commission electricity directive in 1996 required opening of electricity markets for EU-wide private competition.[24] The directive offered two possible ways to go, the negotiated network access on the one hand, and the regulated network access on the other hand.[25] The EU directive was transferred into German anti-cartel law and German power industry law by guaranteeing the right of access to existing networks. The German government was the only one, which decided to establish the institution of negotiated (third-party) network access conditions.

Three agreements were made, the first in May 1998, the second in December 1999, and the third in December 2001.[26] This development stands for a step-by-step learning process, for example, the point-to-point pricing was replaced by access-point pricing, flexibility was increased, benchmarking was introduced, and the contract conditions for household customers were simplified. In their second benchmarking report on the implementation of the internal electricity and gas market, the European Commission states that the electricity prices in Germany decreased due to the complete opening of the market.[27]

Establishing Negotiations in Response to Specific Interests

The opening of the German electricity market for private competition (including third-party access) was organized not by a regulatory agency, but negotiated among the associations of the industry themselves.[28] They were urged to develop network access models via negotiations, with the threat that market access conditions would be regulated by the government. The government preferred the concept of negotiations taking into cognizance the problems associated with asymmetric information.

[24] Directive 96/92/EC of the European Parliament and of the Council of 19 December 1996 concerning common rules for the internal market in electricity (Common Position (EC) adopted by the Council on 25 July 1996).

[25] A third way of a lone single buyer in the electricity market who resells to the others in the market, does only exist in Malta.

[26] Bundesministerium für Wirtschaft und Arbeit 2003, 6 f., and Büdenbender 2003, 4.

[27] European Commission 2003, 7.

[28] Rebentisch 2005, 25 ff., Brunekreeft 2004, 285 ff., Büdenbender 2003, 4 ff., Brunekreeft 2002, 203 ff., and Folle/Schöneich 2002, 249 ff.

Detailed technical and pricing conditions were not given by a large public administration, but were bargained among the parties involved. The agreements were limited in time to allow for revisions, the later agreements were limited up to 2003. It may be assumed that these agreements between the federations of the industries conform with 'good professional practice' of market access. In view of that, a firm's behaviour is accepted, if it conforms to negotiated agreements, whereas abuse would have been penalized by the Cartel Office.

The question has to be raised, why Germany has gone the unique way of negotiated network access conditions. Negotiations, instead of regulations have a tradition in the German power sector. It was argued that due to the information possessed by the government or a regulatory agency being incomplete, firms could identify market access conditions more effectively. This was interpreted as being the more market-oriented solution, and was also seen as an opportunity where the costs associated with the administration of a regulatory agency could be cut.

Furthermore, it was argued that if flexibility is increased,[29] decisions might be reached and revoked more quickly in the private sphere than in the case of a political or administrative rule–making process, sequential learning would be pushed, and unintended outcomes could be corrected expeditiously. Besides this, the threat of regulation exerted pressure on the interest groups negotiating electricity network access conditions among themselves.[30]

However the negotiating parties rather preferred particular old-established interests, while market newcomers felt less represented. For example, the old establishment might be interested in technological improvements of conventional electricity production, whereas the activities of newcomers, e.g. regenerative energy suppliers, may cause structural changes of the network. Thus, there were conflicts among competing interests.

The Fall as a Result of Competition among Interest Groups

From an information economics perspective of asymmetric information,[31] the bureaucrats can be seen as being the principal in a principal-agent-relationship, and the associations of the industries

[29] Bundesministerium für Wirtschaft und Arbeit 2003, 6.

[30] For a discussion of regulatory threat in the German electricity market see: Brunekreeft 2004, 288 and 298 ff.

[31] Levine/Lippman 1995.

as the agents. The latter are better informed. The bureaucrats are searching for information to handle the regulatory problem and, therewith, depend on the informed agent. However, the agents will force their own economic interests, e.g. prevention of new entrants and a stable price level.

Whereas the government was interested in political support, lower administrative costs and more flexibility, and therefore urged the federations of the industries to find network access conditions themselves, the associations of the industries took the chance of a step-by-step opening as much as necessary, but not more than necessary, to get the government's favour. Moreover, the industries lobbied to transform the outcomes of the negotiations into law.[32] This would have strengthened the position of the industries in comparison to the position of the German Cartel Office,[33] but the Cartel Office ignored the outcomes.

In fact, there were interest conflicts among interest groups concerned.[34] Small firms and private household consumers were particularly underrepresented in the negotiations. New entrants who were dependant on getting network access came to be involved in the process of negotiations very late in the day. In 2002 new entrants formed the Association of New Power Supplier (bne) to put pressure on the incumbent network providers.[35] This association was for the first time, involved in the negotiations for the third agreement, when the association had become influential due to its increasing number of members. The market newcomers' association, as well as the German Cartel Office put pressure on the government with the objective of establishing a regulatory agency, creating non-discriminatory network access conditions, and furthering unbundling. Besides this, interest groups were established by new entrants, which put political pressure in the same direction.

At the very beginning, the incumbents lowered their prices, because the market became contestable. The prices fell from 1998 to 2000, and thereafter, rose because of increased wholesale prices and taxes.[36] Brunekreeft notes that among these and other explanations, the threat of regulation had an immediate effect, but definitely lost its

[32] Büdenbender 2003, 20 and 29 ff.

[33] Bundesverband der deutschen Gas—und Wasserwirtschaft 2002, 2.

[34] Büdenbender 2003, 19 ff.

[35] See the associations' internet homepage at *http://www.neue-energieanbieter.de/index.html*, 20 May 2006.

[36] Bundesministerium für Wirtschaft und Arbeit 2003, 13 ff.

effectiveness very soon.[37] He argues that old-established incumbent firms aimed to demonstrate the redundancy of ex-ante regulation. The fact that approximately 30 per cent of the private households and 50 per cent of the industrial customers signed new contracts only with the old incumbent suppliers,[38] whereas only less than two per cent of the consumers changed their electricity suppliers,[39] clearly supports Brunekreeft's argument.

Finally, the German concept of negotiated network access was criticized by the European Commission, the German Cartel Office, and the German Monopoly Commission, whereas the German government, the federations of the power industry, and the federations of other industries supported it.[40] The European Commission criticized the arrangement on the grounds that only less than two per cent of the consumers changed their electricity supplier. The Ministry of Economics in its monitoring report 2003, indicated that the network access costs in Germany were too high. The European Commission in its second benchmarking report 2003 came up with the same result, and referred to the high spread of the prices in different regions of Germany, and the remarkable price reductions in some cases as soon as the anti-abuse proceedings were instituted by the German Cartel Office.[41]

Formation of a Single Network Regulatory Agency

The establishment of a regulatory agency and replacement of negotiated network access conditions was required by the European Parliament and the Council. The 1996 electricity directive was replaced by the European Commission (EC) electricity directive 2003,[42] and the EC regulation on conditions for access to the network for cross-border exchanges in electricity.[43] This new EU electricity network regulation, requiring establishment of regulatory agencies, was

[37] Brunekreeft 2004, 298 ff..

[38] Folle/Schöneich 2002, 258.

[39] European Commission 2003, 27.

[40] Büdenbender 2003, 8.

[41] Bundesministerium für Wirtschaft und Arbeit 2003, 21.

[42] Directive 2003/54/EC of the European Parliament and of the Council of 26 June 2003 concerning common rules for the internal market in electricity and repealing Directive 96/92/EC.

[43] Regulation (EC) No. 1228/2003 of the European Parliament and of the Council of 26 June 2003.

targeted on increasing cross-border exchange, and stands for more harmonization of the member states' regulatory policies.[44]

The German government was urged to establish an independent regulatory agency in the energy sector. The isolated concept of negotiated network access had to be replaced by a regulated network access by 1 July 2004. The regulation could have been done by enlargement of the existing RegTP or by forming a separate power sector regulatory agency. The German Monopoly Commission supported the first move to avoid regulatory capture.[45] On 1 January 2006 a single network industries regulatory agency was established by the name of Federal Network Agency,[46] when the former RegTP was extended and became responsible also for electricity and other network industries, henceforth known by the new name.

The German Green Electricity Regulation

The German government also responded to specific identifiable interests, when implementing green electricity regulation. Ecologically-oriented preferences and specific interests towards environmental protection and ecological sustainability have been institutionalized in the national electricity market regulation. In accordance with EU regulation,[47] the German government transferred support for renewable energies into national law.[48] The German regulation does not copy other member states' implementation of EU regulation. The policy instruments for promotion of green energy differ from member state to member state.

In Germany subjective ecological preferences have been institutionalized, for example, in various lobbying interest groups, the Green Party, numerous environmental regulations, and since 1999, in ecologically-oriented tax legislation. Green-oriented taxation was not implemented until citizens' ecological consciousness had

[44] Boltz 2005, 113 ff.

[45] Monopolkommission 2002, 376.

[46] For detailed information about the German Federal Network Agency see the Internet homepage in English at: *http://www.bundesnetzagentur.de/enid/6c4fa8a2fc9166e54568871 6a65d3c36,0/xn.html*, 20 May 2006.

[47] Directive 2001/77/EC of the European Parliament and of the Council of 27 September 2001 on the promotion of electricity produced from renewable energy sources in the internal electricity market.

[48] Renewable energy sources act (EEG) of 29 March 2000 and EEG of 21 July 2004.

been developed and specific interest groups became influential.[49] Eco-taxes were established after the Green Party and the Social Democratic Party formed their red-green government coalition in 1998.[50] The results of recent empirical investigations hint at the relevance of ecologically oriented energy or CO2 taxes and higher government expenditures for environmental purposes, when arguing citizens individual satisfaction with democracy.[51]

Ecological preferences are also reflected in the German electricity market regulation. Electricity from renewable energy sources, such as wind, solar power, hydropower, biomass and so on, have prioritized network access, and supply of regenerative energies is subsidized.[52] The payment rates increased, when the Electricity Feed Act was replaced by the Renewable Energy Sources Act (EEG) in April 2000. Especially, electricity supply from wind power benefited from grants. From 1999 up to 2004, wind electricity supply quintupled, and solar electricity supply increased tenfold. Germany has worldwide leading positions in installed photovoltaic power capacity and installed wind power capacity.[53] In all likelihood, the German government was responding to particular identifiable interests.

However, renewable energy regulation has not only stimulated new entrants and pushed engagement in technologies, such as photovoltaic, energy transformation, energy storage, combined heat and power generation, fuel cells,[54] decentralized electricity generation, virtual networks,[55] and so on, but also stimulated conventional electricity suppliers to invest in modernization,[56] for instance in carbon dioxide (CO2) reduction, as well as in lobbying activities. In competition with other interests, conventional energy suppliers have incorporated ecological reasoning in their lobbying activities. For

[49] Rucht/Rose 2001, 269 ff., analyse the process of how eco-protest has been institutionalised in the German democratic system.

[50] Ahlheim 2003, 258 ff., and Truger 2001, 135 ff.

[51] Wagner/Schneider 2006, 14 ff.

[52] Federal Ministry for the Environment, Nature Conservation and Nuclear Safety 2005, 8 ff.

[53] For share and structure of renewable energy sources in the EU countries see: Federal Ministry for the Environment, Nature Conservation and Nuclear Safety 2005, 28 ff.

[54] Winter 2005, 48 ff.

[55] Hennig 2005, 38 ff.

[56] Bantle 2006, 18 ff., Kernan 2006, 30 ff., Bantle 2005, 48 ff., and Briese/ Büchsenschütz 2005, 42 ff.

instance, nuclear power suppliers argue their general relevance with ecologically-oriented reduction of CO_2 emissions.[57]

Particular technological progress exerts pressure on network structures. Structural changes of electricity networks are notably forced by new technologies in regenerative energy generation, energy transformation and energy storage. Networks can become virtual because of decentralized electricity generation,[58] which means that there is not *the* electricity network anymore. Thus, economic regulation will be necessary from a normative perspective to guarantee non-discriminatory market entry and competition among competing interests and technologies. But even then, economic regulation will also be the government's response to specific interests, and positive theorizing will be necessary to answer the question of why economic regulation occurs. From a normative perspective the question will have to be answered, how energy suppliers, network providers and customers can benefit from regulatory management.

Conclusion

In putting focus on the national implementation of EU directives, it can be stated, that in all likelihood the German government in their regulatory policy, responded to particular interests. The German national electricity market regulation is not just a copy of regulations in other member states, which all act under the same EU common norms.

A government's response to specific interests was demonstrated in two cases, the short-lived institution of negotiated network access conditions, and the green electricity regulation. Citizens' ecologically-oriented preferences and group interests have been institutionalized in the national electricity market regulation. The German implementation of EU electricity regulation can not only be argued by using normative principles of regulation, however, but also reflects specific interests in the member state. Such an analysis of why economic regulation actually occurs, stands in the tradition of Stigler's and Becker's approach of linking normative and positive theorizing.

[57] Kienle 2005, 20 ff.

[58] Hennig 2005, 38 ff., and Wacker/Schulz/Kurrat 2005, 20 ff.

References

Ahlheim, Michael, 2003, Ökosteuern—Idee und Wirklichkeit, in: Rose, Manfred (ed.), Integriertes Steuer—und Sozialsystem, Heidelberg: Physica-Verlag, 242–67.

Albers, Michael, 2005, Regulierung, Netzzugang, Unbundling: Die europäischen Vorgaben, in: Schwintowski, Hans-Peter (ed.), Verhandelter versus regulierter Netzzugang: Grenzen legitimer Preisgenehmigung für Strom, Baden-Baden: Nomos, 9–19.

Bantle, Christian, 2005, Investitionserhebung 2003: Investitionen in Kraftwerke gestiegen, in: ew—Das Magazin für die Energiewirtschaft 104, issue 1-2, 48–50.

Bantle, Christian, 2006, Investitionserhebung 2004: Mehr Investitionen in Stromnetze, in: ew—Das Magazin für die Energiewirtschaft 105, issue 4, 18–20.

Backhaus, Jürgen G., 1980, Öffentliche Unternehmen: Zum Wirtschaftsrecht, den Funktionen und Rechtsformen öffentlicher Unternehmen, 2nd edition., Frankfurt/Main: Haag und Herchen.

Becker, Gary S., 1983, The Theory of Competition among Pressure Groups for Political Influence, Quarterly Journal of Economics 98, 371–400.

_____, 1988, Public Policies, Pressure Groups, and Dead Weight Costs, in: Stigler, George J. (ed.), Chicago Studies in Political Economy, Chicago, London: University of Chicago Press, 85–105.

Blankart, Charles B., 1980, Ökonomie der öffentlichen Unternehmen. Eine institutionelle Analyse der Staatswirtschaft, München: Vahlen.

Boltz, Walter, 2005, Die europäische Dimension: Aktuelle Entwicklung der Strommarktregulierung auf Ebene der Europäischen Union, in: Boltz, Walter, Holoubek, Michael (eds.), Strommarktregulierung: Aktuelle Fragen aus der Sicht von Akteuren und Betroffenen., Wien: Braumüller, 113–21.

Briese, Dirk; Büchsenschütz, Kay, 2005, Zeit der Entscheidungen in der Energiewirtschaft: Kohle, Gas, Neubau oder Retrofit?, in: ew—Das Magazin für die Energiewirtschaft 104, issue 10, 42–4.

Brunekreeft, Gert, 2002, Regulation and Third-party Discrimination in the German Electricity Supply Industry, in: European Journal of Law and Economics 13, 203–20.

_____, 2004, Regulatory Threat in Vertically Related Markets: The Case of German Electricity, in: European Journal of Law and Economics 17, 285–305.

Bundesministerium für Wirtschaft und Arbeit, 2003, Bericht des Bundesministeriums für Wirtschaft und Arbeit an den Deutschen Bundestag über die energiewirtschaftlichen und wettbewerblichen Wirkungen der Verbändevereinbarungen (Monitoring-Bericht), Berlin, 31 August 2003.

Bundesverband der deutschen Gas—und Wasserwirtschaft, 2002, Antworten des BGW zum Fragenkatalog für die Sachverständigenanhörung des Wirtschaftsausschusses des Deutschen Bundestages zur Novellierung des Energiewirtschaftsrechts am 13. Mai 2002.

Büdenbender, Ulrich, 2003, Verbändevereinbarungen im Energierecht, Köln et al.: Carl Heymanns Verlag.

European Commission, 2003, Second Benchmarking Report on the Implementation of the Internal Electricity and Gas Market, Commission staff working paper, SEC(2003) 448, Brussels, 7 April 2003.

European Commission, 2005, Report on Progress in Creating the Internal Gas and Electricity Market, SEC(2005) 1448, Brussels, 15 November 2005.

Federal Ministry for the Environment, Nature Conservation and Nuclear Safety, 2005, Environmental Policy: Renewable Energy Sources in Figures: National and International Development, Berlin, Internet Update of June 2005, http:/www.erneuerbare-energien.de.

Folle, Rosemarie; Schöneich, Michael, 2002, Der deutsche Weg der Regulierung: Verhandelter Netzzugang und Verbändevereinbarungen, in: Frehmut, Walter; Parak, Christoph (eds.), Regulierung der Deregulierung von Infrastrukturmärkten, Wien: Manzsche Verlags—und Universitätsbuchhandlung, 249–64.

Glaeser, Edward L.; Shleifer, Andrei, 2003, The Rise of the Regulatory State, in: Journal of Economic Literature 41, 401–25.

Hennig, Erik, 2005, Virtuelle Kraftwerke nicht nur für Energieversorger interèssant, in: ew—Das Magazin für die Energiewirtschaft 104, issue 13, 38–40.

Kernan, Peter, 2006, Comeback für saubere Kohle, in: ew—Das Magazin für die Energiewirtschaft 105, issue 3, 30–1.

Kienle, Friedrich, 2005, Appell der europäischen Nuklearindustrie: Faire Chance für die Kernenergie gefordert, in: ew—Das Magazin für die Energiewirtschaft 104, issue 6, 20–7.

Kurth, Matthias, 2003, Privatisierung/Deregulierung/Marktverfassung: Die Sicht der Regulierungsbehörde, in: Perspektiven der Wirtschaftspolitik 4, 341–58.

Laffont, Jean-Jacques; Tirole Jean, 2000, Competition in Telecommunications, Cambridge et al.: MIT Press.

Levine, David K.; Lippman, Steven A. (eds.), 1995, The economics of information 1 and 2, Aldershot, Brookfield: Edward Elgar.

Monopolkommission, 2002, Vierzehntes Hauptgutachten der Monopolkommission 2000/ 2001, Deutscher Bundestag Drucksache 14/ 9903, 28 August 2002.

Peltzman, Sam, 1976, Toward a More General Theory of Regulation, in: Journal of Law and Economics 19, 211–40.

Posner, Richard A., 1974, Theories of Economic Regulation, in: Bell Journal of Economics and Management Science 5, 335–58.

Rebentisch, Manfred, 2005, Fortentwicklung des Energiewirtschaftsrechts: Verhandelter Netzzugang, in: Schwintowski, Hans-Peter (ed.), Verhandelter versus regulierter Netzzugang: Grenzen legitimer Preisgenehmigung für Strom, Baden-Baden: Nomos, 25–31.

Rucht, Dieter; Roose, Jochen, 2001, Zur Institutionalisierung von Bewegungen: Umweltverbände und Umweltprotest in der Bundesrepublik, in: Zimmer, Annette; Weßels, Bernhard (eds.), Verbände und Demokratie in Deutschland, Opladen: Leske + Budrich, 261–92.

Stigler, George J.; Friedland, Claire, 1962, What can Regulators Regulate? The Case of Electricity, in: Journal of Law and Economics 5, 1–16.

Stigler, George J., 1971, The Theory of Economic Regulation, in: Bell Journal of Economics and Management Science 2, 3–21.

Stiglitz, Joseph E., 2000, Economics of the Public Sector, 3rd edition, New York, London: W. W. Norton.

Tiedtke, Andreas, 2005, Demokratie in der Europäischen Union: Eine Untersuchung der demokratischen Legitimation des europäischen Integrationsprozesses vom Vertrag von Amsterdam bis zum Entwurf einer europäischen Verfassung, Berlin: Duncker & Humblot.

Truger, Achim, 2001, Der deutsche Einstieg in die ökologische Steuerreform, in: Truger, Achim (ed.), Rot-grüne Steuerreformen in Deutschland. Eine Zwischenbilanz, Marburg: Metropolis, 135–69.

Viscusi, W. Kip; Vernon, John M.; Harrington, Joseph E., Jr., 2005, Economics of regulation and antitrust, 4th edition, Cambridge, London: MIT Press.

Wacker, Jens; Schulz, Christian; Kurrat, Michael, 2005, Virtuelle Regelkraftwerke mit Mini-Blockheizkraftwerken: Eine wirtschaftliche Utopie?, in: ew—Das Magazin für die Energiewirtschaft 104, issue 17–18, 20–3.

Wagner, Alexander F.; Schneider, Friedrich, 2006, Satisfaction with Democracy and the Environment in Western Europe: A Panel Analysis, CESifo Working Paper No. 1660, February 2006.

Winter, Carl-Jochen,2005, Strom und Wasserstoff—Konkurrenten, Partner?, in: ew—Das Magazin für die Energiewirtschaft 104, issue 3, 48 ff.

8

Lessons from Regulation of Post-reform Power Sector

A Case Study of Orissa

MOHAMED ZAKARIA SIDDIQUI

Introduction

Many Indian states have begun to reform their State Electricity Boards (SEBs) for which broad policy guidelines have been laid down by the union government. The reason for this is the poor financial and physical performance of the SEBs. Though individual states have the option to follow an alternative path of reform, the availability of financial resources from the Centre has been conditioned upon the adoption of the model that the Centre has proposed for states to follow. The model seeks to de-integrate the vertically-integrated SEBs, where separate managements will manage generation, transmission and distribution activities, preferably under the management of private parties. Orissa was one of the first states to bring in comprehensive reforms of this kind in the power sector.

The power sector reform process in developing countries including India generally begins with the introduction of an Independent Regulatory Commission (IRC) along with the de-integration of the publicly-owned vertically-integrated structure into separate entities i.e. generation, transmission and distribution. Potentially competitive segments, generation and distribution, are further horizontally de-

A version of this paper was presented in the Fifth Development Convention at the Centre for Multidisciplinary Research, Dharwar. I am thankful to Dr Vijayamohanan Pillai and Professor K. P. Kannan for their comments and suggestions on the earlier version on this paper. I have also benefited from discussions with Dr Santhakumar.

integrated with the objective of fostering competition among these entities (firms). The IRCs in India are quasi-judicial bodies vested with delegated power so that the state governments are kept significantly away from the decision-making apparatus of the utilities (firms) even when it is publicly owned. The next step is to privatize these de-integrated entities and introduce mechanisms through which firms can compete with each other to serve their clients. In Orissa, following this regulatory orientation, an IRC was established under the name of Orissa Electricity Regulatory Commission.

The distribution system of the Orissa Electricity Board (OSEB) was divided into four regional utilities and was thereafter privatized. The transmission assets remained under public ownership with the Grid Corporation of Orissa (GRIDCO). For the generation sector, the reform document (World Bank 1996) stated that the grant of new generating plants should be based on competitive bidding but no new generation establishments came into being after the introduction of reform. Existing hydro-generation assets were vested with Orissa Hydro Power Corporation (OHPC) and the thermal capacity of the OSEB had to be transferred to the National Thermal Power Corporation (NTPC) to settle the dues of the OSEB with the NTPC. Figure 8.1 shows how OSEB was fragmented (see Appendix for more details of implementation)

In addition to the de-integration, the asset value of the power sector was revalued to double the initial value, the required rate of return that utilities could earn was raised from 3 per cent to 16 per cent and consumption subsidy was completely stopped. Presumably these are the factors that led to manifold increase in electricity tariffs of Orissa immediately after the reforms were initiated. On the other

FIGURE 8.1: PROCESS OF RESTRUCTURING OF OSEB ASSETS

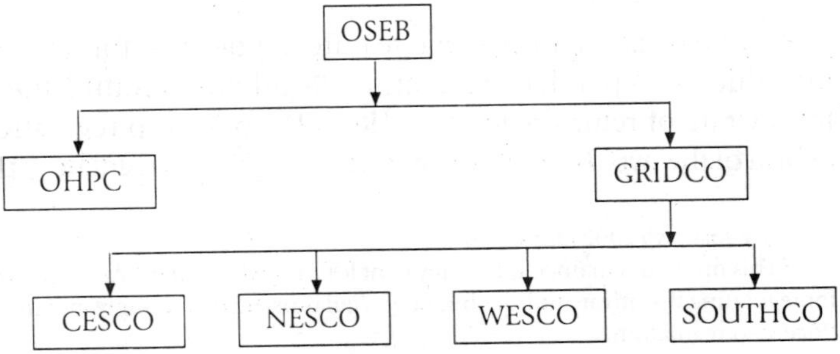

hand, a significant amount of transaction cost in the form of coordination cost and the cost of writing a formal contract between separate entities emerged due to this de-integration.[1]

The objective of this paper is to analyse the impact of power sector reforms on incentives for firms and other stakeholders involved in the electricity sector. To perform this analysis, extensive use has been made of the tariff order as a source of data; in fact it is the main source of data. A tariff order is the document through which most of the regulations relating to tariffs, cost and demand are delivered by the OERC or other similar state-level IRC. The OERC goes through several complex steps while formulating a tariff order. It is the primary responsibility of the regulators to make a realistic assessment of the cost and demand data provided by the licensees or companies falling under their jurisdiction.

This paper maintains that even though it was expected that efficiency gains after the initiation of reform would offset the increase in costs, this did not materialize, as there were some endogenous factors within the reform model itself that led to an increased cost of the power supply. In other words, the reforms were unable to target the serious ailments of the power sector in Orissa. The complex web of perverse incentives that existed in the pre-reform era are still intact and therefore, the generic problems of the power sector like high distribution losses and low cash collection efficiency by the utilities, continue to plague the companies.

The paper consists of six sections including this one. The sections describe the method of regulation; the process of constructing a tariff order; the various issues underlying the tariff order and finally, the section, 'Alternative Strategy to Regulate in the Current Scenario' offers suggestions to improve the regulatory practice.

Method of Regulation

As we noted earlier, the general feature of power sector reforms is to introduce independent regulators. Regulators around the world follow rate of return regulation (RORR),[2] price cap regulation or a hybrid of the two. To be able to engage with OERC's regulatory practice

[1] See Joskow (2002) for details.

[2] This method remained quite prevalent for a long time in the American economy for regulating the private utilities but now regulators are increasingly moving towards Price Cap regulation.

we critically review these methods. The OERC largely follows RORR along with price cap method in a limited way.

Rate of Return Regulation

Rate of Return Regulation aims to regulate profit levels and evolved to balance the interest of investors and consumers. The effort was to achieve a satisfactory balance between the interest of the investors and consumers/voters and at the same time, allow utilities to remain a private regulated monopoly. Williamson viewed RORR as the development of an incomplete long term contractual relationship that offered utilities a fair rate of return based on the capital invested in exchange for the ability to renegotiate the terms of the contract without excessively costly haggling (Williamson 1985:347). The formula for achieving the total required revenue for a utility to serve consumers according to this method, is:

$$\sum_{i=1}^{n} P_i Q_i = CE + s(RB) \tag{1}$$

where P_i and Q_i are the price and quantity of ith commodity produced by regulated utility respectively. CE is current expenditure, RB is rate base i.e., capital employed and s is the rate of return. The left hand side of the expression (1) represents the required revenue of the utility.

This method of regulation is also known as cost plus regulation. This is the oldest method of regulation and has been widely used in the American economy to regulate the investor owned utilities (IOUs). Economists have over time, increasingly criticized this RORR. The Averch and Johnson (1962) model investigated 'profit maximizing monopolist' operating under a rate of return constraint. One of the key assumptions of their analysis is that the allowed rate of return exceeds the actual (market) cost of capital, and they conclude that the firms operating under RORR will employ excess (i.e. more than optimal) capital[3] and thus it will not result in cost minimization. The general lesson we can draw from this model is that if:

1. R (allowed rate of return) > R* (market rate of return with similar risk) then the firm will employ more than the optimal capital, thus leading to an inefficient input combination (overuse of capital).

[3] This phenomenon is usually termed as gold plating in literature.

2. R = R* then the firm will employ the optimal level of capital, thus leading to an efficient input combination (optimal use of factors).
3. R < R* then the firm will employ less than the optimal capital, thus leading to inefficient input combination (under-use of capital).

The inability to deal with the problem of common cost is yet another shortcoming of RORR. Generally in the electricity industry one firm serves two markets. One is competitive and the other is monopolistic. However the capital employed by the firms is utilised for serving both the markets. According to Averch-Johnson, the firm operating under conditions where the regulation of rate of return is higher than the market rate, might have a long run incentive to price below long run marginal cost (LRMC) in the competitive market i.e., sub-optimal pricing to erase the competitors from the market in the long run. Firms may be able to do so because it is difficult for the regulator to clearly attribute what portion the total capital employed should be taken as the rate base for the regulated market and in turn, its revenue. This is basically the case of cross subsidizing the competitive sector with monopoly operation (Braeutigam and Panzar 1989).[4]

Another criticism is that it requires very detailed information for which the regulator has to depend on the monopolist, as there is no other source. So the monopolist has every incentive to misreport and exaggerate its cost component. These limitations led to various alternative regulatory mechanisms of which price cap regulation became the most famous.

Price Cap Regulation

Price cap regulation was initially recommended for British Telecom by Stephen Littlechild (1983). This method basically consists of fixing a floor price that a firm can charge. Once the price is fixed by a particular period, the next period price is indexed to the inflation rate, usually measured by retail price index (RPI), which is then reduced by possible productivity increases (X), as assessed by the regulator. In other words, the actual change in prices will depend on growth in RPI minus growth in X. So the formula for growth of price is RPI–X. This formula has implicit efficiency improvement incentive, because if a utility can outperform X, it can claim all profits occurring due to

[4] This is happening in the French electricity market.

increase in productivity greater than X. This is easy to administer as the price is based on a possible justified cost rather than the actual cost. However, one important limitation of this formula is that it leaves significant information rent with producers while this is not the case in RORR.

Comparison of the Two Methods

Each of these two forms of regulation can be seen as a special solution to the general problem of designing a system of regulation in which the regulator has imperfect information about the cost and opportunities faced by the regulated utility (Laffont and Tirole 1993; Laffont 1994).[5] The regulator specifies the rules that determine the utility's allowable revenue, R, in which:

$$R = b\overline{R} + (1 - b)C$$

where $\overline{R}$ is independent of utility's total cost, C. The term b is the power of regulatory incentive scheme, with b = 0 (the lowest power) corresponding to RORR and b = 1 to a high-powered regulation scheme such as price cap regulation in which utility receives all the benefits of cost reduction. Yet another general formulation of these two regulatory schemes has been done by Joskow and Schmalensee (1986). Their formula is:

$$R_a = R_t + h(R^* - R_t)$$

R^* is the targeted rate of return and R_t is the actual rate of return in period t. h is a positive constant ranging between zero and one. This formula gives us the actual rate of return (R_a) at the new price. If the value h is 1 the formula reduces to RORR and if the value of h is 0 then it is price cap regulation. Various public utilities have been put into this kind of regulation like gas, water and electricity (Viscusi et al. 1995). Regulating electricity in this way seems to be more universal as all countries are trying to bring private participation and competition. The practical implementation will depend on what kind regulatory problem is faced by the industry.

The regulator faces both a moral hazard as well as an adverse selection problem. It is unable to monitor a firm's effort to reduce

[5] Quoted in the *New Palgrave Dictionary of Law and Economics* 1998.

the cost and has less information than the firm about the technology used by the firm. It has two broad goals to promote i.e., to reduce cost and to extract the firm's rent, but these two goals are in conflict. To understand this, let us take the polar cases of RORR and price cap regulation. Now, the fixed price regulation induces the right amount of the effort because it makes the firm, residual claimant for its cost savings. The firm has the socially optimal (100 per cent) incentive for cost reduction as it receives all amounts it saves. On the other hand RORR offers no incentive (0 per cent) for cost reduction, because the firm does not appropriate any of its cost savings.

The logic gets reversed when it comes to rent extraction. Under price cap regulation the rent extracting power is 0 because the firm appropriates any exogenous reduction in the cost. The firm's rent thus, is very sensitive to the technological environment. Since the firm must have a non-negative rent when it has an intrinsically high cost, it obtains a substantial rent when facing an intrinsically low cost. However, the RORR is ideal for rent extraction because any exogenous variation in cost is borne by the consumers.

When the regulator has perfect information about the technology (moral hazard but no adverse selection) the optimal regulatory instrument is price cap regulation. But when the firm has private information about the technology the optimal regulatory scheme is RORR. So effort inducement calls for price cap regulation while rent extraction calls for ROR type regulation. In reality the regulator has to design an optimal regulatory contract, which confronts both the problems, by mixing the elements of regulation (price cap regulation and RORR) in the best possible way (Laffont and Tirole 1993: 40; Laffont 1996).

In the pre-reform era the method of regulation was usually RORR or cost plus regulation as envisaged by the Electricity (supply) Act 1948 and the tariff was decided by the OSEB. In the post-reform scenario also, the method of regulation has remained broadly RORR but now it is for the OERC to make a decision on tariffs relayed in their tariff orders. The Orissa Electricity Reform Act (OERA) 1995, earlier guided the OERC in its regulatory activities, but now the Electricity Act 2003 along with OERA 1995 guides it. Based on these laws, the commission may change its method of regulation if it feels that other forms of regulation may be more conducive to the electricity supply industry (ESI). In the Orissa context we have noted that over time there has been significant amount of variation in the method of regulation ranging from a pure RORR model to a mixture of Performance Based Regulation (PBR) and RORR.

Making a Tariff Order

In the initial stages of making a tariff order, licensees are notified to produce an annual revenue requirement (ARR) proposal to be presented to the OERC. After the licensee submits the ARR, the OERC notifies publicly in leading newspapers of the state, inviting objections to the said ARR. If the ARR does not have the required information, the OERC may again notify the licensee to provide such information. After the OERC has received the objections on ARR, it fixes a date of hearing when the objecting parties, the OERC members, and licensee or any other interested person can attend the proceedings. During the hearing the objectors register their objections and the licensee is supposed to clarify or reply to those objections. After hearing the views of all the stakeholders, the OERC finally approves the suggested tariff structure if it feels that the structure is in conformity with certain pre-decided norms. The document detailing the approval is called the Tariff Order. This process of finalization of the Tariff Order generally takes around three months.

Upon viewing tariff orders as a whole, the first distinct impression is that stakeholders are preoccupied in protecting their own interest. Although there is constant demand to penalize inefficient operation of utilities, objectors do not usually come up with well-researched suggestions to reduce the overall cost of the system. Since, the process of hearing by the OERC offers interest groups a platform to list their stakes, it could be a breeding ground for public action. However there is virtually no such activity and we still await the experience of operationalizing the envisioned involvement of stakeholders.

Issues Underlying Tariff Orders

The analysis of the tariff orders given by the OERC for various years helps us identify significant aspects as well as consequences of regulation. We try to address the major issues involved in tariff orders of bulk supply tariff (BST) and retail supply tariff (RST). For the initial three years starting from 1996–7, the Grid Corporation of Orissa (GRIDCO) was responsible for both transmission and distribution of power. Except for the first year, it has always operated under the regulation of the OERC till date. Here we will examine the major changes which occurred primarily due to regulation. Issues central to the discussion during hearings are mainly to question the GRIDCO's and DISTCOs' proposal for approval of tariff and suggestions to the OERC for better regulation that can reduce cost and thus, tariff in the short run. What seems to be lacking in the hearing process is that no individual or group came up with the suggestion to improve the internal corporate structure of the GRIDCO and DISTCOs in a way that employees at all levels of corporate functioning have incentives to perform better than their erstwhile organization, the OSEB. This question is at the heart of the problem. The literature relating to efficiency and ownership concludes that efficiency of an organization does not depend on public or private ownership but on the level of competition it faces. However, if competition is not feasible then the only way to reduce inefficiency is to improve the incentive structure of the organization so that the whole corporate practice is characterized by transparency, accountability and participation (TAP).

We now move on to discuss specific issues relating to the tariff orders. Broadly speaking, the major problems faced by the sector are high cost of procuring the power required by the state from various generating companies, inappropriate allocation risk and opportunities by the regulator, distribution losses of the DISTCO, low cash collection efficiency of the billed units of power by the DISTCOs, and un-metered consumers.

Cost of Purchase of Power

Power is purchased by the GRIDCO from various state-dedicated sources and central utilities like the NTPC and NHPC. The GRIDCO has to buy power to meet the demands of the DISTCOs. The DISTCOs' requirements are determined by the final demand of consumers plus the distribution losses. I will explain distribution losses a little later; for the moment, let us take it as a proportion of the power purchased by the DISTCOs from the GRIDCO which does not reach the intended consumers. In relation to this I propose to construct a power purchase multiplier to facilitate the understanding of this mechanism.

Let Y be the units of power that is required by the DISTCOs from the GRIDCO to meet the final demand of amount X say, by the consumers. Then:

$(Y - bY) = X$ where $b < 1$, is the distribution loss factor

$Y(1 - b) = X$

Therefore, $Y = \dfrac{X}{1 - b}$

Now differentiating Y with respect to X, we get the Power Purchase Multiplier as

$$\frac{dY}{dX} = \frac{1}{1-b}$$

Power Purchase Multiplier = $\frac{1}{1-b}$

Now if b that is loss factor, is 42 per cent then the value of the multiplier is 1.72. This implies that to satisfy one unit of final demand of the consumers, the DISTCOs will have to buy 1.72 units of power from the GRIDCO. Power Purchase Multiplier is expected to be higher for those DISTCOs, which have higher loads in the low tension (LT) category. Table 8.1 gives the calculation made on the basis of this multiplier.

From Table 8.1 the value of the multiplier gives a better insight into distribution losses than distribution loss figures alone. The table also gives an estimate of money that could have been saved, if the system operated at a normative level (15 per cent) of the distribution loss.

The cost of power purchase has risen to significantly high levels. The OERC has been continuously making changes in the purchase plan of the GRIDCO in order to minimize the cost of power purchase. The OERC has always emphasized that DISTCOs should draw maximum power from the cheapest plants so that the revenue requirements remain at the lowest level, thus leading to lower tariffs. However after the introduction of the Availability Based Tariff (ABT) this problem has to some extent, been further aggravated. ABT is the system of tariff where GRIDCO will have to pay a fixed amount to the generator on the basis of the capacity that the generator makes available to the GRIDCO. It is immaterial whether that capacity is utilised by the GRIDCO or not during the period of the contract.

Power is procured through a contract between the GRIDCO and the generating companies known as the power purchase agreement (PPA). The PPA is signed under the supervision of the Central Electricity Regulatory Commission (CERC) if the generating company falls outside the jurisdiction of the OERC, i.e. the generating company is a central government-owned utility and/or is not operating in Orissa. Initially, the two parties of the PPA are supposed to negotiate and reach an agreement but in case of failure of such negotiations, the CERC will dictate the terms and condition of purchase which should finally be acceptable to the two parties.

TABLE 8.1: POWER PURCHASE REQUIREMENTS WITH ACTUAL AND NORMATIVE MULTIPLIER

	Final demand (MUs)	*Distribution Loss (%)*		*Power Purchase Multiplier*		*Power Purchase (MUs)*		*Energy Savings (MUs)*	*Potential Money Savings* (Rs million)*
		Actual	*Normative*	*Actual*	*Normative*	*Actual*	*Normative*		
1999–2000	5602.83	43.9	15	1.78	1.18	9987.22	6591.56	3395.65	39.23
2000–01	6081.32	43.95	15	1.78	1.18	10849.81	7154.49	3695.32	42.69
2001–02	5772.87	47.47	15	1.90	1.18	10989.66	6791.61	4198.05	48.50
2002–03	6731.779	40.75	15	1.69	1.18	11361.65	7919.74	3441.91	39.76

Note: * This has been calculated by assuming power purchase cost of 115.52 paise per unit for all the years as approved by OERC for GRIDCO's purchase cost

Source: OERC (2002)

Experts (Dhubash and Rajan 2001; Grutoo and Pandey 2001; Morris 2000) are of the view that PPAs are designed in such a way that they harm the interest of the purchasing utility. The standard PPA typically reflects those incentives. The generating companies are generally assured of their returns with virtually no risk as the minimum-mandated performance level (62 per cent of plant load factor PLF)[6] is not that difficult to achieve for any generating company. 'Cost plus' agreements along with conditions of performance indicators induce a generation company to be less concerned about cost minimizing exercises and also cause it to be capital-intensive. This kind of contract is prone to gold plating as the RORR is structured on the capital base. The impact of the PPA is very well reflected in the financial results of NTPC and the buying utilities. It should be noted that NTPC is a well-performing, profit-making corporation. The buying utilities on the other hand, have been suffering losses continuously. This is not to say that all the losses of the buying utilities or the SEBs are attributable to PPAs but this is certainly one of the major factors contributing to losses. Several experts claim that one of the major reasons of financial erosion of the SEBs are PPAs with either the IPPs or the NTPC (Grutoo and Pandey 2001; Kannan and Pillai 2002 and Morris 2000).

The major contention of the reform was to remove the inefficiencies in the wire segment of the business i.e., transmission and distribution. This however, has not yet been addressed. In the absence of these efficiency improvements, purchase requirements are impossible to bring down. The GRIDCO therefore, will continue to suffer losses until efficiency improvements are effected within it and the four DISTCOs of the state.

A typical PPA consists mainly of three parts. One, the determination of fixed charges; two, the standard of physical operation and; three, the variable charges which mainly depend on the usage and price of fuel. Fixed charges have various components and the contents of a PPA often discuss the justification of these components.

Components of Fixed Charges: Capital base, rate of interest on loan, return on equity, depreciation, O and M (operation and maintenance) expenses, interest on working capital, income tax, etc.

[6] PLF is expressed as total amount of electricity actually produced as a percentage of the total units of electricity the plant is capable of producing.

$$PLF = \frac{kWh}{kW * 8760 \text{ Hours}} * 100.$$

Components of Physical Operation: Plant load factor, target availability, satiation heat rate,[7] auxiliary consumption, specific fuel oil consumption.

The problem with such take-or-pay PPA is that the utility will be charged for the full capacity it has contracted, irrespective of the utilisation of that capacity. One way of solving this problem is that the contracted generation capacity should be tradable. In cases where a buying utility is not in a position to utilise her contracted capacity fully for a particular time period, she should be free to trade the unutilised capacity with any other utility, which is in need of the same. Objections to this argument maintain that the GRIDCO should buy all the power and export it so that the burden of capacity cost could be minimized. But such a solution may not be feasible as it requires administrative complexity and involves risk. It may nevertheless be noted that the earlier solution can lead to significant amount of administrative ease, reduction in the risk of the utilities and efficient allocation of generating capacities.

Revenue Risk for the GRIDCO

As mentioned earlier, GRIDCO charges the DISTCOs on the basis of two-part tariff. The point to note is that they do so only to maintain the tradition of two-part tariff. The fixed charges in reality, do not represent the actual fixed costs incurred by the GRIDCO on transmission network and procurement of power. In all tariff orders the demand charges (fixed charges) are lower than the required levels (fixed charges are around 25 per cent of the actual fixed cost). The remaining part (75 per cent) of the fixed cost is added to the variable expenses to arrive at energy charges. The problem with such an arrangement is that the projected sale of the GRIDCO may be more than what GRIDCO actually sells to the DISTCOs while the energy charges are determined by the projected sale. Therefore the GRIDCO in actuality may not be able to realize its required revenue. This is how the demand risk, imposed by the DISTCOs, is borne by the GRIDCO. Also, GRIDCO has to pay the fixed charges equal to the actual fixed cost incurred by the generating utilities. This particular arrangement of tariff reveals that the publicly-owned GRIDCO is being used as shock absorbing organization for Orissa's power sector, as seen in Table 8.2.

[7] Heat Rate is defined, as heat required per unit of generation of power (e.g. kcals/kWh). It serves the purpose of conversion (of fuel to electricity) efficiency parameter in a generating utility.

TABLE 8.2: NORMATIVE AND ACTUAL TARIFF STRUCTURES

Structuring Option	*Demand Charges Rs/kVA/Month*	*Energy Charges Paisa/unit*
Structuring Demand Charges to cover full cost of transmission and all the fixed cost of power purchase. Energy Charges will cover only the variable costs of generation or normative tariff structure.	1057.58	62.07
Actual Charge as approved by the OERC	200	91*

*Actual energy charge for each DISTCO is different depending upon the projection of purchase of energy units by a particular DISTCO. This is the average of energy charges of all DISTCOs.
Source: OERC (2002)

In the above-mentioned case what happens at the end of the financial year is dependent on the following difference, viz., (Y–Y*), where Y is actual units bought by the DISTCOs and Y* is units of electricity expected to be bought by the DISTCOs. If the above difference is positive i.e., the DISTCOs buy more than the expected amount, then GRIDCO will earn profit but if the difference is negative i.e., the DISTCOs buy less than the expected amount, the GRIDCO will run into loss. In addition, this pricing structure has an in-built perverse incentive for the DISTCOs to show high expected purchase of power from GRIDCO while filing the ARR so that energy charges arrived at by the following formula, are low:

$$EC = \frac{(FE - FC) + VE}{ES}$$

Where EC = Energy Charge, FE = Total Fixed Expenses of the GRIDCO, FC = Total Revenue Earning through demand charges, VE = Variable Expenses and ES= Expected Units of Sale of the GRIDCO to the DISTCOs.

There is an inversely proportionate relationship between energy charge and the projected purchase by DISTCOs i.e., higher the projected units of sale, lower will be the energy charge. Therefore it will be in the DISTCOs' interest to buy less units of power than they have actually projected so that they can escape paying for the capacity or the fixed charges. In such a case, the GRIDCO will not be able to cover its required revenue. Therefore the GRIDCO always has a risk of demand uncertainties. One may argue that the DISTCOs should be charged according to their projected energy purchase rather than

TABLE 8.3: POWER PURCHASE OF THE DISTCOs FOR 2002-03

DISTCOs	*Projected*	*Approved(Y*)*	*Actual(Y)*	*Y–Y**
CESCO	4321	4321	4055.75	(-)265.25
NESCO	3023	2291.2	2395.38	104.18
WESCO	3066.54	3066.54	3353.78	287.24
SOUTHCO	1713.71	1682.39	1556.7	(-)125.69
Total	12124.25	11361.13	11361.61	0.48

Source: OERC (2002) all Tariff Orders

the actual purchase. The problem with this solution is that the GRIDCO will have little incentive to be efficient and responsive to the demands of the DISTCOs because it has already ensured its revenue. Table 8.3 helps us understand this more clearly.

We can see from Table 8.3 that the WESCO actually draws more than its projected purchase. However we need to be aware of the fact that the WESCO owned by the BSES, might be operating in collusion with the SOUTHCO and the NESCO, which are also owned by the BSES; ignorance of this clearly misguides the regulators. Clubbing all the BSES companies together, their projected energy purchase is 7803.25 MUs but they have actually drawn only 7305.86 MUs, a difference of around 500 MUs i.e. Y–Y* = (–) 500 MUs. If the regulator had calculated energy charges based on projected energy purchase by the DISTCOs, then the GRIDCO may have suffered a loss of Rs 69.40 crore. It may be true that regulators can correctly estimate the purchase, as can be seen from Table 8.3. The approved purchase units are nearly the same as the actual units purchased in aggregate, but this cannot contradict the fact that there is a significant error in the estimation of company-wise purchase (compare the 3rd and 4th columns in Table 8.3). This means that revenue required by the GRIDCO has been covered but the burden of revenue shared by the DISTCOs is not justified i.e., some of the DISTCOs gain from this; for example, the CESCO and the SOUTHCO, while others lose like the NESCO and the WESCO. In the aggregate the GRIDCO has a small surplus. The important point here is that the GRIDCO's fate is highly dependent on actual purchase of power by the DISTCOs which sometimes may be quite different from the expected quantity.

Another possibility that cannot be ignored is that there may be a deliberate attempt to over-project the purchase of power by the DISTCOs in cases when regulators and the DISTCOs collude. In other words, the DISTCOs might influence the regulators through kickbacks to allow their higher projected purchase for tariff calculation. Therefore, the demand charge should be able to cover the total fixed costs; otherwise there is a possibility of opportunistic behaviour by the purchaser and seller of the power including the regulator.

Dealing with Depreciation

The allowed rate of depreciation can have a significant impact on the tariff. During the initial years the OERC simply adopted the earlier rates. It was a well-known fact that the asset values were simply re-valued without any physical addition to the capital stock. For example, if an asset of Rs 500 is simply re-valued at Rs 1,000 without any addition to capital at the discretion of the government with depreciation rates remaining constant, then the value of depreciation will be quite high because the base was re-valued. Let us take the depreciation rate as 5 per cent; then the depreciation amount before revaluation would be Rs 25. In the post-revaluation scenario it will be much higher at Rs 50. Such a situation emerged with the 1997–8 tariff order of the GRIDCO. The OERC could have mitigated a part if not the full impact of the revaluation of assets by heavily reducing the depreciation rates. This realization came to the OERC only after a few years of operation. Thus for the financial year 2003–4, the OERC gave the above reason to calculate the depreciation amount based on considerably lower rates than the earlier ones.

Liquidity Crisis in the Power Sector

The GRIDCO faces a huge liquidity crisis because the DISTCOs are not able to pay on time. The GRIDCO however, has to pay its dues to generating companies on time. Disproportionate distribution of opportunities and challenges or responsibilities of the Orissa ESI will ultimately turn out to be unsustainable in the long run. So far, there has been no attempt from the regulator's side to ensure that the liquidity problem is solved. The liquidity problem emerges from the inability of the DISTCOs to collect money efficiently as mandated by the OERC. Initial ARR filings were based on the assumption that immediately after the DISTCOs are in operation, billing-to-collection efficiency would be 100 per cent as envisaged by the Staff Appraisal Report (World Bank 1996). Failure of this led to the non-payment of dues to the GRIDCO which in turn, could not pay its dues to the generating companies on time. On the suggestion of the Kanungo Committee Report, the OERC, starting from 2003, has based its regulatory activity on aggregate commercial and technical (AT&C)[8] losses, which takes into account distribution losses, collection inefficiency, rather than just distribution losses (see Siddiqui 2004, Chapter 3 for details of AT&C loss).

Issue of Distribution Losses

When electricity passes through wires some part of it is lost. The precise number of units of electricity lost in this manner depends upon the electrical resistance of the wire and the amount of electricity that is being transferred through the wire. Distribution loss can never to reduced to zero because it is an intrinsic property to distribution of electrical power over wires. In addition to this loss, some amount of electricity is stolen through human intervention like hooking, bypassing meters and by other ingenious methods. These losses are usually termed as commercial losses. Therefore the elements comprising distribution losses are commercial losses and technical losses. Distribution loss is one of the most important and bewildering parameters concerning the Indian power sector. With the introduction of the restructuring process in some of the states, the actual amount of distribution losses have been revealed to be much higher than generally shown by their erstwhile SEBs, who usually conceal these losses by describing them as the consumption by unmetered consumers—usually agricultural and domestic consumers. The phenomenon of widespread theft has also been emphasized. But here I am only going to focus on the issue of regulatory effectiveness. There was a huge gap in the proposed and approved loss levels. The regulators were usually adamant on keeping the approved losses at 35 per cent level. The OERC also provided the DISTCOs with the incentive that any cost savings beyond the 35 per cent level would be the firm's profit. For example, a particular DISTCO is able to operate at a loss level lower than 35 per cent, say 32 per cent. The OERC will however, continue calculate the revenue requirement of the DISTCO assuming 35 per cent distribution loss. The cost-saving effected due to the improved performance (3 per cent) will be the profit of the DISTCO. But none of the DISTCOs could

[8] The Kanungo Committee Report has coined AT&C loss as distinct from the conventional distribution loss to capture the totality of loss, both technical as well as commercial owing to non-billing, non-collection, theft, etc. Formula for AT&C loss is $[1 - (b.c)].100$ where $b < 1$ is distribution efficiency factor and $c < 1$ is efficiency of cash collection.

FIGURE 8.2: DISTRIBUTION LOSSES OF THE DISTCOs

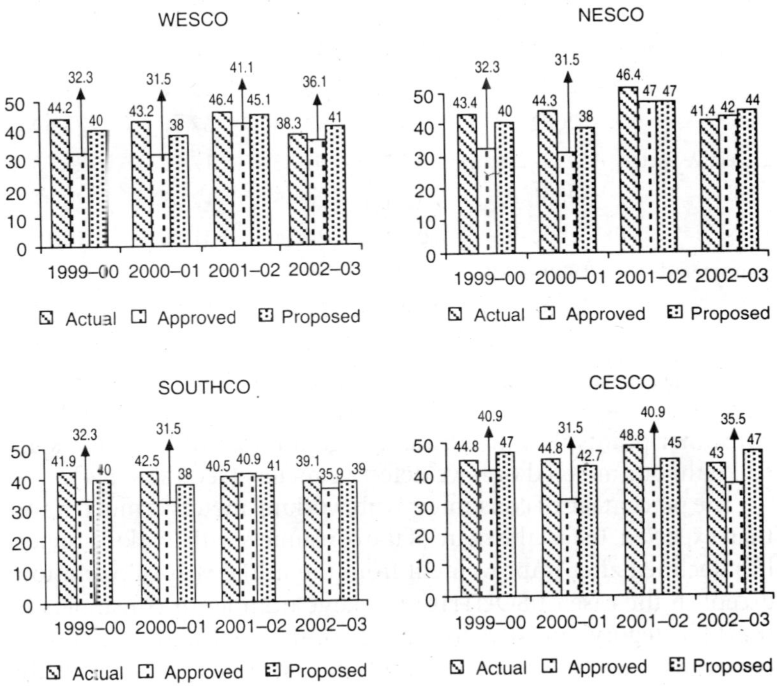

respond to this incentive scheme as their actual losses were still very high. Ultimately the World Bank resolved the issue in 1998, by stating that 35 per cent loss level benchmarked by their study, was an unachievable target under the given conditions. Therefore, the OERC raised its target of loss levels to around 42 per cent for all the DISTCOs. But even then the DISTCOs' distribution loss levels remained higher than the 42 per cent mark (see Figure 8.2).

Issues of Information Asymmetry

For effective regulation, a regulatory body no matter how expert and independent, needs access to reliable information to make sound decisions. This includes information about the needs and priorities of consumers, firms and other stakeholders, as well as about the performance of the regulated firms; alternatively demand and cost information. It is also known that to get reliable information regarding demand 100 per cent metering is needed at all feeder levels and

TABLE 8.4: METERING STATUS OF THE DISTCOs (PERCENTAGE)

		CESCO	*NESCO*	*WESCO*	*SOUTHCO*
Working meters	1999–2001	39.78	47.09	60.90	68.22
	2001–02	57.15	46.04	69.40	72.11
	2002–03	53.47	52.08	67.77	78.62
Defective meters	1999–2001	40.14	31.83	17.12	25.03
	2001–02	28.38	26.45	12.03	20.97
	2002–03	30.90	24.74	11.76	16.11
Unmetered	1999–2001	20.07	21.07	21.98	6.75
	2001–02	14.47	27.51	18.57	6.92
	2002–03	15.62	23.18	20.47	5.27

Source: OERC, all the tariff orders of DISTCOs from 1999 onwards

consumer points. But in Orissa, a large number of consumers are still either unmetered or have defective meters (see Table 8.4).

The percentage of consumers with working meters is much lower than expected. In fact the share of the consumers with working meters has declined after improvement from the initial year of operation, except in the case of SOUTHCO. A large number of consumers in the LT category (mostly domestic, commercial and agricultural consumers) are still unmetered. Overall, only 62 per cent of the consumers have working meters in Orissa which is quite low especially when agricultural consumers, for whom metering is the most challenging, constitute only 3.13 per cent (in 2001) of the total number of consumers.

On account of this the information asymmetry between the regulator and the regulated firms has widened, working to the advantage of regulated companies. If metering is not universal, data regarding distribution loss cannot also be considered reliable. As a result, performance benchmarking becomes difficult, which again works to the advantage of the companies in cases when the regulator grants the benefit of the doubt to the companies. This problem gets aggravated when all the DISTCOs are operating in a collusive environment. It is highly possible for companies to extract information rent in such situations, when the regulatory expertise and technological capabilities are in their infancy.

My earlier study (Siddiqui 2004) has shown that immediately after the reforms, the generation sub-sector improved significantly because it was easier to get information, and incentives were aligned favourably to the generation companies. A similar dramatic improvement however, did not take place on the distribution side. This inability to improve the situation in relation to distribution was because of the possibility of severe information rent extraction and also since incentives were not aligned in ways where companies could narrow down the information asymmetry. Part of the information asymmetry is maintained because regulators do not give incentives to bring about technological innovation. For example, if proper incentives were designed to introduce a computerized system of meter-reading, it would be possible to forecast demand accurately and far more easily. Therefore the regulators have to be careful about the innovations that can make the process more transparent and provide reliable information. Although tariff orders direct the DISTCOs to achieve 100 per cent metering, the OERC has not enforced any financial penalty until now on those who have not done so.

One of the important factors which helps the DISTCOs to misreport consumption data by different categories, is the non-existence of 100 per cent metering at consumers' level. It is easy for the DISTCOs to dump the consumption of one category into another consumption category and they have an incentive to do so because if they report higher consumption in the LT categories they are allowed to operate at higher AT&C losses. In addition to this, they earn unreasonable revenue (rent) from this process. Suppose a consumption of quantity Q of industrial consumers was dumped as consumption of domestic consumers, the following profit or rent can be earned by any of the participants in the sale i.e., company, employee, consumer, or all of them together, if they are in a collusive environment.

Rent = $(P_i - P_d) \times Q$ where P_i is industrial consumers tariff and P_d is the tariff for domestic consumers.

Earning such a rent is possible only when there are price differences between different categories (necessary condition). The enabling factor for this to happen is the absence of metering (sufficient condition). If these price differences disappear there will be no incentive to delay the process of metering. However as long as this price difference (cross-subsidy) exists, companies will have an incentive to delay metering. In the near future it is highly unlikely that these price differences will disappear. The only option for the regulators therefore, is to provide enough incentives to the DISTCOs to implement metering in 100 per cent of the cases. This will eliminate the enabling factor by which the DISTCOs earn rent.

Pandey and Morris (2004) has shown that after metering was done in some of the distribution circles in Madhya Pradesh, there was a dramatic improvement in the distribution loss and cash collection efficiency. Power purchase requirements reduced and ultimately, an improvement was effected in the financial performance of the circles. This was possible because of the aggressive metering campaign conducted by determined officers, coupled with support from top political offices. It was also argued that a publicly-owned organization has comparative advantage over a private organization for the implementation of such reforms. Privately-operated DISTCOs may not be an efficient agent to implement this reform because this cannot be done by the DISTCOs alone and needs the help of several other supportive institutions e.g., police administration, political offices and the society at large. It is easier for publicly-owned distribution companies to seek co-operation from other public institutions and implement it.

Therefore the first step of the regulators should be to make sure that the necessary infrastructure needed to reduce the information asymmetry is implemented at the fastest possible rate because each moment lost entails loss of welfare. To achieve this, regulators need to increase the intensity of incentive on metering. Currently, incentive intensity is applied on distribution loss but not on metering and voltage of wires that help to reduce distribution losses.

Discrimination against Publicly-owned Company

When reforms were initiated, it was agreed in principle that all the companies involved in Orissa's power sector would get the same rate of return irrespective of their ownership. But the manifold increase in the price of power compelled the Kanungo committee to look at sources for reducing the tariff. In order to do that, it recommended that the GRIDCO and the OHPC, publicly-owned companies, should not be allowed to earn any 'rate of return'; they should only cover their fixed and variable costs. This, it was felt, would reduce the revenue requirements of the two companies, which ultimately would translate into lower tariffs at retail level. The commercial principle was compromised to keep prices low; there is little difference in the mode of thinking of the policy makers in the post-reform scenario. Since the goal of deriving benefits from the efficiency improvement is far from being realized, we see only inappropriate ways of reducing cost i.e., through financial manipulations.

Alternative Strategy to Regulate in the Current Scenario

As already explained, the regulatory strategy to promote efficiency and rectify the misallocation of resources has been based on the advice of the World Bank. The structure was established by the Orissa Electricity Reform Act 1995, which based itself on earlier laws like the Electricity Supply Act 1948 and the Indian Electricity Act 1910. The Electricity Act 2003 became the OERC's guiding principle after its advent. This change in structure has resulted in at least some significant changes. The mode of regulation broadly, is RORR at all levels i.e., generation, transmission and distribution, although there is also an element of PBR. The major advantage of the PBR is that it may be tailored to suit the parameters of performance that the regulators choose to impose on the regulated utilities (Sankar and Ramachandran 2000). This form of regulation is well-suited to the Indian conditions as PBR can help the regulators target specific matters of performance, in that, incentives can be designed to impact particular parameters, while being sensitive to the costs and benefits associated with the regulation. In a sense, the task being performed by regulators in India is quite non-conventional in nature. Their efforts are directed towards making the utilities run in a commercial way rather than introducing competition into the sector. Most of the utilities in India are near financial bankruptcy, and therefore, the foremost challenge for the regulators is to convert financial deficits into a reasonable surplus. Regulators have also learnt that changing the structure is not going to help as much as expected, as evident from the Orissa experience. It has also been experienced that regulating the utilities on the basis of broad parameters like distribution losses only, has not helped until now. The Dhabol Power project debacle and the California energy crisis have revealed that the private sector has never really missed a chance to make use of the weaknesses of the rules of the game (Dubash and Rajan 2001; Kannan and Pillai 2002 and Phadke and Rajan 2003). It should also be borne in mind that an incentive may not work in cases where the individual or parties affected under the incentive scheme do not have the capacity to respond to incentives i.e. incentives will work provided the companies are not already adversely selected. The experience until now suggests that both the government and the private sector have failed to bring about the desired change and therefore, the answer to problems of the ESI has to be cautiously given. What seems to work are the targeted improvement programmes for different performance indicators; this philosophy is current in the Accelerated Power Development and Reform Programme (APDRP) initiated by Ministry of Power (MoP) wherein they plan to reduce the AT&C losses. What is proposed here is to take this philosophy to a broader level. Below, we discuss some of the issues to be addressed by the above-mentioned measures.

Maintaining Reliability

Reliability is one of the most important parameters from the consumer's point of view. Low reliability of power supply has become a political issue. Regulators need to assign DISTCOs to operate with a particular level of reliability at which it must supply power to a particular region or circle of distribution. Different categories of consumers are generally connected to the same wires, so the regulator may resort to differential pricing mechanism for different categories of consumers enjoying same the level of reliability. For example, in urban areas the commercial consumers and household consumers are connected to the same wires and therefore, they enjoy the same level of reliability. In other words, reliability is a non-excludable commodity for all the consumers connected to a given wire.

Regulators can also prioritize hours of the day at which different categories need the highest reliability in case of shortages. In urban areas, consumers at high-tension (HT) and extra high-tension (EHT) end are industries, which require the highest reliability during office hours of the day. On the other hand, commercial and household consumers at the LT end may require highest reliability during non-office hours. It is understood however, that the commercial sector will need power at all points of time more desperately than any other group. But given a choice of having high reliability immediately before and after office hours or at other points of time outside of office hours, they may prefer the first alternative. Nothing can be said with certainty about such prioritization of reliability in the absence of a comprehensive survey, which is beyond the scope of the present study. But for our purpose it is important to understand that such prioritization is indeed possible, and can be adopted by the regulators after a comprehensive survey, to mitigate the problem of shortages in the short run.

The cost of system reliability is dependent on tensions at which power is provided. There can be some kind of cross-subsidy mechanism among the different groups served at the same tension as well as other tensions. Studies suggest that tariff should be based not only on the amount of electricity consumed, but also on the reliability level at which electricity is consumed (Moorhouse 2001). But providing different reliability levels to individual consumers according to demand may not be possible with the current technology of metering. All the consumers connected to a particular feeder will enjoy the same level of reliability. One should keep in mind that such a pricing regime is possible only when the metering is also capable of rationing the electricity. This is not possible in near future as, even simple meters are not installed and even if installed, a large proportion of them are not in working condition.

It is important to note that not only is the cost of electricity supply inversely related to the voltage at which electricity is supplied, but also the reliability. Marginal cost of reliability reduces as the voltage at which an additional unit of reliability has to be ensured, increases. On the other hand, the categories that demand higher reliability generally consume electricity at the high voltage end. These categories can therefore, be charged higher than the actual cost of reliability. This possibility of extracting a surplus from such consumers is beneficial as it can be transferred to the other consumer groups with a low capacity to pay, mainly agricultural and domestic consumers. They can regulate the reliability of the supply through the code of supply (as by the Electricity Act 2003).

The high demand for reliability from industrial consumers can be confirmed from the emergence of the Captive Power Producers (CPPs) in Gujarat and Orissa. The industrial sector appears to be deprived of high reliability because of the political pressure on utility to supply power to households without controlling the high distribution losses. Ramesh et al. (1990) shows that the usage of captive power generation facilities by industries is at the maximum level during the agricultural seasons. This has led to the vicious circle of the higher tariff for subsidizing category of consumers (Figure 8.3). The falling reliability in supply has forced the industrial consumers to seek alternative sources of power. As a result, the demand for electricity by the consumers groups, which cross-subsidizes the other groups of consumers, has reduced. This has in turn, led to the need for further increase in the price of electricity to be paid by groups that bear the costs of subsidy, so that enough revenue is generated to

FIGURE 8.3: VICIOUS CIRCLE OF LOW QUALITY OF POWER SUPPLY

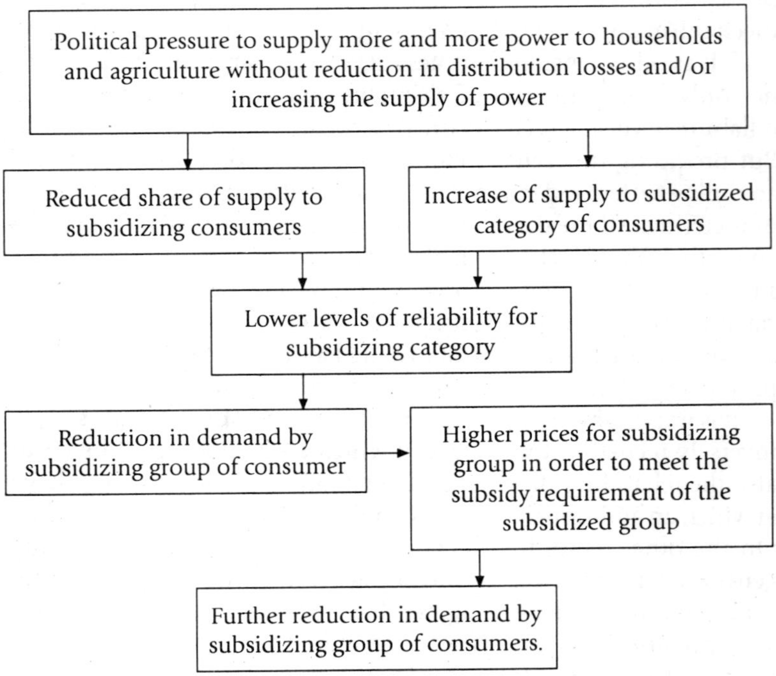

subsidize lower end consumers. Low reliability coupled with high prices has further induced consumers who bear the costs of subsidy, to opt for other sources of power. This cycle thus, goes on until the picture becomes totally unbearable!

Demand for Reliability

The cost of having higher reliability than that provided by the incumbent utility is extraordinarily high. Here we take a category of consumer as one consumer group i.e., domestic, agricultural, commercial and industrial consumers: If we assume that all consumers of one group have common preference for reliability, it is possible for one to perceive the likely shapes of the demand curves for the reliability (Figure 8.4). Consumers would like to bid higher prices for the higher level of reliability i.e., positively sloping demand curve. But different categories will have different levels of willingness to pay. Thus the price elasticity of demand and the area under the

FIGURE 8.4: DEMAND FOR RELIABILITY FOR DIFFERENT CATEGORIES

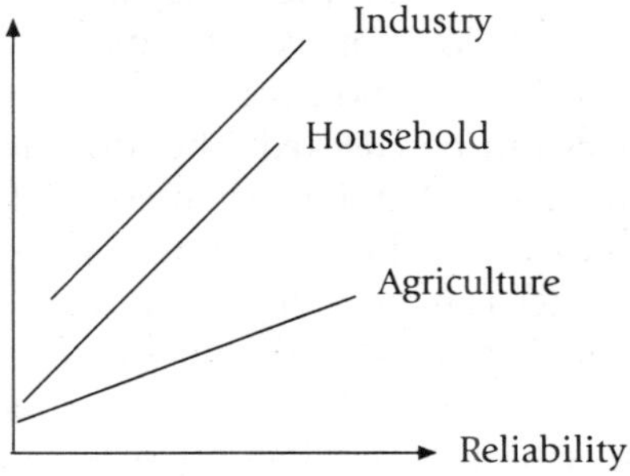

demand curve i.e., the utility will be different for different categories of consumers.

Intuitively, it is clear that higher reliability is preferred by different categories of the consumers at different time intervals of the day. Industrial consumers are expected to have the highest willingness to pay for reliability. On the other hand, agricultural consumers have the lowest willingness to pay. This does not mean that such consumers can be ignored. We need to be aware of the development externality of electricity consumption in rural areas. Rural supply of power might be instrumental in bringing about rural industrialization and increase in agricultural productivity and possibly, even promote the habit of reading. In fact policy should try and influence the demand curve in such a way that if agricultural consumers are willing to pay more, they are able to derive more utility from a higher level of reliability compared to what they get presently. This can happen if the rural population becomes aware of the potential benefit that can be derived from increased reliability of power. The story for the household consumer lies somewhere in between the two extremes of the industrial consumer and the agricultural consumer.

Reducing Distribution Losses

In the case of Orissa, companies have not been able to stand up to the expectation of the regulators. They have not found ways to reduce losses as per the regulator's order. Now in such a situation the regulator assumes the role of an executive director, as it needs to focus on the disaggregated parameters crucial in minimizing distribution losses. For example, technological improvements in metering, computerized billing and transformer capacities may help in reducing commercial losses along with increasing the transparency of the system. By improving the mix of low voltage (LV) and medium voltage (MV) wire lengths in the distribution network, the technical part of the distribution losses can be checked. The MoP has already adopted this approach under the APDRP, which presently focuses on reducing the distribution losses by closely monitoring the above parameters (MoP 2002). Under this programme, utilities are provided with financial assistance based on their achievements relative to the target fixed in the previous period. One of the major reasons for very high cost of purchase is the huge distribution losses of the DISTCOs. Here we propose some ways to regulate the sector so that the chaotic state of affairs prevailing in the sector can be arrested.

The strategy of controlling the distribution losses should be well spelt out. One of the major sources of the high distribution loss is theft of electricity. If we take account of the non-payment of the power sold i.e., collection inefficiency, then this figure is much higher. The revenue recovery of even the recorded electricity sold is not 100 per cent.

Controlling Theft

Educating Consumers: Educating consumers may be one of the important factors, which can lead to reduction in theft in the long run. Simple estimates by the regulatory commission about possible reductions in the tariff in the absence of theft can be publicized through various mechanisms like schoolchildren conveying the message to parents, using electronic media etc. The basic idea here is to make people realize the amount of resources that are being wasted.

Political Willingness: Improvement in the quality of power seems to be an impossible dream unless theft is arrested. Hooking is a social phenomenon in Orissa while industry steals power with greater sophistication (Parayas 2002 and Mahalingam 2002). The control of theft of electricity is highly dependent on the level of political willingness. Kannan and Pillai (2002:82) have highlighted that the culture of theft enjoys the patronage of the SEB officials and this holds true even in privatized regimes. In fact, the non-payment of the utility bills is not only because of the inability of the consumers to pay, but also largely because of their attitude. We see that most of the defaulting consumers are public organizations and people with political influence. At the same time, utility employees are not very serious about collecting bills. Surprisingly, even after defaulting on payments these consumers continue to get power. This is possible only because of the political pressure on the SEBs to continue the supply of electricity for electoral mileage. This kind of informal pressure on DISTCOs or SEBs from politically influential individuals to supply power to commercially unattractive sections of consumer results in the worsening quality of supply to categories which cross-subsidize the other categories. This induces them to go for CPP as shown in Figure 8.3.

Individual Incentives for Reporting Theft at Various Levels: There is a need to introduce third party intervention in the process of reporting theft. The DISTCOs or SEBs should involve the general public in controlling theft. There should be some sort of incentive scheme for reporting the theft of electricity that takes care of both incentive compatibility and participation constraint (Laffont and Martimort 2001). It is highly likely that the substance of the problem in the distribution segment of the electricity sector originates in the fact that policy does not take these kinds of constraints into consideration.

Incentives for Employees

The incentive for employees to perform better can be designed at various levels. Lack of employees' accountability has been a major factor responsible for the huge losses in power utilities in India. The low productivity of the employees as well as their collusion with thieves of power has been the main source of the AT & C losses. Employees can work contrary to the motives of the organization only when they are sure that the terms of the employment cannot be enforced. Given the past experience of enforcement, employees perceive that they cannot be fired easily even if they are caught red-handed with trying to 'fix' electricity bills or stealing power. Also, the perceived probability of being caught is extraordinarily low and the expected cost of being caught therefore, as the product of these two factors, is lower still.

Another important factor responsible for low productivity of the employees in SEBs, including the OSEB or DISTCOs in privatized regime, is the centralized decision making process. Ruet (2002) gives a detailed account of how rigid these boards are. There is a lack of budgetary allocation for employees even at high levels, which can be instrumental in a cost minimization exercise. Further there exists a long chain of approval prior to the execution of a field officer's recommendation for change or repair of equipment. Such a cumbersome process demoralizes even the most dutiful of individuals. Therefore organizational rigidities and flaws in the employment contract along with a very low cost of being disloyal to the organization make employees inefficient.

The alternative design of the employment contract should be such that incentives are in line with the goal of the organization. One strategy would be to link the remuneration of the employees with their productivity (Kannan and Pillai 2002:41–2). The current fixed level of payment gives little incentive to put in more effort. The mere act of going to work is enough to entitle an employee to a wage. One of the reasons why private firms have more labour productivity than the government companies is because incentive intensity is higher in private firms, and there is nothing to stop a public firm from introducing similar incentive intensity (Corneo and Rob 2003; Kannan and Pillai 2002). On the other hand, if employees are to be more responsible they have to be given decisional as well as financial autonomy. If this is done then they do not have to go through the long list of approvals in order to implement a change they decide on.

Conclusion

A critical examination of the incentive effects of the rules 'governing' the electricity sector indicates that misallocation of risks, as well as costs and benefits among the stakeholders of the power sector in Orissa is widespread. The risks and costs are heavily loaded on the publicly-owned transmission company GRIDCO, a situation that is typical of Public Private Partnership (PPP) contracts. The contractual obligations in PPPs are decided in such a way that public organizations have to take a majority of the risks, an experience that seems to be common across various developing countries (Bell 2003). One way to approach this problem in relation to the Indian case is to think of it in the following manner: in a democratic society people in political power try to maximize their economic gains from such power in the short run, as they are not sure of this power after the next election. As a result, private players provide kickbacks to the politician in power, in exchange for favourable contractual terms and conditions which will ensure a future stream of income (Rose-Ackerman 1996, 1999; Hall 1999).

The agenda of reforms was to improve the performance of the power sector by restructuring the sector in a way that would provide motivation to individual firms or consumers to act in a manner that would further the interest of the sector as a whole and the economy at large. However evidence shows that such restructuring has not changed the incentive structure to orient the sector in the desired direction. It needs to be realized that we may restructure a particular sector, but no improvement can be expected unless appropriate changes in the incentive structure are engineered. The GRIDCO is still the single buyer of electricity like OSEB; the only change that has occurred is that the final consumer is being served by set of firms that virtually form a monopoly de facto, the DISTCOs rather than one big monopoly, the OSEB.

The lack of proactive and critical research on the regulatory aspect of the Orissa's power system in most academic circles as well as the media, has made the regulator complacent. A careful look at the process of regulation reveals that the application of incentive intensity in any particular parameter of the power sector is not a principle that guides the OERC. Thus all forms of the marginal benefit principle seem to be more or less absent from the act of regulation. In order to ensure transparency in the system, the principle of fixing the incentive intensity should be common knowledge. The persistence of huge information asymmetry between the regulator and the DISTCOs is largely because of lack of initiatives taken by the regulator. It is also evident from this discussion that changes in inter-firm relations effected by restructuring the assets of power sector in Orissa did not lead to changes in intra-firm relations, a change that was crucial to effect desired changes The internal corporate structure of firms involved in transmission (GRIDCO) and distribution of power (DISTCOs) has remained largely unaltered. We therefore, conclude that the restructuring of the electricity sector has introduced further complications in the system without reducing the earlier problems that were ailing the utilities.

Appendix

Restructuring of OSEB Assets

a) The Talcher Thermal power station of the OSEB was transferred to NTPC (3 June 1995).
b) The OSEB was corporatized into the Grid Corporation of Orissa (GRIDCO) with wiring and distribution functions and the Orissa Hydro Power Corporation (OHPC) in charge of the hydropower projects (1 April 1996).
c) The Orissa Electricity Regulatory Commission (OERC) established (August 1996).
    a) Issued seven tariff orders till date
    b) Level of cross subsidy is being reduced
    c) Tariff has experienced a huge hike
d) The Orissa Power Generation Corporation (OPGC) which was established in 1984, got privatized in 1998 with transfer of 49 per cent of stake to the private operator, AES consortium, for Rs 603 crore.
e) The distribution and retail supply of electricity was vested in four distribution companies initially as wholly owned subsidiary companies of the GRIDCO, namely the Central Electricity Supply Company of Orissa Limited (CESCO), the North Eastern Electricity Supply Company of Orissa Limited (NESCO), the Southern Electricity Supply Company of Orissa Limited (SOUTHCO) and the Western Electricity Supply Company of Orissa Limited (WESCO). Three of these distribution companies i.e. except the CESCO were privatized on 1 April 1999 (acquired by BSES) and the CESCO on 1 September 1999 after divestment of its 51 per cent share (acquired by AES consortium, a global power company from US but now the CESCO is administered by a government official as AES backed out from managerial responsibility of the company). The GRIDCO received Rs 1.6 billion for 51 per cent of the stake of the distribution companies (DISTCOS). While the GRIDCO retains only high voltage wiring business under single-buyer model. Figure 8.1 (main text) depicts the process of restructuring of the Orissa Electricity board (OSEB).

References

Averch, H. and L. Johnson, 1962, 'Behaviour of Firm under Regulatory Constraint', *American Economic Review*, vol. 52, pp. 1053–69.

Bell, M., 2003, 'Regulation in Developing Countries is Different: Avoiding Negotiation, Renegotiation and Frustration', *Energy Policy*, vol. 31, no. 4, pp. 299–305.

Braeutigam, R. R. and J. C. Panzar, 1989, 'Diversification Incentives Under "Price-based" and "Cost-Based" Regulation', *RAND Journal of Economics*, vol. 20, no. 3, pp. 373–91.

Corneo, G. and R. Rob, 2003, 'Working in Public and Private Firms', *Journal of Public Economics*, vol. 87, pp. 1335–52.

Dubash, N. K. and S. C. Rajan, 2001, 'Power Politics: Process of Power Sector Reform in India', *Economic and Political Weekly*, 9 January.

Grutoo, A. and P. Pandey, 2001, 'Power Sector In Uttar Pradesh: Past Problems and Initial Phase of Reform', *Economic and Political Weekly*, 4 August.

Hall, David, 1999, 'Privatisation, Multinationals, and Corruption' PISRU Reports, Report number: 9909-U-U-Corrup.doc, Public Services International Research Unit, University of Greenwich. Also available at *http://www.psiru.org/reports/9909-U-U-Corrup.doc*.

Joskow, P. L., 2002, 'Electricity Sector Restructuring and Competition: A Transaction Cost Perspective' in Broussseau E. and J. M. Glachant (eds.), *The Economics of Contracts*, Cambridge University Press, Cambridge.

_____ and R. Schmalensee, 1986, 'Incentive Regulation of Electric Utilities', *Yale Journal on Regulation*, vol. 4, pp. 1–49.

Kannan, K. P. and V. M. Pillai, 2002, *Plight of Power Sector in India: Inefficiency, Reform and Political Economy*', Centre for Development Studies, Trivandrum.

Laffont, J. J., 1994, 'The New Economics of Regulation Ten Years After', *Econometrica*, vol. 63, no. 3, pp. 507–38.

_____, 1996, 'The French Electricity Industry' in Gilbert R. J. and E. P. Kahn (eds.), *International Comparison of Electricity Regulation*, Cambridge University Press, Cambridge.

_____ and J. Tirole, 1993, *Theory of Incentives in Procurement and Regulation*, The MIT Press, Cambridge, Mass.

Littlechild, S. C., 1983, *Regulation of Telecommunication's Profitability*, HMSO, London.

Mahalingam, S., 2002, 'The Great Power Robbery', *Frontline*, vol. 19, no. 6, 16–29 March.

Moorhouse, J. C., 1991, 'Competitive Markets for Electricity Generation', *The Cato Journal*, vol. 14, no. 3.

MoP, 2002, 'Structuring Of APDRP, Reform Framework and Principles of Financial Restructuring of SEBs', *Report of The Expert Committee on State Specific Reforms*, Ministry of Power, Government of India, September.

Morris, S., 2000, 'Regulatory Strategy and Restructuring Model for Gujarat Power Sector', *Economic and Political Weekly*, 3 June, pp. 1915–28.

OERC, 2002, 'Bulk Supply and Retail Supply Tariff orders', *www.orierc.org*.

Pandey, A. and S. Morris, 2004, 'The Beginning of Distribution Reforms in West Madhya Pradesh: A Report' in Morris, S. (ed.), *India Infrastructure Report 2004*, Oxford University Press, New Delhi.

Parayas, 2002, 'HT Energy Audit: The Crucial Starting Point for Curbing Revenue Loss', Prayas Occasional Report, Energy Group, Prayas, Pune, February.

Phadke, A. and R. C. Rajan, 2003, 'Electricity Reforms in India: Not too Late to go Back to the Drawing Board', *Economic and Political Weekly*, 19 July.

Ramesh, S., K. Thakural and B. Kaul, 1990, 'Non-utility Captive Generation for Power Sector Planning in India', *Energy Policy*, vol. 18, no. 9.

Rose-Ackerman, Susan, 1996, 'The Political Economy of Corruption: Causes and Consequences', World Bank Public Policy for the Private Sector Note No. 74, Washington DC: The World Bank.

_____, 1999, *Corruption and Government: Causes Consequences and Reform*, Cambridge University Press, Cambridge.

Ruet, J., 2001a, 'Winners and Losers of the SEB Reforms: An Organisational Analysis', Occasional Paper, French Research Institute in India, New Delhi.

Sankar, T. L. and U. Ramachandran, 2000,'Electricity Tariff Regulators: The Orissa Experience', *Economic and Political Weekly*, 27 May, pp. 1825–34.

Siddiqui, M. Z., 2004, 'Power Sector Reforms in Orissa: Regulation and Impacts', unpublished M.Phil dissertation, Centre for Development Studies, Thiruvananthapuram, also available at Jawaharlal Nehru University, New Delhi.

Viscusi, V. K., J. M. Vernon and J. E. Harrington, 1995, *Economics of Regulation and Antitrust*, The MIT Press, Cambridge, Mass.

Williamson, O. E., 1985, *The Economic Institutions of Capitalism*, Free Press, New York.

9

Small Investor Protection and Issues in Corporate Governance

An IT-enabled Approach to the Decision Making Process of Firms

MURALI KALLUMMAL

Introduction

Globalization and liberalization have brought in additional challenges to governments across the globe. These new challenges largely arise from the increased role of the private sector in the developmental activities on the one hand, and on the other hand, owing to the withdrawal of governmental activities from areas categorized/perceived as commercial/production-oriented in nature. Although the above-mentioned factors are the two prime factors for the additional challenges, the manifestation of the latter takes various shapes depending upon the existing structure and 'maturity' of the sector under consideration. These challenges have had similar dimensions, be it in countries like the United States facing some of the biggest corporate frauds seen in the recent past, or in the least developed countries like Bangladesh facing corruption associated with donor grants and aid programmes.

Efforts in the direction of creating better systems of governance have been addressed at various levels. The initial credit may be attributed to creating a stable, predictable and transparent environment for trade in goods under the GATT Agreement signed in 1947. However, initiatives in areas like indebtedness, environment concerns, wildlife protection and nuclear arms proliferation have also seen considerable progress over the years. In these areas, some of the plurilateral agreements have provided an initial foundation for the process of multilateralism. The process of progression from plurilateral to multilateral levels of harmonization would require substantial reorientation of national systems to incorporate the divergence in ground realities. The decision-making processes would require substantial rethinking and would have to be addressed in the current context.

Although these initiatives have provided a beginning to understanding the value of 'co-ordination' and 'co-operation', there are substantial issues which require immediate attention. Some of these have emerged in the process of 'learning by doing'. However, the experiences over the last two decades have shown that such harmonization initiatives have adopted common approaches to address governance-related challenges. The central theme in devising methods to addressing such conflicts has been through a decision-making process which is highly centralized. One of the best examples is the Bretton Woods institution that has failed to deliver satisfactory results largely due to its highly centralized decision making, thereby delineating it further away from the diverse reality.[1] The simple solution therefore, is in devising new and dynamic approaches which incorporate the growing relevance and need for globally harmonized systems, while simultaneously incorporating local decisions and challenges. While this may look like a rather simple solution, it should be taken as an overall principle for creating a balance between global and local priorities. The challenge ahead is to bring countries from diverse backgrounds to a common platform so as to facilitate better and co-ordinated decisions and thereby avoid a precipitation of crisis.

The issue of corporate governance is one of the areas wherein developing and developed countries have to work together to find a common ground. However, any such efforts towards harmonization would need to be addressed through a balanced approach incorporating national and global standards. At the outset, there is a need to recognize the fact that existing corporate governance structures across the globe are the product of a complex interaction of cultural, legal, corporate and capital needs. Hence, the evolution of various systems has resulted in diverse structural outcomes with different levels of maturity. Any structural transformation as part of the harmonization process at the national level would need to address some of the emerging realities of transition.

Since the 1980s, there has been considerable pressure on developing countries' financial markets to move to harmonized

[1] Stiglitz (2002).

structures closer to those seen in the so-called 'Anglo-Saxon' model. This was to be achieved through a process of 'disintermediation' of capital flows at the national and international levels. Such activities have taken two distinct paths leading to liberalization of capital markets across the developing countries. The first path adopted across the developing or 'emerging economies' has been to promote the mobilization of financial resources through the capital markets[2] and the second has been through the liberalization of the capital account, thereby allowing a free flow of capital. By the end of 1990s, the East Asian financial and economic crisis of 1997 posed a serious challenge to the whole process and a few developing countries including India adopted a cautious approach in the second generation reforms (capital account convertibility).

Further, recent market events and scandals across the 'Anglo-Saxon' systems clearly demonstrated that there is no single perfect model to pick from and there is always a need to make market interventions to make models suitable. The important consideration therefore, should be that any form of governance structure should address issues like transparency, responsibilities, accountability and should be flexible enough to incorporate new changes. In this paper, I would like to suggest a new approach to address the problem of small investors in India and across developing countries. The paper provides an information technology-enabled solution to better the decision-making process across big and small firms which participate in the capital market. In short, the proposed model involves an effective application of democratic principles using internet-based technology.

Across the emerging markets,[3] there was a conscious move towards increasing the role of capital markets in capital mobilization as against the traditional channel of public sector banks since the 1980s. In the case of India, such a transformation was brought about through the removal of Controller of Capital Issues (CCI) (Ministry of Finance, GOI) and induction of Securities Exchange Board of India (SEBI) in July 1992, as the capital market regulator. Owing to these policy-

[2] The process of removal of intermediaries (banks) between the saver (household and the other two sectors) and the investor (firm/government) through the popularization of capital market is known as 'disintermediation'. Such initiatives were considered to be efficient and effective in creating better financial systems.

[3] Emerging markets are those economies which have been seen as potential markets for international investors and are defined so by the private investment hand of the World Bank, the International Financial Corporation (IFC).

driven changes, the financial system provided both the corporate firms and the household investors[4] with multiple investment opportunities. In this short span of hyper-activity in capital markets, India has witnessed an equity boom never to be repeated in the manner and the form in which it happened then. Although such macro-trends can be justified as the so-called cyclical patterns observed across various markets, the equity boom and the following bust brought to the forefront, the presence of weaknesses (large both in number and amount) in the small investor protection mechanism. A large majority of new firms which raised capital through public issues during this period went untraceable and created a substantial amount of 'dead capital'.[5]

It is important to mention in this context that while in the banking sector non-performing assets (NPAs) are used as a performance indicator, there are no estimates of the extent of dead capital created in the capital markets in India alone. More than a decade later in 2006, not a single company has been made liable to pay for the dead capital which they vanished with. The latter is a direct outcome of vanishing companies which issued public shares during the first half of the 1990s (1992–6). From the capital market point of view, these vanishing companies have eroded the confidence of small investors. This loss of confidence has been clearly reflected in the composition of household sector saving pattern (see Table A9.1 in Appendix).

Globalization is catching up quickly and the Indian financial market is gearing itself to integrate with regional stock exchanges like the Sri Lankan stock exchange. Weak investor protection would be disastrous and therefore, needs suitable remedies. Clearly, there is a need to address such issues immediately to provide for a viable domestic channel of intermediation in an increasingly globalizing era of capital flows. The fundamental and critical need for such financial sector governance has been clearly demonstrated by the external capital market-led crises seen among the emerging markets of East and Southeast Asia in 1997.

[4] Of the three sectors, public, private and household, the household sector has on an average, been the single largest contributor to total savings (GDS) in India. As this sector has been the highest contributor to total GDS since the 1950s, the patterns reflected in this sector will have substantial socio-economic and macro implications.

[5] Dhar and Kallummal (2002).

Capital Market-based Financial Intermediation in India: A Brief History

Until the mid-1980s, the dominant view across the developing countries was the neo-Keynesian argument that led to policies for keeping interest rates low in order to promote capital formation in selective sectors in the economy. This led many countries to adopt a highly interventionist financial system, with government controls on the methods of raising finance for investment and for directing it to desired channels/sectors. These interventions were in the nature of fiscal and monetary controls like taxation, credit rationing and interest rate controls.

It was Keynes[6] who proposed the idea of government intervention to create effective demand in the post-war period and further suggested an intermediary status for government to keep speculative elements in check. Subsequently, studies by Copeland (1952), Goldsmith (1969) and McKinnon (1973) confirmed the links between the real sector and the financial sector. These ideas were given high priority and led to the widespread adoption of state-intermediated financial systems for funding investment from the 1960s to the 1980s. The theoretical underpinning and various economic and political compulsions led to policies which aided the growth of credit-based financial intermediation (banks) across the developing countries during these two decades.

However, by the 1980s there was a substantial reversal in many of the polices which promoted the banking sector. These changes were largely influenced by the work of McKinnon[7] and Shaw,[8] which highlighted some of the lacunae of highly intermediated economies, whose financial systems they referred to as one of 'financial repression'. They argued that the seriousness of 'government failure' in command and control regimes was of a higher consequence than 'market failure', and advocated alternative policies in support of financial liberalization. Adding to this was the changed approach of the Bretton Woods institutions towards the increasing debt situation across the developing countries. As a result, many economies which followed the advice of the 'Fund' witnessed an unprecedented rise in domestic capital market activities.

[6] Keynes(1939).
[7] McKinnon(1973).
[8] Shaw(1973).

In the case of India, these changes were witnessed immediately after the Gulf War of the early 1990s. The 1990s appear to be a transition phase in the industrial financing landscape in India, with a reduced role being played by the banks as an intermediary between savers and borrowers and the private corporate sector gaining direct access to the savers of the household sector.[9] Ex-post, one could say that momentarily the capital market had undone the positive effect on the saving culture built up over generations by the banks in India.[10] With the emergence of a new channel for households to park their savings in the form of financial assets, these changes also affected the banks. The new issue market rose to prominence as a substitute for bank and Development Financial Institution (DFI) during this transition phase. This process of 'disintermediation' has serious implications for industrial development through its impact on industrial financing (see Figure A9.4).

Structure of Capital Market in India

The modern capital market in India is one of the oldest in the Asian region. Even though the relative importance of this market has varied during its long history, the Indian capital market has, over the years, evolved into an important segment of the financial system. The Indian financial system can be pictured as seen in Figures 9.1 and 9.2. The sub-categories of the Indian financial market can be represented as the credit, money and the capital market segments. Of the three, the money market has a very short span of operation history when compared to credit and capital markets. Of the two prominent sub-categories, we are more interested, in this paper, in the capital market. The capital market can be further classified into two sub-categories: the 'primary' New Issue Market (NIM); and, the 'secondary' market.

The NIM has direct influence on capital formation as it is through this market that firms mobilize capital for investment activities through public issues.[11] Public issues can again, be further categorized

[9] The household sector is one of the most important sources of savings in India. Reserve Bank of India, 'Report of the Committee to Review the Working of the Monetary System', (Chakravarthy Committee), Bombay, 1985.

[10] Studies like: Joshi (1999); Ajit and Bangar(1997).

[11] The primary market is the segment where only new securities of equities, debentures, etc. are issued by companies, while the secondary market is the segment which provides liquidity to the investors in the primary market, through trading in the existing stocks of companies.

FIGURE 9.1: FLOW CHART SHOWING VARIOUS ORGANS OF FINANCIAL MARKET

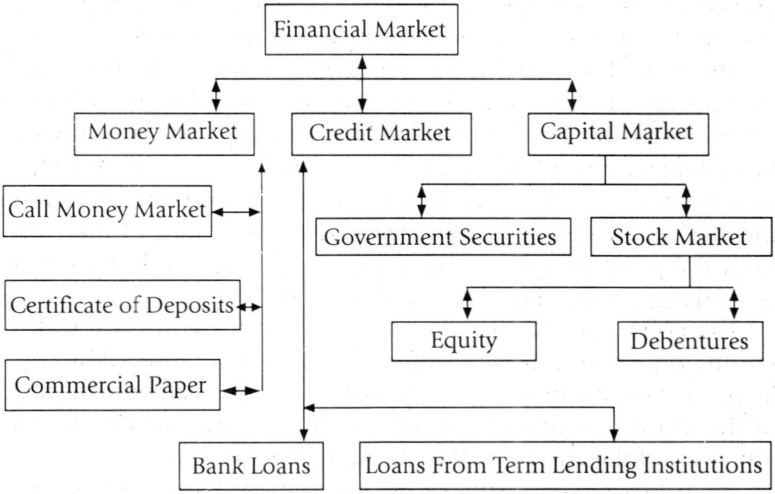

FIGURE 9.2: FLOW CHART SHOWING CONSTITUENTS OF CAPITAL MARKET

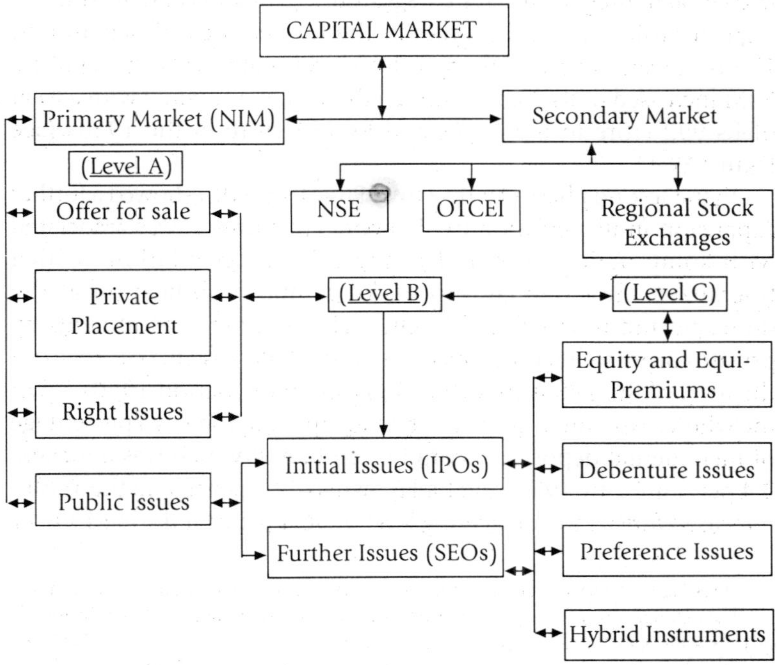

Note: Here, levels 'A' and 'B' categorize the channels which may be used by a firm for raising capital, and level 'C' classifies the various instruments which may be used by the firm for raising capital through any of the channels mentioned in levels 'A' and 'B'.

as 'initial public offerings' (IPOs) and 'seasonal equity offerings' (SEOs) or 'further public issues', based on whether the company is making a public issue for the first time or not (see Figure A9.3).[12]

The NIM developed as an important source of financing for the industry in India in the 1980s and the 1990s. This growth was aided by public polices, product innovation and the growing institutionalization of the market. Besides, the 1990s saw a sea change in some of the fundamental factors which influence the growth of the NIM at a wider geographic level. The importance of the NIM from the point of view of governance, arises from this increased potential as an alternative financial channel.

The policy changes have influenced both the corporate sector seeking capital and the investor supplying capital at the domestic level.[13] Following liberalization, three broad phases can be identified in the growth of capital markets in India, based on the various initiatives of the government to promote this market.

In the first phase, a remarkable growth in the NIM was observed in the 1980s. This followed the relaxation of controls on various capital market activities in different stages during this decade, leading to a greater role for market forces in the limited area of debentures. The proposed investments by private corporate firms through the NIM increased to Rs 23,357 crore in the 1980s compared with a total of Rs 992 crore in the 1970s and Rs 285 crore in the 1950s (see Figure A9.1).

In the second phase (1991–2 to 1996–7), the NIM showed a further expansion in its performance. However, this time it was associated with some major structural changes in the regulations which liberalized the complete process of capital mobilization at the domestic and international levels.[14] The proposed investments by private corporate sector firms through the NIM rose massively from the level of the 1980s to Rs 98,648 crore in the period 1990–6. On the whole, asset intermediation by the capital market as a percentage of incremental deposits of commercial banks, which was a meagre 3.4 per cent in the 1970s and had grown to 22.7 per cent in the 1980s, increased further to a staggering level of 56.4 per cent during 1990–1

[12] See Figure 9.2 for a detailed picture of the various constituents of the capital market.

[13] A detailed analysis of the various phases of the policy changes and their influence on the evolution of the capital market in India has been carried out in Kallummal (1999).

[14] The ADRs and GDRs represented the opening up of Indian capital market activities which allowed companies to mobilize funds in international capital markets like New York and London.

to 1995–6. This was achieved with a marginal rise of four percentage points in total household asset holding. During this period, the share of household assets in shares and debentures increased to 8.3 per cent (1990–6) from 4 per cent during 1985–99. This clearly suggested a movement in the financing of private corporate firms away from term loans and bank loans to stock market-based funds, suggesting a process of disintermediation.[15]

A third distinct phase is the post-1996 period when both the primary and secondary markets have shown substantially depressed performances when compared to the earlier period. A partial explanation to this phase can be found in the Harshad Mehta scam and the global recession subsequent to the Asian financial crisis. However, a fundamental weakness also lies in the large number of vanishing companies, a fact which came to light towards the end of equity boom of the early 1990s. The vanishing of companies led to a sharp drop in the confidence of small investors in the capital market, as is evident from the sharp drop in the contribution of shares and debentures in the total financial assets of households during 1996–2002.[16]

As discussed above, the 'market-based financing' of industrial investments in a liberalized economy can be through the domestic capital market (mainly, the NIM) or the external capital markets (through ADRs and GDRs issued in a foreign stock exchange or through foreign investors' long-term equity investment in domestic firms—FDI). Both these markets compete in terms of cost and accessibility. Their relative shares in corporate financing would greatly depend upon the policies and objectives of the liberalization process which influence the strategies of firms and variations in them would have different economic implications. The Indian capital market failure of the late 1990s (confidence crisis) did not lead to a situation similar to the East Asian financial crisis only because of the relatively high domestic nature of the confidence crisis.

Even though the external markets for industrial investments are an important segment for a developing and capital-scarce economy like India, the neglect of sentiments in the domestic market could be a wrong policy in the long run. Studies on international capital flows reveal an increasing proportion of short-term capital flows relative

[15] See Kallummal (1999).

[16] See Table A9.1 in Appendix for the sharp decrease in the proportion of financial assets held by the household sector in the form of share and debentures in India during 1996–2002.

to long-term capital flows from the industrialized countries to the developing countries,[17] indicating a larger proportion of capital flows in the form of portfolio funds compared to productive capital. The external markets for industrial investments are also characterized by additional risks like foreign exchange risk. Thus, in economies which have an excessive reliance on external capital markets and which are dominated by increased flow of finance capital in comparison to productive capital, a recession or a fall in confidence in the host economy could have serious implications for its industrial development. Studies on countries like Mexico, Argentina, Chile and the Southeast Asian countries have shown the extent of damage this channel can cause in times of crisis and low confidence levels. With the separation of ownership and control[18] in the case of public limited companies, there is a greater risk of outflows in case of an expected crisis, further complicating the situation. It is for this reason that the development of the domestic capital market takes on significance as an alternative investment channel for investors and as a channel for financing industrial development.

Depending on its usually long-term nature, many developing countries have been relying excessively on FDI to supplement domestic industrial capacity and to further export growth. However, excessive reliance on even such external capital can lead to adverse consequences for industrial development, as in this case too, foreign investors look for a 'favourable' investment climate in the host countries and may turn out to be inconsistent. The implications of excessive reliance on external capital following financial liberalization for industrial structure and growth are reflected in the crises of Mexico and the southern Cone countries and the recent crisis in Southeast Asian economies, which went ahead with further integration into the international financial markets. These events highlight the in-built tendency of market failures in such a financial system, and the possible adverse effects on production, distribution and overall welfare. A buffer to the external risks and uncertainties in a liberalized set-up could be the promotion of stable domestic capital markets.

[17] Ghosh and Sen (1998).

[18] The separation of ownership and control is core to the role of stock markets in an economy, both at the domestic and international levels. Control, here, refers to the irreversible part, the investment decision made by the manager. Ownership level is where liquidity and irreversibility are in operation for the shareholder. Efficiency would then depend on the level of interaction between the manager at the control level and shareholder at the market level.

Besides, the alternative of a domestic capital market is very important in countries like India, which have a large middle class segment as savers and a very low average firm size in the corporate sector. A well-developed domestic capital market could be used to tap these large sources of capital for productive investments in a liberalized market.

Socio-economic Factors and Equity Boom of the 1990s

Although most of the growth in the NIM in the 1980s was due to an increase in debenture issues, the role played by equities even during that period cannot be underestimated. In the early 1990s, however, the role played by equities became much more significant. This is clearly exhibited in Figure A9.1. While equities[19] accounted for 10 per cent of the total value of NIM in 1989, their share increased to 66.5 per cent by 1994. Similarly, in terms of numbers, the share of equities rose from 77 per cent of the total number of issues, to 91 per cent during the same period. Hence, the period between 1990–5 can be referred to, as being characterized by an equity boom.

However, since the market was dominated by existing old companies during the 1980s[20], it becomes crucial to understand how this boom occurred in the early 1990s. A number of factors enter into the explanation. These include: a) the foreign exchange crisis; b) secondary market activities; c) changes in the attitudes of investors from semi-urban areas, and d) decreasing bank credit and lower public sector investments in comparison to total production in the economy etc. Needless to say, some of these factors are inter-related. This section seeks to highlight the role of these factors.

The government's liberalization attempts created a sense of euphoria and a significant change in expectations in the market. This opened up the NIM as a source of capital for the deficit sector, even though an active role was still being played by intermediaries like banks, insurance firms and developmental financial institutions. This led to a growth in equity issues during 1992–6. The growth in equities was also due to the liberalization of equity pricing and the initial under-utilization of this source of financing by a large body of private and public limited companies.

Since the early 1980s itself there had been signs of a change in investor attitude towards the capital market. The market which

[19] Equities here include premium issues also.

[20] As suggested by the large number of debentures issued during the period of 1980s.

remained a predominantly speculative investment alternative in a few metros showed signs of dispersion to other parts of the country. An increase in the participation of investors from smaller cities and towns became visible (see Table 9.1).[21] The number of shareholders in India increased from 0.24 crore in 1980 to 0.90 crore in 1986 and finally reached nearly 1.35 crore in 1992, pointing to an increasing trend from the 1980s which continued through the 1990s.[22] Simultaneously, there was an increase in the number of stock market-related support organizations like brokerages, registrars and merchant bankers. A study conducted by the Society for Capital Market Research and Development, New Delhi, showed that places which were outside the top 25 metros in India in terms of shareholder percentage to total population, registered an increased investment activity in NIM along with an increase in the number of shareholders. The combined share of these towns and cities increased from 16.9 per cent of total shares in 1983–4 to 26.6 per cent in 1992 i.e. an increase of 57.4 per cent points over 1983–4. Most of the small towns and cities (1060) also showed a 2 to 3 per cent increase in the number of shareowners during this period.[23]

The change in the investment habits of the smaller towns can also be explained by the movement in the household sector's asset composition in the 1990s. The shift was largely in favour of assets like NBFC deposits and investments in shares and debentures of the private corporate sector. The effect of the movement of household savings away from bank deposits, combined with increased government borrowing from commercial banks reflected in increased banking sector investments in government securities and resulted in decreased credit availability from the banking sector for the private corporate sector, after 1987. This trend was aggravated by the problem of increasing NPAs in the banking sector, which led many commercial banks to turn cautious in their lending.

As mentioned earlier, the 1990s were characterized by a greater interest in primary markets rather than secondary markets. At an impressionistic level, this was evident in the spread of stock market-related activities, from the floors of stock exchanges to the pavements in many metro cities across the country. The number of stockbrokers, merchant bankers and investors increased during this phase.

[21] Gupta et al. (1994)
[22] ibid., p. 3.
[23] ibid., p. 31.

Although there was a large increase in market capitalization, the growth is also attributable to a rise in the number of companies listed in stock exchanges after the 1980s. The number of stock exchanges that had increased from five to eight between 1946–70, increased further from 12 in 1984 to 20 in 1991, and finally to 28 in 1995. There was also an increase in the number of firms listed at various stock exchanges, thus increasing the possibilities for trading activities and leading to an increase in market capitalization.

The growth of regional stock exchanges, by increasing accessibility and liquidity, had a major impact on the 'confidence' of the investor, and led to an expansion of the so-called 'equity culture' in India. The increase in listing in the regional stock exchanges led to a growth in total paid-up capital in the market and the opening up of a new channel for raising capital for the existing and new companies listed in the stock market. The analysis of companies which mobilized capital during 1996 revealed that a large part of these companies were existing private limited companies which transformed themselves into public limited companies by way of public issue of capital.

A study by L.C. Gupta notes that the increase in activity in the primary market was accompanied by a rise in the participation of investors. The study reveals that shareowner incidence (i.e., the number of shareowners in total population) increased to 1.5 per cent in 1992–3 from a meagre 0.4 per cent in 1983–4. The study also found that the western region of India had a shareowner incidence almost three times higher than the other regions of the country.[24]

TABLE 9.1: GEOGRAPHICAL INCIDENCE OF SHAREOWNERS IN INDIA

(In percentage)

Major Cities	*Percentage of Shareowners Accounted for by each City*		
Year	*1992*	*1983–84*	*Difference*
Mumbai	27.3	35.3	-8.0
Kolkata	8.6	10.0	-1.4
Delhi	8.3	9.5	-1.2
Ahmedabad	7.6	7.4	0.2
Chennai	3.5	3.9	-0.4
Rest of India	44.7	33.8	10.9
Total	55.3	66.2	-10.9

Source: Gupta et al., p. 4.

[24] Gupta et al. (1994).

The distribution of share ownership in 1992 as revealed by Table 9.1 points to a strong urban bias and metropolitan concentration, which would have contributed to speculative tendencies in the secondary market. However, the share of the five major cities in total share ownership dropped from 66.2 per cent in 1983–4 to 55.3 per cent in 1992–3, pointing to the increasing significance of other smaller towns and cities across India and the spread of the equity and debenture culture. The difference between these two periods reveals that Mumbai faced the maximum drop in incidence, of 8 percentage points, while Kolkata and Delhi faced a drop of less than 2 percentage points and Chennai less than half of a percentage point. While the incidence of share ownership in big cities was decreasing, that of small ones like Ahmedabad was rising, albeit marginally. This tendency did contribute to the growth of the NIM across the country in the 1990s, especially through expansion into smaller towns and rural areas, from where surplus funds could be garnered through this channel and directed into investment.

The 1990s was also a 'phase of expansion' in terms of growth in various support institutions[25] associated with the NIM and the number of support institutions in the market increased drastically. For example, the number of merchant bankers increased from 120 in 1989–90 to 1099 in 1995–6, while the number of registrars increased from 46 to 307 over the same period. The largest increase was recorded among brokers. Their number increased from 517 in 1989–90 to 4795 in 1995–6. These phenomenal increases were *inter-alia* due to: a) an increase in demand for their services in the market; and b) changes in the policy of the government to promote these institutions. The growth in support institutions was contributed to by an increase in the participation of public sector commercial banks, financial institutions and large corporate houses in the 1990s, especially in the merchant banking and brokerage business. Large and small public sector commercial banks came to account for a major share of the merchant banking market.[26] The participation of large corporate houses in the brokerage business was another feature of the 1990s. The RBI opened

[25] Support institutions here refer to stock brokers who help in ensuring marketability and liquidity of secondary shares, and registrars and merchant bankers who help in the process of public issues.

[26] The Praxis Report rated various public sector banks as the top performers in the merchant banking business.

up this activity by liberalizing the restriction on corporate firms' participation in brokerage activities. This was done to ensure better management, reduce speculative activity and also to safeguard the interests of large corporate companies which faced the brunt of the inefficient brokerage system in India. This change in the composition of support institutions was possibly one of the reasons for the increase in confidence of the general investor.

However, the expansion of the new investor base during the boom of 1989–96 has since then, witnessed a downward trend due to the decreasing number of IPOs and seasonal equity offerings (SEOs) and also due to a confidence crisis which erupted due to vanishing companies. Even so, due to perceived low interest rate regime expectations, the capital market and other non-banking sectors have continued to attract capital flows from the household sector even after the equity boom of 1989–96. In the post-1996 phase, structural shifts occurred within the capital market with a movement away from direct investment in equity, debenture and hybrid instruments to indirect investments through channels like the mutual funds. Such trends have not been able to revive the confidence levels to sustainable levels.

Thus, the Indian financial market is in turmoil, especially since the banking sector has also been affected by the vagaries of markets. Increasingly, the banks are shying away from private lending and are also lending well above the PLR and investing in fixed-return assets like government gilted securities (see Table A9.2). Further, the domestic capital market lacks the confidence of small investors. The combined effect of these factors would starve Indian industries of safe and cheap domestic capital. This may lead to increasing dependence on external capital mobilization, while within the domestic economy, the household sector would continue face the dilemmas of lack of investment opportunities. Hence, it is important to restore the confidence of the small investor in the capital markets and this can only be achieved through radical changes in the decision making process of firms and effective implementation of existing regulation of investor protection.

Dominance of Small Firms in the Equity Boom of the 1990s

A study of the firms that participated in the NIM between 1989–95 based on the size of paid-up capital revealed that liberalization of capital, market led to an increased participation by small firms.[27] This trend was in part, explained by the transformation of many small firms which existed as private entities into public limited companies during this period. The data[28] revealed that small firms (with an investment less than Rs 10 crore) were the dominant participants in the NIM during the 1990s. This category accounted for nearly 88.1 per cent of the total firms resorting to the NIM during the CCI period, though this share dropped to 82.3 per cent after liberalization. This decrease in the share of small firms was largely due to the increase in the share of medium sized firms (Rs 10 to 40 crore), which rose from 10.6 per cent to 14.2 per cent over this period. Large firms (Rs 40 to 100 crore).which accounted for 1.4 per cent of the total in the CCI period increased marginally to 2.6 per cent in the post-CCI period. Thus during the equity boom, the capital market supported firms which would have otherwise faced considerable amount of restrictions under a regulated credit market under banks. This supports the argument that the capital market would help the expansion of small firms, which is the most natural outcome given the relative low average size of firms. This increase in capital mobilization by small firms would have been healthy but for the vanishing companies list.[29]

While in terms of size, the data suggested a preponderance of small firms, (Table 9.2) the age-wise[30] analysis revealed a predominance of middle-aged firms (5 to 20 years old) belonging to the 10 to 20 year category, which accounted for 45.2 per cent of the total firms in the CCI period and 48 per cent in the post-CCI period (Table 9.3). The middle-aged firms were followed by young firms (less than 5 years old), which also accounted for a high share of 43 per cent and 43.6 per cent, during the respective periods. Old firms (above 40 years old) were not only less visible, but also registered a decrease in

[27] The classification of the firms was based on the amount of expected post-issue paid-up capital given in the prospectus. Of the available indicators, this comes closest to an indicator of the size of firms, once they are operational.

[28] The data collected by the researcher from the Delhi Stock Exchange library for 3127 public issues resorted to by firms between 1989–95. This sample accounted for nearly 77 per cent of the total population of public issues in India during this period.

[29] One of SEBI's press notifications of the missing companies suggested a figure of 660 firms, mainly belonging to agro products and plantation industries. See for details, the *Hindustan Times*, Friday 21 December 2001, New Delhi.

[30] Age is taken as the number of years that have elapsed since the time a firm was incorporated as a private limited company (year of incorporation of an issuing firm is given in its prospectus) to the year of its participation in the NIM.

TABLE 9.2: SIZE-WISE DISTRIBUTION OF FIRMS

Years	*1989*	*1990*	*1991*	*1992*	*1993*	*1994*	*1995*	*Total*
Small firms (No.)	97	76	85	242	395	684	955	2534
% age share	91.5	91.6	81.7	81.8	80.0	79.1	87.3	83.3
Medium (No.)	9	7	15	45	86	150	120	432
% age share	8.5	8.4	14.4	15.2	17.4	17.3	11.0	14.2
Large (No.)	0	0	4	9	13	31	19	76
% age share	0.0	0.0	3.8	3.0	2.6	3.6	1.7	2.5
Total	106	83	104	296	494	865	1094	3042

Source: Extracted from the sample data.

TABLE 9.3: AGE-WISE DISTRIBUTION OF FIRMS

(In percentage)

Age of Firms	*1989*	*1990*	*1991*	*1992*	*1993*	*1994*	*1995*	*Total*
Young	44.9	43.1	41.1	39.3	38.5	39.1	57.2	999
Middle Aged	44.9	41.4	49.3	51.4	53.5	51.1	35.9	958
Old	10.1	15.5	9.5	9.3	8.0	9.9	6.9	181
Total	69	58	73	183	301	591	863	2138

Source: Extracted from the sample data.

share during the liberalized phase. This composition confirmed the earlier conclusion of increased NIM participation by a large number of firms graduating from private to public limited company status.

Another observed trend was the rise in pre-issue paid-up-capital; this was observed from the analysis of change in equitization between the CCI and post-CCI periods.[31] This also suggests that there was an increased participation of existing firms or an increase in the number of firms with higher contribution from promoters in the NIM.

This can happen in two ways: First, through an increase in inter-corporate investments in pursuit of objectives like financing of new projects via new companies by existing public limited companies, through channels like firm allotments; and second, an increase in the transformation of private companies (family-owned businesses) into public limited companies.

[31] Kallummal (1999).

In India, as seen in the above section, the household sector (small investor) and small firms participated in the capital market in a big way. The 1990s saw an equity boom involving small players (household investors and small firms) and it was one of the biggest in terms of total capital mobilized, in the history of Indian capital markets. It also supports the argument that the Indian capital market can meet the domestic capital investment activities.

Given this significance, it would be important to attract the missing small investors and small firms back to the primary market (NIM) to create a healthy investment culture (for a detailed analysis on various charactertics of a 'firm' like private versus public, size-wise and age-wise refer to Tables A9.3, A9.4 and A9.5). However, there is a need to learn from the mistakes of the equity boom of the 1990s. This would only be possible if some fundamental changes occur with regard to two important issues: firm-level decision making process; and, stronger regulator control so as to restrict the incidence of fly-by-night operators. It is in this context that we would like to propose a new approach to the annual general body meeting—a mandatory body for decision making for a listed firm—to be reformed so as to make it more democratic. Such efforts would go a long way in restoring the confidence of small investors in capital markets. The next section highlights some of the salient features of the proposed model.

Information Technology-enabled Approach and Effective Firm-level Decisions

Protection of the investment activities of the household sector is vital since the household sector constitutes nearly 70 per cent of the gross domestic savings (GDS) in India. While household sector investment activities in the banking and financial institutions (deposits) are regulated and supervised by the RBI, similar investment activities through the capital markets are largely at the mercy of the management of the firms, in which the investments are made. Unlike banks, the decision-making process in firms is largely non-transparent and less democratic. The only forum available for investors within the firm's decision making structure is the Annual General Body Meetings (AGMs) that are mandated by the Companies Law in India (for public listed companies). Due to various reasons, it has been found that the small investor gets neglected in this important forum for decision making.

However, the possibility for creating a healthy investment culture will increasingly depend on the assimilation of both small investors and small firms in the governance activities of the NIM. A healthy investment culture will contribute and decide the stability of capital markets, which in turn, will determine the protection of investors and sustainability of fund availability. Two factors related to the existing approach to AGMs which hinder this are the financial viability of small investors attending such meetings (geographical distance and associated costs) and the existing biases favouring the medium and large investors. These two limitations need to be overcome if there has to be sustained increased participation of small investors to the mutual benefit of both the investors and firms.

In joint stock companies, governance can take effect through reforms in the conduct of the AGM, the supreme decision-making body which meets at least once a year. The AGM decides on the matters stipulated in the Companies Act such as the acceptance of the financial statements and proposed dividends, the release from liability of members of the Board of Directors and the President and the CEO, the election of the members of the Board of Directors and Auditors, and the compensation paid to them, etc. The decision taken at AGMs can influence many activities like management and proper arrangement of the operations, scope and size of the operations etc. These include the acceptance of the goals of the firm and the main strategies for achieving them, the acceptance of action plans, the definition and acceptance of control policies, the acceptance of the organizational structure of the firm, and the nomination of the President and CEO, his deputy and the members of the Executive Board and the monitoring and evaluation of their performance.

The AGM elects a Chairman and a Vice Chairman of the Board as well as other Board Members; these would be in accordance with the Articles of Association of the firms. The AGM decisions have implication on the various committees and the executive board, which support the President and the CEO. The Executive Board considers all matters essential for the corporate management, for example corporate and business area strategies, budgets, corporate synergies and themes, acquisitions, divestments, matters relating to the corporate image, interim reviews, principles for important investor relations, bonus plans as well as leading principles for human resources policy.

On the whole, the AGM provides a unique opportunity for every stockholder of a company to participate and contribute by exercising his or her consent or vote. Each of the shareholders (preferential and ordinary) commands influence equivalent to his or her respective share in the total paid-up capital. The effectiveness of increased participation of small investors is more effective in situations wherein the shareholding pattern is diversified (see Table 9.4).

With the increasing role of capital markets in India, the proportion of companies falling the first category 'C'[32] (mentioned in Table 9.4) is fast decreasing and is being replaced by firms with diversified holding pattern falling under categories 'A' and 'B'. Although the increased merger and acquisition (M&A) activities during the late 1990s and towards the early years of this decade have reversed the diversification of shareholding to some extent, the need for an improved system of decision making is still important. Effective participation of small investors in AGM would be directly beneficial for companies with diversified shareholding and therefore it calls for an immediate rectification of the existing lacunae of the present system of decision making.

TABLE 9.4: DIVERSIFICATION OF SHARE OF SMALL SHAREHOLDERS AND EXTENT OF INFLUENCE IN THE PROCESS OF DECISION MAKING

(Share of stock in percentage)

	Company A	*Company B*	*Company C*
Large Shareholders (Preference and Ordinary Share)			
Larger Shareholder (1)	11.0	30.0	50.0
Larger Shareholder (2)	6.0	20.0	15.0
Larger Shareholder (3)	4.0	10.0	15.0
Larger Shareholders (n)	2.0	11.0	10.0
Total share (1 to n)	30.0	71.0	90.0
Small Shareholders (Ordinary Shares)			
Small Shareholder (1)	2.0	1.0	1.0
Small Shareholder (2)	1.0	2.0	1.0
Small Shareholder (3)	2.0	1.0	1.0
Small Shareholder (4)	1.0	3.0	0.5
Small Shareholders (m)	1.0	4.0	0.5
Total Share (1 to m)	70.0	29.0	10.0
Paid-Up-Capital	100.0	100.0	100.0

[32] Also known as family-owned companies, seen in the 1980s and 1990s across the Asian continent.

Lacunae of the Existing System

1. Besides the economic reasons behind effective participation, the companies were also found to be avoiding the general shareholders while holding their AGMs. The means used are many, for example, some companies hold such meetings away from the region of their small shareholder concentration. Another strategy used by managements is to hold meetings on the same dates as other major companies' AGMs, thus putting common shareholders in considerable difficulty.

2. At the AGM, there are class formations based on shareholding, especially between large shareholders (insiders) and small shareholders. On many occasions, the small shareholders are neglected as a group in the decision making by way of physical alienation from participation. The effect of the old system is critical because without the general consent of small shareholders, the management of companies belonging to 'A' category manage to get the resolution passed.

3. All the above lead to a gradual loss of confidence of small investors in the functioning of corporate firms in the country. Such a trend will severely affect the investment pattern in the capital markets (both direct and indirect channels) and lead to a decreased participation of domestic real investments in comparison to speculative investments. This may lead a situation wherein domestic investors may opt to resort to the secondary market (speculative) investments while neglecting primary market participation. Such a trend would precipitate a situation wherein external investors would find active secondary market investment scope in India, providing ample ground for speculative gains. In the long run, this would hamper the relationship between saver and investor, built over the last half-a-century.

Alternative Proposals and Possibility for Information Technology Intervention

Alternative proposals for effective participation of small shareholders can be achieved through the application of information technology and internet in AGMs. To make it simple, let us call it the Computerized Response Sheets (CRS) approach (Figure 9.3). The objectives are to achieve: effective participation (response); effective decision (democracy) and effective accountability (transparency), without causing additional economic cost in terms of both money and time for firms and investors. The model could be explained in the following steps:

Firm-level Functions

Step I: As in the case of the existing system of AGM, firms would be required to prepare a list of issues which need clearance at the General Body Meeting. These questions can be either be posted to the individual shareholders in the form of a questionnaire with space for individual responses or hosted at a common site (Central Authority) on the internet for online voting.

Two channels can be followed for getting the response: C2: where the companies send the questions to the central authority and then collect the results from the central authority. In this channel the companies pay for the total services of the central authority. Second, C1: where the companies send the questions to the central authority for the preparation of the response sheet and then post the same with the questions (or host at the central authority web address) to individual shareholders for voting. The shareholders send the voted answer sheet back to the companies, and the companies in turn, send

FIGURE 9.3: CRS APPROACH TO DECISION MAKING IN FIRMS

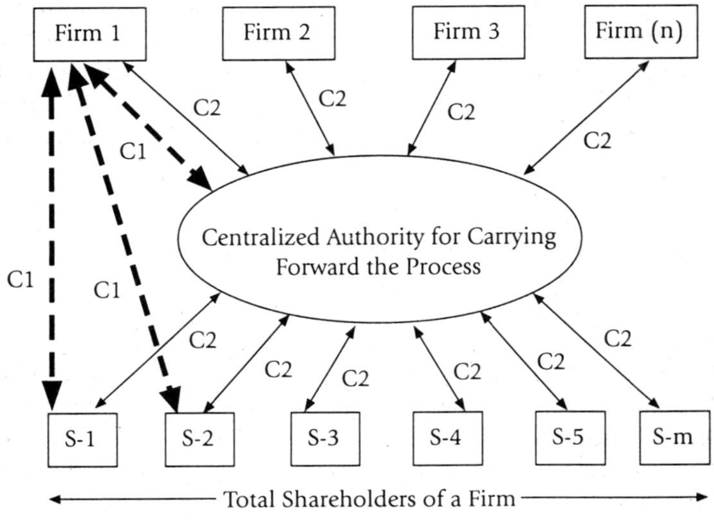

the complete set of responses to central authority to get the final tally of responses.[33]

Step II: The Computerized Response Sheet (CRS) prepared for voting can take two forms; first, a general format, and second, a customized format. It should be left to the companies' discretion, but only the centralized authority should be allowed to print the response sheets. The CRS can either be got in bulk by the respective companies from the centralized authority and be posted directly to the shareholders, or the centralized authority itself can post to the shareholders, on behalf of each company. The CRS should be coded so as to make sure cross-voting across the companies can be avoided. All aspects of protection of the identity of voters should be addressed.

Step III: The CRS should be responsible for the complete process. A final copy of the annual report and decisions taken by the companies based on the results should be sent to the centralized authority for verification purposes.

Structure of Centralized Authority

It is advisable that a central authority be present for carrying out such activities to increase the neutrality and effectiveness of the process. The centralized authority could be a body managed by the government with representation from various interest groups like banks, financial institutions, business houses and associations, brokers, and general citizens. This organization could be placed directly under the SEBI for overall effectiveness of policies and decisions taken with respect to capital markets. All activities should be performed in a set time frame and there should be a set time for completion of the various activities to be carried out by the centralized authority and the companies (see Figure 9.3). Such a structure would help in building a healthy database for aiding both competition and investment policy-related activities.

The centralized authority should maintain absolute professional secrecy regarding the results of responses and questions put by the companies. But in case of any discrepancy with respect to the results, the centralized authority should make public, the results for the larger interest of shareholders. The language used for CRS should be Hindi

[33] The C2 is the better channel of the two as there is no chance of any bias entering the process.

or English; however, more languages could be used depending upon the dispersion of investors.

Benefits of CRS

CRS is a foolproof system to monitor the decision making of corporate firms, and ensure the proper representation of small investors and to thus protect their interests. In addition, it offers advantages in terms of cost and time, for both investors as well as the companies. This system could also be operationalized through internet facilities provided at the regional stock exchanges and for individual internet connection holders. With increasing Internet usage in India, the operationalization of such an approach would be workable. A similar approach has already been suggested in the new corporate reforms package for companies in Japan. The process would also lead to the building of a database for effective monitoring of competition and other investment-related policy decisions. It would also help in strengthening the supervisory function of SEBI by consolidating the effectiveness of already proposed Central Database for Market Participants and Investors ('MAPIN' Database, 2003).[34]

Conclusion

Following the initial phase of the Indian liberalization process which involved the de-licensing of a large number of industries and trade liberalization, subsequent changes focused on fiscal restructuring, banking sector reforms, and liberalization of the capital market. Although India has been cautious to avoid full convertibility and full-fledged external sector liberalization, the country substantially liberalized its domestic capital markets in 1992. This led to a rush of private corporate companies into the NIM and to a shift from a credit-based system to a capital market-based system of corporate financing. These changes were hastened by the decrease in budgetary support for a large number of public sector financial institutions. As a result, the domestic capital market has come to play an important role in the financial system.

The structural shift in corporate sector resource intermediation following capital market liberalization led to many unwarranted episodes like the Harshad Mehta scam in the secondary market and

[34] SEBI (2003)

the vanishing companies in the primary market. These negatively affected the confidence level of small investors in the capital markets, as these investors lost a substantial part of their savings and led to creation of dead capital. It brought issues in corporate governance to the forefront, which now have direct implications for the protection of small investors in the capital market.

As discussed earlier, corporate governance is no different from the larger issue of balancing the public concerns with that of the private interest. In the case of governance issues related to small investors, it is required to address the concerns from diverse angles: one, the public concern of a 'saver'; two, the private concern of being an 'investor'; and, simultaneously the private interest of the firms operating in an open market. This involves considerable deliberation and debate before any institutional structure is created. However, what is clear from the magnitude of problems across various existing economic and political systems is that there is no perfect model or system. Governance needs to be addressed locally with ingenuity and dynamism so as to check crisis situations.

Past experience and knowledge will go a long way in providing fundamental approaches to build upon. Technology (for speed) and access to information can help in the identification of early signs of crisis or degeneration. We should put in place structures that are neutral, by incorporating all stakeholders in order to balance the rights of each player. It is important to incorporate the recent advances in information technology to make governance more effective as these would address speed and access issues more effectively. In this context, the suggested model on the conduct of AGMs would go a long way. Combined with the proposed 'MAPIN Database' of SEBI, it would facilitate the creation of a powerful database on the capital market and its interface with stakeholders. It would also help in promoting a sustained flow of investments into capital markets by promoting participation of both small investors and small firms. However, it should be mentioned here that by no means it should be viewed that capital market is the sole channel for resource intermediation in an economy. A two-sector model involving both banks and capital market only would help in building a fundamentally strong domestic financial intermediation regime.

Appendix

TABLE A9.1: CHANGES IN FINANCIAL ASSETS OF THE HOUSEHOLD SECTOR (PERCENTAGE SHARE)

Period/ Year	*Average Financial Asset (Cr.)*	*Curr-ency*	*Bank Deposit*	*Non–Bank-ing Dep-osit*	*Life Insu-rance Fund*	*Provi-dent and Pens-ion Fund*	*Claims on Govt.*	*Shares and Debe-nture*	*Units of UTI*	*Trade Debt (Net)*
1970–79	5296	13.9	45.6	3.0	9.0	19.6	4.2	1.5	0.5	2.7
1980–85	19524	11.1	41.1	5.4	7.2	16.9	11.6	3.9	1.5	1.3
1986–89	39037	12.4	38.0	4.0	7.9	18.1	11.9	4.0	3.6	0.0
1990–96	106469	10.8	32.9	8.4	9.5	17.8	8.0	8.3	5.1	–0.8
1996–2002	233266	8.6	38.2	3.8	12.4	20.6	14.2	3.4	0.2	–1.5
				Yearly						
1996–97	15851	8.6	32.1	16.4	10.2	19.2	7.4	4.2	2.4	–0.4
1997–98	171740	7.4	43.1	3.9	11.3	18.8	12.9	2.6	0.3	–0.4
1998–99	207390	10.5	38.3	3.8	11.3	22.4	13.6	2.5	0.9	–3.3
1999–2000	239058	8.7	34.7	3.7	12.0	22.6	12.1	6.4	0.8	–0.8
2000–01	256735	6.9	36.9	4.8	13.3	21.3	15.2	2.8	–0.4	–0.7
2001–02	291406	9.7	37.8	2.9	14.2	18.0	17.1	3.0	–0.6	–2.1

Source: RBI, *Handbook of Statistics on Indian Economy*, Government of India.

TABLE A9.2: DISTRIBUTION OF OUTSTANDING CREDIT OF BANKS ACCORDING TO INTEREST RATE RANGE

Interest rate range	*1996*	*1997*	*1998*	*1999*	*2000*	*2001*	*CGR*
Less than 6%	5.4	4.6	4.0	1.5	1.5	1.0	–28.6
6% and above but less than 10%	1.0	1.0	0.9	0.9	0.4	0.3	–21.4
10% and above but less than 12%	3.1	2.9	3.0	5.5	8.3	8.9	23.5
12% and above but less than 14%	13.7	10.0	24.7	10.6	17.8	23.3	11.2
14% and above but less than 15%	31.4	39.0	25.4	10.1	13.1	15.8	–12.8
15% and above but less than 16%	14.8	13.5	13.3	17.2	18.0	17.7	3.6

(*contd.*)

(*Table A9.2: contd.*)

Interest rate range	*1996*	*1997*	*1998*	*1999*	*2000*	*2001*	*CGR*
16% and above but less than 17%	4.9	4.5	10.6	20.4	19.7	19.1	31.3
17% and above but less than 18%	12.0	9.0	6.7	15.0	10.3	6.5	-11.5
18% and above but less than 20%	7.6	9.2	7.1	13.1	8.1	4.8	-8.8
20% and above	6.1	6.3	4.3	5.6	2.8	2.6	-15.7
Total loans & advances	100.0	100.0	100.0	100.0	100.0	100.0	0.0
Total	4767771	5523900	6755563	1308890	1514558	1908167	-16.7

Source: RBI, *Handbook of Statistics on Indian Economy*, Government of India.

Table A9.3: Distribution of Firms Based on Operation as Private and Public Limited Companies

Sl. no	*Public age (#)*	*Total Age Of Firms (*)*									
		< 2	*2 to 5*	*Young*	*5 to 10*	*10 to 20*	*Middle Age*	*20 to 40*	*> 40*	*Old*	*G. Total*
1.	Less than 2 years	753	611	1364	418	205	623	50	6	56	2041
2.	2 to 5 years	0	234	234	143	52	195	19	7	26	457
	Young	753	845	1598	561	257	818	69	13	82	2498
3.	5 to 10	1	0	1	191	66	257	20	0	20	278
4.	10 to 20	0	0	0	0	70	70	19	3	22	92
	Middle-Aged	1	0	1	191	136	327	39	3	42	370
5.	20 to 40	0	0	0	1	0	1	46	3	49	50
6.	Above 40	0	0	0	0	0	0	1	25	26	26
	Old	0	0	0	1	0	1	47	28	75	76
	Grand Total	754	845	1599	753	393	1146	155	44	199	2944

Note: * = Age calculated from the year of incorporation of the firm to the year of public issue.

= Age calculated from the year of attaining public limited status to the year of public issue.

Source: Based on the survey results.

TABLE A9.4: SIZE OF FIRMS AND FIRM ALLOTMENTS IN A PUBLIC ISSUE

Size of firms	*1989*	*1990*	*1991*	*CCI*	*1992*	*1993*	*1994*	*1995*	*Post CCI*
< 5 crore	27.92	31.72	25.81	28.5	25.04	16.63	22.16	30.21	23.5
5 to 10 cr	35.4	51.67	43.3	43.5	28.66	21.22	26.26	32.49	27.2
10 to 20 cr	41.75	35.67	46.5	41.3	32.53	26.76	30.37	36.09	31.4
20 to 40c cr	56	43	58	52.3	38.54	27.54	27.71	28.55	30.6
40 to 100 cr	0	0	33	11.0	25.2	5	35.45	13.5	19.8
Above 100 cr	0	0	18	6.0	0.25	6.6	36.33	38.22	20.4
				Broad classification of firms					
Small	31.7	41.7	34.6	36.0	26.9	18.9	24.2	31.4	25.3
Medium	48.9	39.3	52.3	46.8	35.5	27.2	29.0	32.3	31.0
Large	0.0	0.0	25.5	8.5	12.7	5.8	35.9	25.9	20.1

Source: Based on the survey results.

TABLE A9.5: AGE OF FIRMS AND FIRM ALLOTMENTS IN A PUBLIC ISSUE

Age of firm	*1989*	*1990*	*1991*	*CCI*	*1992*	*1993*	*1994*	*1995*	*Post CCI*
Less 2 years	39.9	42.9	31.5	38.1	34.9	22.2	28.8	34.4	30.1
2 to 5 yr	35.0	38.9	35.0	36.3	32.3	22.5	29.0	32.6	29.1
5 to 10 yr	26.8	32.3	31.4	30.2	26.1	19.1	23.6	30.8	24.9
10 to 20 yr	13.9	7.8	11.6	11.1	18.1	14.7	18.7	27.3	19.7
20 to 40 yr	5.3	10.9	4.3	6.9	15.9	12.0	18.7	20.9	16.9
above 40 years	0.0	0.0	31.0	10.3	20.0	8.5	12.4	17.1	14.5
				Broad Classification of the Firms					
Young	37.4	40.9	33.2	37.2	33.6	22.4	28.9	33.5	29.6
Middle Aged	20.3	20.0	21.5	20.6	22.1	16.9	21.1	29.0	22.3
Old	2.7	5.5	17.7	8.6	17.9	10.3	15.5	19.0	15.7

Source: Based on the survey results.

FIGURE A9.1: GROWTH OF PRIMARY MARKET IN INDIA: DEBENTURES VS EQUITY

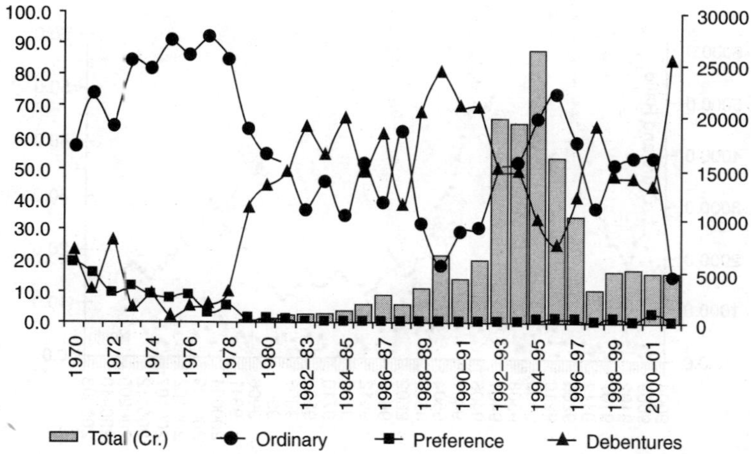

Source: RBI, *Handbook of Statistics on Indian Economy*, Government of India.

FIGURE A9. 2: CORPORATE FINANCING AND THE TRENDS IN THE PRIMARY MARKET IN INDIA: (1970–2001)

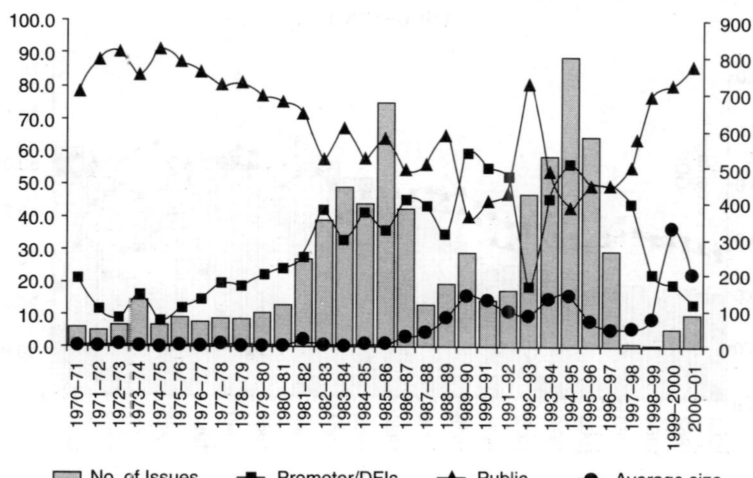

Source: RBI, *Handbook of Statistics on Indian Economy*, Government of India.

FIGURE A9.3: RELATIONSHIP BETWEEN SECONDARY MARKET AND PRIMARY MARKET IN INDIA

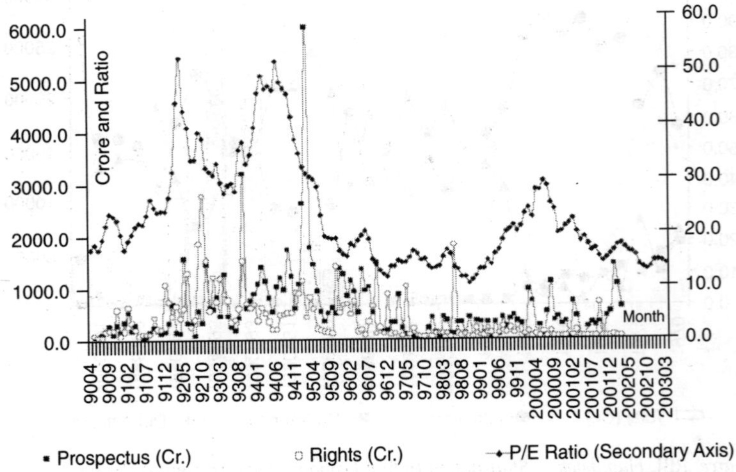

Source: RBI, *Handbook of Statistics on Indian Economy*, Government of India.

FIGURE A9.4: SAVING AND INVESTMENT RELATED ACTIVITIES IN INDIA: 1960–2001

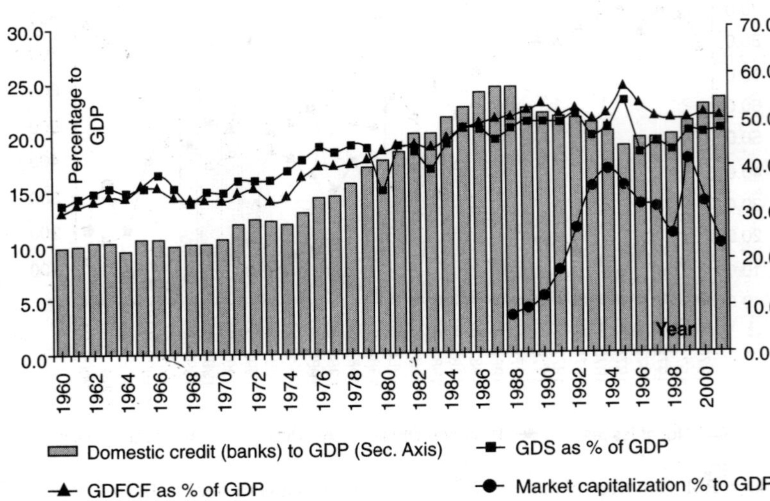

Source: World Bank, *World Development Indicators 2003*, CD.

References

Ajit, D., and R. D. Bangar, 1997, 'Banks in Financial Intermediation: Performance and Issues', Reserve Bank of India, Occasional Papers, vol. 18, nos. 2&3, September.

Dhar, Biswajit and Murali Kallummal, 2002, 'Capital Inflows and Effects of Market-Driven Investments: A Focus on the Southeast Asian Crisis', RIS Occasional Paper No. 66, Research and Information System for the Developing and Other Developing Countries, New Delhi.

Ghosh, Jayati and Abhijit Sen, 1998, 'Capital Flows and Macro-Economies: A Historical View', Deepak Nayar (ed.), *Economy as Ideology and Experience*, Frank Cass & Co Ltd, London.

Gupta, L. C., Naveen Jain and Yash Kulshreshtha, 1994, *Shareowners' Geographic Distribution: City-wise, Urban-rural and State-wise*, Society for Capital Market Research and Development, Delhi.

Joshi, P. N., 1999, 'Banking Sector Reforms: The Other Side of the Coin', *Economic and Political Weekly*, March, vol. 34, no.14, pp 797-8.

Kallummal, Murali, 1999, 'Disintermediation and Private Corporate Financing: An Analysis of the New Issues (Primary) Market in India', unpublished Ph.D. Thesis, Centre for Economic Studies and Planning (CESP), JNU, New Delhi.

Keynes, J. M., 1939, 'The Process of Capital Formation', *Economic Journal; Collected Writings of John Maynard Keynes*, Vol. 26, (ed.) D. E. Moggridge.

McKinnon, R. I., 1973, *Money and Capital in Economic Development*, The Brooking Institutions, Washington DC.

SEBI, 2003, 'Discussion Paper on Development of Central Database for Market Participants and Investors ('MAPIN' Database) in Indian Security Market', also at *http://www.sebi.gov.in/commereport/*.

Shaw, E. S., 1973, *Financial Deepening in Economic Development*, Oxford University Press, New York.

Stiglitz, J. E., 2002, *Globalization and Its Discontents*, W. W. Norton and Company, New York.

10

An Enquiry into Insurance Regulation

The Interaction of Investment and Price Regulation

AJIT RANADE AND RAJEEV AHUJA

Introduction

India is a relative newcomer among developing countries that have liberalized their insurance markets. For more than four decades in the life business, and almost three decades in non-life, insurance had been a state monopoly in India. The business has seen good growth, but perhaps less than its counterparts in Asia. Insurance is a USD 20 billion business in India, and together with banking services, adds over 8 per cent to India's GDP. Gross premium collection is about 3.2 per cent of the GDP and is growing between 15 and 20 per cent per annum. India also has the highest number of life insurance policies in force in the world, with the total investible funds with the Life Insurance Corporation of India (LIC) constituting almost 8 per cent of the GDP. Yet more than three fourth of India's insurable population has no life insurance cover. Health insurance of any kind is negligible, and other forms of non-life insurance are much below international standards. The Indian insurance sector was opened in the year 2000 to new private entrants into life and non-life businesses who now coexist with the state-owned LIC and four general insurers. The Insurance Regulatory and Development Authority (IRDA) has several regulatory functions including setting up entry norms, issuing

A version of this paper was presented in the Fifth Development Convention at the Centre for Multidisciplinary Research, Dharwar. I am thankful to Dr Vijayamohanan Pillai and Professor K. P. Kannan for their comments and suggestions on the earlier version on this paper. I have also benefited from discussions with Dr Santhakumar.

licences, standardizing procedures regarding intermediaries, etc. Also, it promotes public education and awareness campaigns regarding insurance so as to enable healthy growth of the insurance sector. It is the development[1] brief of the IRDA which makes it a different proposition from the conventional insurance regulators.[2] In fact in developing economies like China, India and Sri Lanka, the insurance regulation involved a two-step process.[3] The first step was to orchestrate the entry of private sector players, and having done that, the second step was to ensure sound functioning of the market. The first step involved thinking about an appropriate market structure, the number of players to be allowed and entry norms, while the second step involves solvency regulation and market regulation. Solvency regulation is mainly about capital adequacy and restrictions on investments based on the risk of the institution product profile. Market regulation involves supervision of products, pricing, contract details, other trade practices, grievance redressal and so on.

In this paper we examine the issue of ensuring solvency, or financial soundness of insurers through the imposition of price floors and restricting their investments in risky assets.[4] In the following sections we briefly touch upon issues in solvency and premium regulation. In

[1] See Pant (1999) for critical evaluation of this clause in the IRDA Bill.

[2] The conventional insurance regulation and supervision has mainly aimed to protect the interests of the insurance-buying public. In fact the basic objective of insurance supervision is to ensure that insurers will have financial resources required to pay all claims as they become due, and insurers will treat consumers in an equitable manner in all financial dealings. This is accomplished first by ensuring that policyholders and beneficiaries are given a fair and reasonable treatment by insurance firms and insurance agents, and second by ensuring the financial soundness of the firms themselves and their capital, reserves and investments.

[3] As a part of their on-going financial sector liberalization, many developing countries such as China, Sri Lanka and India are at varying stages of liberalizing their insurance markets. In order to improve competitiveness of China's insurance industry, the Chinese government broke monopoly power of the state-owned PICC by allowing the entry of Ping An Insurance Company (PAIC) in 1988 and of China Pacific Insurance Company (CPIC) in 1991. Since then the government has been gradually opening up its domestic insurance market. However, Chinese insurance market is still dominated by three domestic insurers. Their combined share is about 98 per cent of the market share. Even though the PICC share has declined from 98 per cent to 74.4 per cent, it still remains the largest insurer in China (for details see Qu 1998). In Sri Lanka the insurance industry was liberalized for private participation in 1986. Insurance business in Sri Lanka is also quite concentrated among the eight insurance companies operating in the industry.

[4] For an overview of other regulatory issues in the context of insurance regulation in India, see Ranade and Ahuja (2000).

the section, 'A Simple Model' we show through the use of a simple analytical model, that as far as solvency is concerned, a separate price floor as a regulatory requirement is redundant, and is subsumed by a single investment restriction which imposes a minimum share of premium collections to be invested in 'safe' assets. We illustrate our model through some numerical simulations in the section, 'Simulation Results'. A separate rationale for price regulation from a developing country perspective is provided in the section, 'Justification for Price Regulation' and the final section concludes the paper.

Solvency Regulation

Solvency regulation of which capital adequacy is a major component, is to ensure the financial soundness of insurers. The need for it arises due to costly information and by agency problems (limited liability diminishes incentive to maintain safety). To check against solvency risk, regulators require that insurers maintain a minimum amount of capital to meet their financial obligations. Capital adequacy regulation is applied almost everywhere in the financial services industry. Besides capital adequacy requirements, solvency regulation includes additional restrictions on investments, reinsurance, reserves, asset-liability matching and so on. Capital and reserves act as a cushion against unexpected increases in liabilities and decreases in the value of assets. Capital is also used to fund rehabilitation or liquidation with minimal losses to policyholders and claimants in case of bankruptcies. Restrictions are also placed on the ownership of insurance companies in several countries, to limit influence and contagion effects in case of insolvencies.

Rate (Price) Regulation

The issue is whether to impose a price floor, or price ceiling, or both, on premiums. The justification for price floor is that price competition in insurance can be unhealthy as it might bring some firms close to insolvency or bankruptcy, which in turn, can cause a panic and 'bank run' type of domino effect. High rates of inflation can also lead to premiums being insufficient to cover claims and hence, might justify price floors. On the other hand, price ceilings are justified because of the presence of consumer search costs that impede competition and result in excessive prices and profits. The flip side of insurers' underwriting business is asset management. The competitive advantage of insurers lies in their skill in securing high returns on their investments. This may call for aggressive, possibly risky investments. All financial institutions vie for attracting the same pot of household savings. Regulation of investments of all financial institutions, including those of insurance firms is a common feature worldwide. This is to ensure that firms do not invest excessively in risky projects. There is however, a clear trend away from detailed investment regulation and towards prudential norms especially in developed countries. But neither detailed investment regulation nor complete freedom to insurance firms in determining their investment portfolio is deemed desirable. This is because on one hand, all investments in completely safe assets would deprive the buyers of insurance, of higher return (reflected in a lower premium rate). On the other hand, full freedom in defining the investment portfolio may adversely affect solvency and claims settlement when firms invest in risky assets. There exists thus, an optimal level of investments between risky and safe assets. This has a bearing on the pricing of insurance products. What is this optimal mix? We show this optimal mix in the model presented below.

A Simple Model

We assume the expected utility maximizing agent (i.e. the insuree) who has a concave, twice differentiable utility function of money, U; and has (money) income of W and W–L in good and bad state respectively. Let p be the probability of the bad state. The agent has an option of buying insurance against loss in the bad state. However, the insurance company invests the premium it collects in both risky and safe assets. Let δ denote the fraction of the premium it invests in safe assets. The agent then faces another risk of getting back only part of his claim in the bad state. This risk, denoted by (1–r), emanates from the risky investments of the insurance company. While some investments in risky assets are utility enhancing for the agent, the same if done in excess, may actually diminish the agent's utility. There exists the optimal value of δ that maximizes agent's utility. We show this formally below. Suppose the following insurance contract is offered by an insurer to the agent:

i. buy any coverage, denoted by D at price q; and

ii. receive in bad state, the coverage amount D with probability (1–r) and with probability r receive coverage amount $\delta * q * (D/p)$ (this comes from the zero profit condition shown below).

Given this, the optimal coverage level is one that maximizes agent's expected utility.

$$EU = (1 - p)\, u(W - q\,D) + p\,(1 - r)\, u(W + (1 - q)\,D - L)$$
$$+ p\,r\,u(W - L - q\,D + \delta\, q\,(D/p)\,) \qquad (1)$$

Under competitive conditions expected profits of a firm would be driven down to zero. Hence, the zero profit condition would be:

$$r\,[\max(\delta\, q\, D - p\, D, 0)] + (1 - r)[\delta\, q\, D + (1 - \delta)\, q\, D\, R - p\, D] = 0$$

The risky asset assumed here has return of R with probability (1 – r), and 0 otherwise. The zero profit condition becomes,

$$r\,(0) + (1 - r)[q\,D\,(\delta + (1 - \delta)\,R)) - p\,D] = 0$$

or

$$q\,D\,\delta + (1 - \delta)\,R = p\,D$$

Solving explicitly for q,

$$q = p/(\delta + (1 - \delta)\,R)$$

Differentiating q w.r.t δ yields,

$$dq/d\delta = -\,p(1 - R)/(\delta + (1 - \delta)\,R)^2 > 0 \qquad (2)$$

The first order condition that follows from the maximization of (1) is,

$$q\,(1 - p)\,u'(W - q\,D) = (1 - r)\,p\,(1 - q)\,u'(W + (1 - q)\,D - L)$$
$$+ r\,(\delta - p)\,q\,u'(W - L + q\,(\delta/p - 1)\,D) \qquad (3)$$

Proposition:
Given parameter values W; L; R; r; p; q there exists δ such that $0<\delta<1$ which maximizes agent's utility.

Proof:
Evaluate objective function (EU) at the optimum D. Differentiate this valuation function with respect to δ using envelope theorem we get,

$$V = [\,(1 - p)\,u'(W - q\,D) + (1 - r)\,p\,u'(W - L + (1 - q)D) +$$
$$r\,p\,u'(W - L - q\,D + q\,\delta\,D/p)\,]\,(-\,D\,dq/d\delta) + r\,p\,u'$$
$$(W - L - q\,D + q\,\delta\,D/p)\,(q\,D/p + \delta\,D/p\,dq/d\delta) \qquad (4)$$

At δ = 1, p = q which implies D = L

This in turn implies $u'(W - q\,D) = u'(W + (1 - q)\,D - L) = u'(W - L + q\,(\delta/p - 1)\,D)$

$$V|_{\delta=1} = u'(W - q\,D)\,(-\,D\,dq/d\delta) + r\,p\,u'(W - q\,D)$$
$$(1 + 1/p''\,dq/d\delta)\,D$$

$$V|_{\delta=1} = u'(W - qL)L\, dq/d\delta\, (r - 1) + r\, p\, u'(W - qL)L \quad (5)$$

$$V|_{\delta=1} = u'(W - q\, L)L\, [(r - 1)\, dq\, /d\delta + r\, p] \quad (6)$$

for $V|_{\delta=1} < 0$, $(r - 1)\, dq\, /d\delta + r\, p < 0$

or

$$(dq/d\delta)\, (1 - r) > r\, p$$

Substituting $dq/d\delta$, and since $R > 1$ we get the following condition,

$$V|_{\delta=1} < 0 \Leftrightarrow (R - 1)\, (1 - r) > r$$

Now, we derive a condition for which $V|_{\delta=0} > 0$

$$\text{At } \delta = 0,\ q = p/R$$

At $\delta = 0$, $u'(W - q\, D) < u'(W - L - q\, D)$ and $u'(W - L + (1 - q)D) < u'(W - L - q\, D)$ but $u'(W - L + (1 - q)D)$ could be greater or less than $u'(W - q\, D)$ depending on the optimal value of D which could be higher than L since price of insurance could be lower than actuarially fair price.

$$V|_{\delta=0} = [(1 - p)\, u'(W - q\, D) + (1 - r)\, p\, u'(W - L + (1 - q)D) + r\, p\, u'(W - L - q\, D)]\, (- D\, dq/d\delta) + r\, p\, u'(W - L - q\, D)\, (qD)/p$$

For $V|_{\delta=0} > 0$; we have the following condition

FIGURE 10.1: EXPECTED UTILITY AND PROPORTION OF INVESTMENTS IN SAFE ASSET: U (X) = $\sqrt{x}$

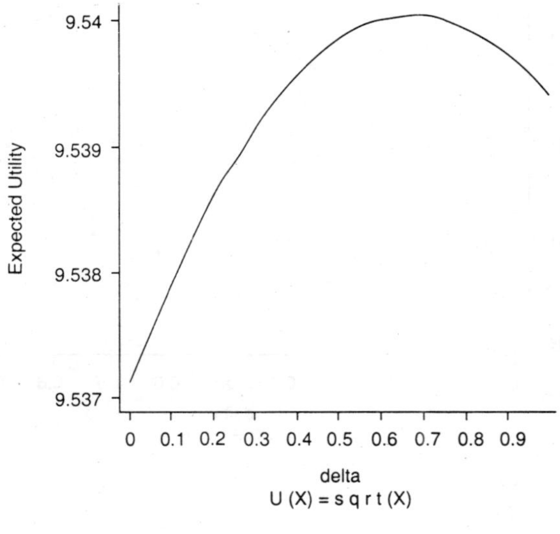

$(dq/d\delta)\ [(1 - p)\ u'(W - q\ D) + p\ \{(1 - r)\ u'(W - L + (1 - q)D)$
$+ r\ u'(W - L - q\ D)\}] < r\ p\ q\ u'(W - L - q\ D)$

$$dq/d\delta\,|_{\delta=0} = -\ p\ (1 - R)/R^2 > 0 \qquad (8)$$

Substituting $dq/d\delta\,|_{\delta=0}$ we get

$(R - 1) < r\ q\ c\ R^2$

This then is the condition for $V|_{\delta=0} > 0$
where,

$c = u'\ (W - q\ D - L)/[(1 - p)\ u'\ (W - q\ D) + p\ \{(1 - r)\ u'$
$(W - L + (1 - q)D) + r\ u'\ (W - L - q\ D)\}]$

Simulation Results

The figures 10.1, 10.2 and 10.3 show the simulation results for three different utility functions. We work with the following three utility functions: (a) $u(x) = \sqrt{x}$, (b) $u(x) = \log x$, and (c) $u(x) = 1-\exp^{-\rho x}$. The parameter values assumed are: W = 100, L = 36, p = 0.25, r = 0.1, and r = 0.01. However, the value of R is varied to obtain a concave shape of the curve (to rule out corner solution). Accordingly, the

FIGURE 10.2: EXPECTED UTILITY AND PROPORTION OF INVESTMENTS IN SAFE ASSET: $u(x) = lnx$

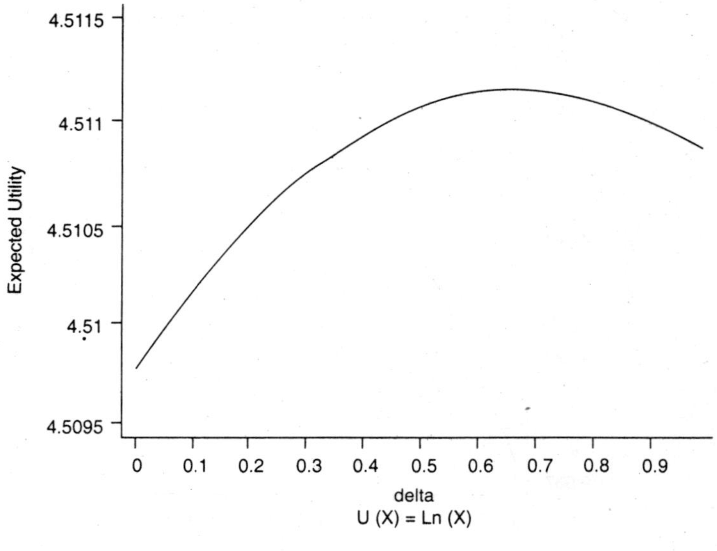

FIGURE 10.3: EXPECTED UTILITY AND PROPORTION OF INVESTMENTS IN SAFE ASSET: $u(x) = 1 - e^{-\rho x}$

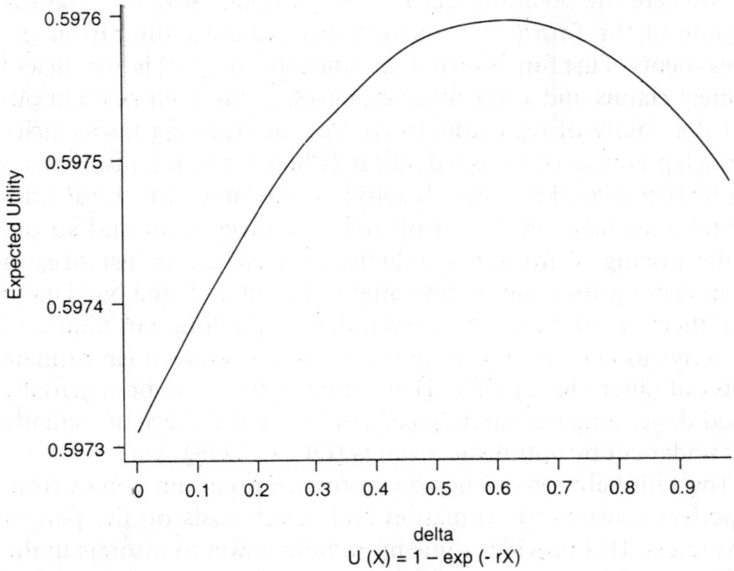

value of R in case (a) is 1.12, and in case (b) and (c) is 1.13. In all these figures, we show that there exists a particular value of δ at which the expected utility of agent is maximized.

Justification for Price Regulation

Traditionally, insolvency concerns in a competitive insurance market were sought to be addressed through price/premium regulation and costly information (Finsinger and Pauly 1986). In the insurance business, loss or claims liabilities are not known until later in the future. It is argued that in a competitive set-up there is a tendency for insurers to under-cut each other leading to the premium falling dangerously below the actual cost. This in turn, results in insolvencies.[5] Hence,

[5] Insolvency in case of insurance though not uncommon, has been rather low worldwide. In the US context, Klein (1995) reports that approximately 20 insurers failed every year in the period 1976–84, compared to an annual average of 70 failures for the period 1984–93. Still these figures are fairly small relative to the size of the industry (less than one per cent of the total companies in operation).

there exists a rationale for the regulator to impose a price floor to prevent the market from imploding.[6] However, while there may be cases where the premium becomes so insupportably low that the income of the firm (even where the income accruing from the investments of the firm is included in the total income) is insufficient to meet claims and cover other expenses, it has been pointed out that the ability of regulators to control the resulting insolvencies through premium controls is doubtful (Chandler 1998). Insolvencies can be better checked through solvency regulation which includes capital adequacy, restriction on reserves, investment and so on. Under-pricing of insurance is better understood as instances of insurers not possessing or obtaining sufficient and credible data to base their premium on. Moreover, due to the long tail nature of property/casualty insurance contracts, insurers know their ultimate costs only after a long period. Hence, pricing that must be actuarially based depending on the frequency of loss and its severity actually gets under-cut by optimistic insurers (OECD 1998).

The rationale for ceilings on insurance premium comes from imperfect consumer information and search costs on the part of consumers. This provides some monopoly power to insurers in the market. Moreover, since it is costly to ascertain risk characteristics of consumers, informational advantage accrue to insurers who are well entrenched in the market. This too accords some degree of monopoly power to the already established firms (Klein 1995). Developing countries like India are facing a regulatory challenge in devising an appropriate set of regulations in the conduct of insurance business. These countries are characterized by low consumer sophistication, weak contract enforcement, unreliable or absence of data base, shortage of trained personnel, low professional standards and so forth. Besides these factors, the OECD 1998 report also lists other factors that pose a supervisory challenge in developing countries. It may take time before some of these hurdles can be overcome. Until such time standardization of insurance contracts may be desirable at least in the initial stages of opening up of their markets to private insurers. Contract standardization has both its costs and benefits. But it is believed that a good range of standardized contracts can

[6] Insolvency of an insurance company could be due to a number of reasons such as inadequate reserves, poor monitoring and enforcement of reserve requirements by the regulator, poor investment decisions, fraud by management, and non-payments of claims to insurance companies by reinsurers.

minimize the associated costs. Price regulation may even be needed in case of mandatory coverage to effect cross-subsidization consistent with certain social objectives or in case of assigned risk pool meant for high risk people who find it difficult to get/buy coverage. Thus, even though premium regulation cannot address solvency concerns, it may still be warranted in a developing country context.

Conclusion

In this paper we develop a model to demonstrate that there exists an optimal mix of safe and risky investments that the insurance company must undertake. While an over-cautious approach towards investments of insurers may deprive the policyholder of higher returns that goes with risky investments, excessive assumption of risk through risky investments would expose policyholders to different kind of risk i.e., risk of claims default. A fine balance between these two tendencies is one of the crucial functions of a regulator. Left to themselves insurers may deviate from this optimal mix. Hence, there arises the need for regulating investments of insurance firms. We also argue that price regulation cannot address insolvency concerns. These concerns can best be addressed through other regulatory devices such as capital adequacy norms, reserve requirements, asset-liability match etc. Furthermore, we argue that developing country characteristics such as less sophisticated buyers, weak contract enforcement, absence of database for setting of premium rates, and social/equity considerations requiring cross-subsidization call for explicit regulation of premium rates and contract standardization at least in the initial stages of their regulatory development.

References

Chandler, Seth, 1998, 'Insurance Regulation', B. Bouckaert and G. De Geest (eds.), *Encyclopedia of Law and Economics*, Edward Elgar, Cheltenham.

Finsinger, J and M. Pauly, 1986, 'Introduction', in Jorg Finsinger and Mark Pauly (eds.), *The Economics of Insurance Regulation*, St. Martins Press, New York.

Klein, R. W., 1995, 'Insurance Regulation in Transition', available at *http://www.naic.org/geninfo/about/regutra3.htm*.

OECD, 1998, 'Competition and Related Regulation Issues in Insurance Industry', Committee on Competition Law and Policy, DAFFE/CLP(98)/20, OECD.

Pant, Niranjan, 1999, 'The Insurance Regulation and Development Bill: An Appraisal', *Economic & Political Weekly*, vol. XXXIV, no. 45, 6–12 November, pp. 3166–9.

Qu, H., 1998, 'China Insurance Market: Competition and Regulation', *Singapore International Insurance & Actuarial Journal*, vol. 2, no. 2, pp. 19–62.

Ranade, A. and R. Ahuja, 2000, 'Issues in Regulation of Insurance', *Economic & Political Weekly*, vol. XXXV, no. 5, 29 January.

Savage, Lawrie, 1998, 'Re-Engineering Insurance Supervision', World Bank Working Paper No. WPS 20, World Bank, Washington DC.

Winter, Ralph A., 1988, 'The Liability Crisis and the Dynamics of Competitive Insurance Markets', *Yale Journal on Regulation*, pp. 455–99.

Wright, Kenneth M., 1992, 'The Life Insurance Industry in the United States: An Analysis of Economic and Regulatory Issues', World Bank Working Paper No. WPS 857, The World Bank, Washington DC.

11

Telecom Liberalization

A Case Study of India's Experience with Regulation

RAJAT KATHURIA

Introduction

Infrastructure services, unlike many other commodities cannot be effectively traded in markets. There are several characteristics that make it unlikely that socially optimal and economically efficient prices and quantities will be delivered through the market. Investments are large and lumpy, implying significant scale economies in operations. Further, because of different classes of users, issues relating to cross-subsidy of one category of users by another need to be addressed.

Until the mid-1990s, telecommunication services in India were provided by an incumbent monopoly, the Department of Telecommunications (DoT), which was seen as the best method of overcoming the market failure resulting from the characteristics of telecommunications. Recently as technological and economic change made the reintroduction of competition seem consistent with the goals of collective welfare, new forms of institutional design and regulatory policy evolved across the world and were sought to be established in India through the introduction of competition in the telecommunications sector.

Introduction of competition, especially in the presence of a large incumbent public sector monopoly requires setting of an independent regulator and a set of regulatory rules. These rules should specify rules for entry. They should outline the extent of competition permissible and ensure interconnection between new and previous service providers. They should list equipment approval procedures. They should connect pricing to cost to quality of service. They should set up clear subsidy arrangements and describe exit guarantees. They should also establish clear procedures for conflict and dispute resolution and most important, conduct continuous monitoring and surveillance that rules are followed.[1]

In this broad sense of 'regulation', we are not far from 'telecommunications policy'. The commonly accepted function of regulation in telecommunications refers to an independent regulator, which governs the operations and pricing of telecommunications companies, that is, 'regulates' them. The regulatory mandate varies, but most regulators are charged to approve tariffs, ensure consumer protection and quality of service, resolve disputes between various interests including customers and service providers, and often, ensure competition that is neither predatory nor cartelized. Some regulators are empowered to control entry into the market through licensing Others may be mandated to ensure the productivity and/or the rate of return on investment of the regulated companies.

Paul Joskow's list of regulatory goals for infrastructure, while referring to a 'monopoly', addresses in strictly economic terms, the objectives underlying infrastructure regulation in any market structure:[2]

Making sure that the monopoly charges consumers reasonable prices for services
Inducing the monopoly to provide services efficiently
Using the level and structure of prices to induce consumers to make efficient use of services offered
Providing additional incentives to attract additional capital to the sector
Achieving income distribution goals through the level and structure of prices.

In most jurisdictions, the frame of activity of the regulator is set out by the legislature through statute. The executive sets and communicates telecommunications policy, while the regulator uses its powers to implement the policy on a day-to-day basis. The concept of an independent regulatory agency operating with transparent procedures, obligated to make decisions based on a logical evaluation of the facts in light of its statutory responsibilities and subject to judicial review, may not be easy to create. As Paul Joskow states, 'Regulatory institutions necessarily take time to create and mature,

[1] Mody et al. (1993).
[2] Joskow (1998).

and their independence and credibility are established on the basis of both their legal foundations and their actual behavior when faced with difficult decisions that involve substantial interest group controversy'.[3] William Melody describes independence not as independence from government policy, but rather as independence to implement policy without undue interference from politicians or industry lobbyists.

Regulatory governance has emerged as an area of concern across the world. As regulation becomes essential, the establishment of independent regulatory institutions becomes important. The International Telecommunications Union (ITU) reports that there are now over 84 independent regulatory agencies in the world, whereas earlier there were only ten.

This paper is about the challenges of establishing independent regulatory agencies in the telecom sector in India. The paper adopts a case-based approach in that it explores the problem through a few legal cases that have been contested in the telecom sector in India. It is noteworthy that litigation started in the sector even before the Telecom Regulatory Authority of India (TRAI) was established and it continues to be an endemic part of sector development. The paper does not cover every piece of the vast litigation in the sector, but only a few major ones. Through these cases it attempts to demonstrate that litigation has been used and much 'abused' by *all* service providers to promote narrow self interest at the cost of sector development. Had the standards of institutional governance been higher the pace of development of India's telecom infrastructure would have been considerably faster.

The National Telecom Policy (NTP) 1994

Telecommunications was not perceived as one of the key infrastructure sectors for rapid economic development during the formative years of the Indian economy. The relatively low levels of investment in the sector affected the quality, quantity and range of services provided. In 1994, telephone density in India was less than one telephone per hundred persons, while the world average was 14.[4] The situation today is vastly different. Telecom infrastructure is considered to be one of the crucial requirements for ITESBPO.

[3] Joskow (1998).

[4] *World Telecommunication Development Report*, ITU, 1999.

The change in attitude toward telecommunications was first set out in the NTP document in 1994. NTP 1994 stated that in order to realize the goals of India's new economic policy (1991), it was necessary to have world-class telecommunications infrastructure. 'It is [therefore] necessary to give the highest priority to the development of telecommunications service in the country.'[5] The NTP 1994 thus focused on telecommunications for all and telecommunications within reach of all; universal service covering all villages as early as possible at affordable and reasonable prices; quality of telecom services to be of world standard; India to emerge as a major manufacturing base and major exporter of telecom equipment and defence and security interests to be protected. To achieve these objectives, the policy acknowledged the pivotal role of private investment and therefore NTP 1994 envisaged the setting up of an 'independent' regulatory body, the TRAI.

Although the policy specified the creation of a regulator, the latter was not set up until 1997. Meanwhile, implementation of the 1994 policy was carried out by the DoT. This was faulty institutional design since it gave DoT an enormous advantage over private operators. It was later to prove to be a thorny legal matter in regard to the newly-created regulators powers to give directions to a policy maker that also combined the role of a service provider. This aspect is described in detail in the section 'Initial Years of the TRAI'.

In August and September 1995, the first eight mobile licences began commercial operations in Delhi, Mumbai, Kolkata and Chennai.[6] The basic or fixed service licences[7] were not as keen to sign license agreements as their mobile counterparts, because they would be in direct competition with the DoT, who was also responsible for implementing policy. By early 1996, the DoT had issued letters of intent to a few of basic service licences.

The regime devised by DoT to implement the policy was naturally skewed in its favour, especially as it related to it service provision functions. The DoT and its counterpart in Mumbai and Delhi, Mahanagar Telephone Nigam Limited (MTNL) recognized that one way to increase the cost of operations of new entrants was to deny or delay access to interconnection. Interconnection is the lifeblood of

[5] NTP 1994, Ministry of Communications, Government of India, New Delhi, see *www.dotindia.com*

[6] Each Metro service area was limited to two mobile providers.

[7] In this paper Basic, PSTN and Fixed services are used interchangeably and refer to what is commonly known as landlines.

all modern communications systems. In order for communications systems to be effective, they must interconnect with other systems. Interconnection includes both the commercial and technical arrangements under which service providers connect their equipment networks and services to enable their customers to have access to customers, services and networks of other service providers.[8]

Optimal interconnection arrangements help increase the network effect or the value of a communications system. The incumbents' dominant position in the early phase of reform gave them an enormous advantage in interconnection matters. The DoT and MTNL used this advantage to negotiate interconnection arrangements with private licences that included terms and conditions that were heavily in their favour. Private licences had no other option but to deal with the incumbents because private licensees were forbidden to directly interconnect among themselves. Therefore, traffic from one private network and another private network had to be routed through DoT and MTNL switches. In addition all national and international long distance calls had to be transmitted exclusively through DoT networks in its capacity as the monopoly long distance carrier and interconnection charges were to be borne totally by the new entrants.

The effects of unsatisfactory interconnection can undo much of the benefits of good regulation in other areas. Thus, the benefits of private entry can be neutralized by a dominant incumbent, especially in the absence of a regulatory body. Unchecked, the DoT relied on unilateral internal orders in deciding the manner in which private licences could interconnect to its networks and the process of fresh entry into the nascent telecommunications sector. In fact, the genesis of the TRAI lies in the bidding process for the grant of basic services licences and the litigation that followed the grant of the first set of cellular licences under NTP 1994.

The bid process for basic services in Circles was marred by complaints of lack of transparency. This applied to crucial provisions relating to operator selection and led to mutual accusations of failure to meet contract commitments. Among the transparency-related issues was a post-bid decision by the DoT imposing a cap on the number of Circles that could be awarded to one bidder. For this purpose, the Circles were categorized into 'A', 'B' and 'C' types depending on the size of operations. It was announced that not more than three circles

[8] See TRAI, Register for Interconnect Regulation (No. 2 of 1999), s2(iv), Telecom Interconnection Register Regulation.

('A' plus 'B' categories) would be allowed per operator[9] on grounds of curbing monopoly. New entrants challenged the government and the DoT and questioned the process of awarding basic service licences. This gave rise to a legal struggle in the Delhi Science Forum and others vs Union of India[10] case which also questioned the legality of the government's cellular licensing process that was underway at that time.

The litigation delayed entry of competition in the sector and the Supreme Court agreed that there had been a delay on the part of the government to establish an independent regulatory agency. Between the time of the filing of writ petitions, and the date of delivery of the judgment, the Telecom Regulatory Authority of India Ordinance, 1996 had been promulgated. The Supreme Court analysed the said Ordinance and held that:

> The existence of the Telecom Regulatory Authority with the appropriate powers is essential for the introduction of plurality in the telecom sector. The National Telecom Policy is a historic departure from the practice followed in the past century. Since the private sector will have to contribute more to the development of the telecom network than DoT / MTNL in the next few years, the role of an independent telecom regulatory authority with appropriate powers need not be impressed.[11]

The creation of the new regulatory agency was a significant event in the need to establish an institutional framework capable of achieving the objectives of NTP 1994. A key defect of the existing policy was its failure to recommend the creation of a regulatory body. After some litigation, the need for such a body was recognized and with the creation of TRAI, DoT surrendered its regulatory role, although it retained policy making, licensing and operations within the same organizational boundaries.

Initial Years of the TRAI

The Telecom Regulatory Authority of India Act (TRAI Act) 1997 established the TRAI in January 1997, with a view to providing an

[9] This factor ought to have been considered and clarified to bidders before the bids were invited. Interestingly, NTP 99 sets no limit on the number of Circles or Service Areas that a single operator could take up.

[10] See Delhi Science Forum and others vs. Union of India and another (1996) *Supreme Court of India Company Law Journal* 47:2 (April-June 1996).

[11] Delhi Science Forum vs Union of India.

effective regulatory framework and achieving adequate safeguards to ensure fair competition and protection of consumer interests. To achieve the objectives of the TRAI Act, TRAI was given the power to issue directions to service providers, make regulations, notify tariffs by Order and adjudicate disputes arising between the Government (in its role as service provider) and any other service provider. More details are provided in Annex 1.

The passing of the TRAI Act had been long delayed in the legislative process. It is quite possible that the DoT did not want a regulator with teeth. Regulation of the industry would imply in practice, focus on the incumbent and even 'reform' of the incumbent provider in terms of its operations especially towards the new entrants. The TRAI was soon plunged into adjudicating between the DoT and cellular mobile circle licensees. It began with DoT hiking PSTN[12] to mobile tariffs in Circles upto Rs 10.00 per minute, making it 24 times more expensive than PSTN to PSTN calls, thereby making such calls unattractive. Since 99 per cent of all PSTN lines were either with DoT and MTNL this would diminish calls to mobiles and encourage PSTN to PSTN calls, adversely hitting the private cellular operators' revenue. Another source of friction between DoT and the new entrants was the limited number of points of interconnection offered to the private operators by DoT, to connect to the latter's network. This was an example of predatory conduct by the DoT that sought to drive up prices for cellular services.

In the litigation that followed, TRAI determined that the DoT did not have the right to charge a huge premium to its customers for PSTN to mobile calls. The tender documents floated by the DoT (and on the basis of which it had received the bids) specified that the tariff for the service provided by the licensee 'shall be subject to the regulation by TRAI, as when such an authority is set up by the Government of India'. Further, with respect to the contention of the petitioners regarding connectivity, the TRAI held that 'subject to the technical integrity of the network and technical feasibility, operators should not be denied points of interconnect and multiple GMSCs as they require for their optimal and efficient operation of their networks'.[13] In effect, TRAI reversed the DoT's order that unilaterally raised fixed to mobile tariff, and ruled that the DoT must provide greater interconnection to private entrants.

[12] Public Switched Telecom Network, also known as Basic Service or Fixed Service.
[13] Aircel Digilink and others vs Union of India and others, TRAI Petition 1, 1997.

In another case regarding non-payment of licence fee by private licensees who accused the DoT of delaying clearances prior to commercial launch, TRAI stated:

> The TRAI Act has been promulgated in the context of national objectives of acceleration of rural and urban telephone penetration; attraction of private capital—national and international—to upgrade telecom infrastructure and economic growth enabled by a developed communications infrastructure. Investors in order to have confidence to invest in the sector require an assurance that the DoT does not combine in itself the dual role of the regulator and the monopoly operator, that an independent authority plays a watchdog role of regulator under internationally accepted regulatory practices. The distinction sought to be made by the respondents [DoT] in regard to their role as licensors for receiving license fee divorced from their obligations as incumbent monopoly network operators for providing interconnection etc is totally unsustainable in the circumstances. This stance would also in part defeat the legislative intent of the setting up of this authority namely speedy settlement of disputes between DoT and the service providers.[14]

These decisions marked the beginning of an antagonistic relationship between the TRAI and DoT. Partly it was due to the fact that the DoT seemed to think that TRAI was deliberately hostile to it and perhaps more importantly, it was due to the DoT's inability to accept the competitive model after having operated an unbridled monopoly for such a long time. The inevitable loss of market share prompted MTNL's entry into the cellular market in Delhi and Mumbai, the two most lucrative telecom markets at that time. The DoT gave such a licence to MTNL, without consulting TRAI. In the litigation that followed, TRAI remarked:

> In a multi operator environment, an independent evaluation of the economic needs for a new service provider is a condition precedent for on the one hand maintaining investors' confidence and on the other achieving public policy objectives. This is particularly so at this point in India when the Government in the DoT combines itself the roles of a licensor policy maker and service provider.[15]

The TRAI held that as a precondition to exercising its licensing powers, the government had to ask TRAI for its recommendations. The DoT was not pleased with this interpretation and filed an appeal in the

[14] Fascel Ltd. and others vs Union of India and others.

[15] Bharti Cellular and others vs Union of India and another.

Delhi High Court. The dispute related to whether in exercise of its powers to regulate 'service providers', the TRAI could regulate the functioning of the government as a licensor and whether it was mandatory for the government to seek its recommendations with regard to matters covered in the Act. The case was the Union of India vs Telecom Regulatory Authority of India in the High Court of Delhi and was decided in July 1998. In this case, it was clearly held that the question of grant or amendment of a licence by the Central Government acting in its capacity as the licensor falls outside the jurisdiction of the powers of the TRAI. Further it held that it was not mandatory for the Government to seek the TRAI's recommendations. The folly of this judgement lay in the fact that issues which were subject to frequent change and review, for example tariffs, were also a part of the licence conditions and by implication, beyond the jurisdiction of the newly established regulator. That the terms and conditions of the licence are inviolate and not subject to 'review' by TRAI could not have been the intent of the legislature if it were serious about lifting the quality of telecommunications in the country to world class levels. The judgment also failed to recognize that the TRAI was a body equipped with professional capability to give expert advice on licensing issues to the Government.

The Telecommunications Tariff Order 1999

Although the High Court judgment held that the TRAI had no power over licensor-licensee disputes, its powers of specifying the tariff regime remained intact. After going through a comprehensive consultation procedure covering service providers, consumers, policy makers and parliamentarians, the TRAI issued its Telecommunication Tariff Order (TTO) on 9 March 1999. The order was a landmark for infrastructure regulatory agencies in India in terms of attempting to rebalance tariffs to reflect costs more closely and to usher in an era of competitive service provision. The chief features of the tariff order were substantial reductions in long distance and international call charges, increase in rentals and local charges and steep reductions (an average of about 70 per cent) in the charge for leased circuits.

For basic services, the TRAI demonstrated that tariff re-balancing was necessary to prepare the market for competition. A small proportion of the subscribers account for a major share of call revenue, and these subscribers would be the subject of competitive churn when private sector operators enter the market. Loss of such customers would have a significant effect on the revenue situation of the incumbent, making it difficult to meet the objectives of Universal Service Obligation (USO) and network expansion. Thus, while tariffs have to be reduced for the services that are priced much above cost (e.g., long distance and international calls), tariffs for below-cost items need to be increased. Such a re-balancing exercise is common when preparing the situation for competition. Otherwise, competition will result in a decline in above-cost prices without any compensating charge in the below-cost prices.

The methodology of specifying tariffs included the following feature to impart flexibility. For certain services, the TRAI specified particular tariff levels while for several others, it showed forbearance. Even for services for which tariff levels were specified, the framework included the possibility of providing alternative tariffs. The tariffs specified by the TRAI form a package that was termed the 'standard tariff package'. Besides the mandatory standard tariff package, the service provider was free to provide any 'alternative tariff package'. Since the standard tariff package is always available to the customer, any alternative tariff package had to be better in order to attract any customer. Therefore, the standard tariff package provided a minimum guarantee to the customer. In one sense, it specified the peak expenditure level for the customer, with the alternative tariff packages being attractive only if the expenditure involved in them was lower than that for the standard tariff package. This method of flexibility was adopted because of the growing tendency in telecom markets to provide different tariff combinations for various baskets of services.

In the case of basic telecom tariffs, changes in certain tariffs (e.g. rental, domestic long distance and international call) were to be phased in over a period of three years. For cellular mobile, tariffs were restructured because the prevailing rentals were low and call charges were high. This resulted in a tariff structure that dissuaded usage and loaded the subscriber base. Thus, call charges were reduced and rentals were increased. The methodology clearly included licence fee as costs and showed that a high licence fee translates into higher tariffs.

Standard monthly rental for mobile cellular was increased from Rs 156 to Rs 600, but the maximum call charge was reduced from a peak of Rs 16.80 per minute to Rs 6 per minute. The service providers were allowed to give alternative tariff packages which resulted in lower tariffs. Leased circuit tariffs were decreased in order to encourage the use of telecom by business and bulk users, and to provide a competitive stimulus to such users through the use of leased circuits. Since there was a major systemic change encompassed in the tariff changes, it was not possible to be definite about any eventuality. Thus, the framework included in the annual review of the situation, TTO 1999 evoked considerable protest from a number of quarters, including the DoT. The DoT was extremely reluctant to implement TRAI-determined tariffs for various reasons, including presumed revenue loss[16] and did everything to prevent implementation of the Tariff order. The exhortations delayed implementation briefly, but the order was implemented *in toto* by May 1999.

In the Explanatory Memorandum to TTO 1999, the TRAI had stated that implementation of Calling Party Pays (CPP)[17] would follow later due to technical considerations involved in upgrading the incumbent's network to allow for new billing systems. After consultation, the TRAI announced its final decision on CPP including the crucial aspect of the regime that raised the price of PSTN (fixed line) to mobile calls. A portion of the increased charges were to be paid to the cellular provider for completing the call on its network. The ratio for sharing was fixed at 2:1 in favour of mobile. The target date for implementation of this regime was 1 November 1999. The DoT and MTNL had both made submissions to the TRAI that the regime would result in revenue losses and sought a change in the ratio that according to them, favoured mobile providers at the expense of PSTN providers.

A consumer organization, Telecom Watchdog, filed a public interest litigation against CPP in the High Court of Delhi claiming regulatory capture of the TRAI by private cellular operators. The MTNL also challenged the arrangement due to a presumed and significant negative impact on revenues. In court however, MTNL adopted a different approach and argued that the licence agreement made no mention of any termination charges payable by PSTN operators to mobile operators and in the light of the earlier High Court judgment of 1998, maintained that the TRAI had no power to modify the licence agreement even under the garb of tariff fixation. In January 2000, the High Court struck down the introduction of the CPP regime as specified by the TRAI on the grounds that it did not have the power to revise licence conditions nor to set revenue sharing terms. One

[16] See TRAI, Explanatory Memorandum to Telecommunication Tariff Order (TTO) March 1999.

[17] CPP is a regime where the called party does not have to pay to receive calls; instead a termination charge is paid to the terminating service provider through an inter-operator revenue share arrangement.

implication of this judgement was that the TRAI's powers did not extend to fixing the terms and conditions of interconnection, but were merely limited to monitoring the terms already defined in the licences. At best, it could monitor a revenue share arrangement mutually agreed by both parties. If this interpretation was left as it is, it would have affected the ability of the regulator to intervene in interconnection matters. In the amendment to the TRAI Act that followed, the Government expressly confirmed the power of the TRAI to regulate interconnection arrangements.

The TRAI (Amendment) Act 2000

Successive court decisions had watered down the powers of the TRAI critical to independent regulation for a viable and competitive telecommunications sector. Thus, the court decisions established:

i) that the government was not required to seek a recommendation from the TRAI before issuing additional telecom licences
ii) that the TRAI did not have the power to adjudicate disputes between the licensor and licensee
iii) that the TRAI did not have the power to alter provisions in the licence agreements
iii) that the TRAI could not make regulations on revenue sharing, without these being negotiated between service providers.

On 24 January 2000, an ordinance amended the TRAI Act 1997 and altered a number of aspects. For example, the adjudicatory role of the TRAI has been separated and has been provided to a Telecom Dispute Settlement and Appellate Tribunal (TDSAT).[18] This Tribunal has been provided the powers to adjudicate any dispute

i) between a licensor and a licensee;
ii) between two or more service providers; and
iii) between a service provider and a group of consumers

The TDSAT has been given additional powers compared to the powers that had been given to the erstwhile TRAI. For example, it can settle disputes between licensor and licensee. Further, the decisions of the Tribunal may be challenged only in the Supreme Court.

The remaining functions of the TRAI have been better defined and increased, for instance with respect to powers relating specifically

[18] In its present form, the CCI Bill also envisages the dispute settlement function to be performed by the Communications Dispute Settlement Appellate Tribunal (CAT).

to interconnection conditions. The TRAI now has the power to 'fix the terms and conditions of inter-connectivity between the service providers' (TRAI (Amendment) Act 2000), instead of 'regulating arrangements between service providers of sharing revenue from interconnection' (TRAI Act 1997).

The new legislation signalled an attempt to re-establish a credible regulator. The government would be required to seek a recommendation from the TRAI when issuing new licences. The adjudication of licensor-licensee disputes would be undertaken by an independent tribunal specialized in telecom. In terms of interconnection arrangements, the TRAI was given powers to override the provisions of licence agreements signed with the DoT. However, while there has been an increase in the powers of the Authority (other than dispute settlement), the Act has led to a weakening of the guarantee that was provided in the previous Act with respect to the five year working period for the TRAI Chairman and Members. This statutory guarantee was done away with, and the revised Act provides for less stringent conditions for removal of any Authority Member or Chairman. The term of the Authority was reduced from five to three years.[19]

Interestingly, the new Act conferred upon the TRAI powers that court decisions had established it did not have. Maybe the statute was not drafted properly in the first place and gave room for alternative interpretations. This provided an opening for service providers to use litigation to pursue their own narrow interest.

Wireless in Local Loop and Limited Mobility

The new TRAI would grapple with a new competition issue almost as soon as it was created. In February 1999, the TRAI had protested the government's intentions to permit MTNL and the DoT into mobile without a TRAI recommendation. In June 1999, MTNL announced a 'limited mobility' service in Delhi based on Wireless in Local Loop (WLL) technology, with tariffs identical to basic services rates, a flat Rs1.2 for the first three minutes of calling time. The TRAI intervened asking MTNL for the basis for a 'limited mobility' service to which MTNL claimed that they already had a licence for the WLL service,

[19] In a letter to the Minister, the TRAI Chairman has sought extension of the tenure of the Authority from three to five years as is the case with other regulators, *The Hindu*, 15 August 2006.

and that the limited mobility offering was merely an attempt to put the technology, at the disposal of those who might want 'a poor man's phone, offering value for money' targeted at the 'very low end of the cellular subscribers'.

In September 1999, when it became clear that if the MTNL licence permitted it to offer mobile services, the same would necessarily be true of the licences of the private basic services licensees, the DoT amended the MTNL licence to cover mobile explicitly. The new provision made MTNL's mobile licence 'technology neutral'. The fixed line players brought to the attention of Government of India as well as the TRAI the fact that CDMA technologies being used by fixed line players, can also be used to provide mobility. They demanded to be allowed to offer mobility services as a part of their fixed line licence.

In October 2000, the DoT advised the TRAI of the cost advantages of hand held instruments over fixed wireless instruments (Rs 6,000 against Rs 15,000) and sought the TRAI's recommendation with respect to:

> ... scope of Area of hand held subscriber terminals under Wireless Access System operations, the basis for assigning WLL frequency and the amount of entry fee and spectrum charges as a percentage of revenue to be charged from the Basic Service Operator for extending the above facility in respect of existing as well as future Basic Service Licensees, so as to ensure a level playing field with the Cellular Operators.[20]

In the run-up to January 2001 when the TRAI made recommendations to the government on Wireless in Local Loop with Limited Mobility (WLL(M)) as part of the Basic Service licence, extensive consultations were held with all stakeholders, including with the Parliamentary Standing Committee on Communications. Cellular operators were opposed to WLL(M) mainly on two grounds. First, they argued that WLL(M) was a 'backdoor entry' for basic service in the mobile market and secondly, permission to offer mobility under the basic service licence would violate the terms of the mobile licence. Amidst the widespread controversy that this episode generated, the TRAI provided its recommendations to DoT that mobility be permitted for basic service, but it be restricted to the Short Distance Charging Area (SDCA). The rationale was to allow operators to use new technology to increase penetration in a cost effective manner. Mobility was viewed as an additional or value addition to the Basic

[20] *www.trai.gov.in.*

Service in order to increase the attractiveness of the service to customers. While allowing limited mobility under the Basic Service licence the government granted concessions to CMSPs in order to provide for a level playing field between the licences (See Annex II for concessions).

Cellular Mobile Service Providers (CMSPs) challenged the decision dated 25.1.2001 of the DoT allowing Fixed Service Providers (FSPs), also referred to Basic Service Providers (BSP) or Basic Service Operators (BSO) to provide mobility to subscribers with Wireless Access Systems limited within local area i.e. SDCA in which a subscriber is registered. The decision was challenged on various grounds particularly, that the decision was against the NTP-99, tender documents and licence agreements of both the service providers. The CMSPs' contention was that allowing BSPs with limited mobility would encroach the field exclusively occupied by them.

The TDSAT dismissed the petition particularly on the ground that granting limited mobility in WLL [WLL (M)] was a matter of policy of the Central Government which they could not review. On an appeal filed by the CMSPs in the Supreme Court the order of the Tribunal was set aside and the matter remanded to the Tribunal. In a 2:1 judgement, the TDSAT once again dismissed the petition of CMSPs. Although the matter was once again taken to the Supreme Court, it died a natural death with the introduction of the unified access licence, which is discussed below.

The dissenting voice in the 2:1 divided opinion given by the TDSAT was that of the Chairperson. He was extremely critical of the role of the government and especially the TRAI, in supporting the introduction of the hybrid limited mobility service. This was the beginning of many bruising collisions between the TRAI and TDSAT between 2003 and 2005 which were strategically used by stakeholders to delay reform. This is further discussed in section 'Question of Legitimacy'.

Meanwhile, operational implementation of the restriction of mobility became awkward and difficult for the TRAI as operators used ingenious ways of offering full mobility to customers while seemingly remaining within the letter of the new licence conditions. The TRAI has admitted that:

> ... artificial restrictions [would] encourage service providers to find loopholes in licensing regime and they will use technology or loopholes in networks/ regulation to by-pass such restrictions. One such recent case is the mobility under WLL(M) where the limited mobility within SDCA, granted to the operator has been converted into almost an All-India roaming by the operator registering the subscribers almost all over the country by using call-forwarding

and multiple registration. Such aberrations lead to disputes and litigation which hamper the growth of telecommunication sector. Ultimately no one gains, since the ability of the technology should not have been restricted in the first place by means of a technology neutral license[21]

In the litigation-intensive scenario that threatened to undermine the institutional structure, the TRAI recognized the need to settle the mobility issue across different licence types by proposing a unified licence regime for basic and cellular operators. This regime covered both the access services and proposed that the scope of the licence be enlarged to include all services at a later stage. The TRAI maintained that the shift to a unified licensing regime was not at odds with NTP 1999 because the CMSPs at the time of migration to revenue share regime, had accepted a multipoly regime. According to the TRAI, the restriction on the number of CMSPs by the licensor due to limitations of availability of spectrum at a particular time, was not to be claimed as a contractual right. NTP 1999 stated:

> The Licensee shall forego the right of operating in the regime of limited number of operators after 01.08.1999 and shall operate in a multipoly regime, that is to say that the Licensor may issue additional licenses for the Service without any limit in the Service Area where the Licensee Company is providing Cellular Mobile Telephone Service.[22]

The unification of access licences successfully ended the crippling litigation in the sector.

Question of Legitimacy

While the level playing field issue relating to WLL (M) may have got settled after protracted litigation and government intervention, litigation continued to be used as an instrument of strategic involvement by service providers. Conflict between regulatory institutions can be used to strategic advantage by self-serving service providers, while coordination between the agencies can effectively blunt such strategic attempts. For example if a service provider is convinced that chances of successfully challenging a TRAI or government order are high, it will do so.

One danger of augmenting competition in the telecommunication market in India has been the lack of coordination between newly

[21] Recommendations on Unified Licensing, TRAI, 27 October 2003, *www.trai.gov.in.*
[22] Ibid.

established regulatory agencies. The role of the TRAI in issues relating to passing tariff orders and interconnection regulations are defined under section 11 (2) of the TRAI (Amendment) Act 2000. These orders and regulations can be challenged by operators in the TDSAT. Soon after the Amendment to the TRAI Act in 2000, the TRAI made the Telecommunication Interconnection (Reference Interconnect Offer) Regulation 2002. It was challenged in TDSAT, which held that the TRAI could not amend the terms and conditions of interconnection since these are embedded in the licence. Similarly in another case where the TRAI issued a direction in 2003 to all service providers to establish direct connectivity, TDSAT set aside the direction, again citing that the TRAI could not vary terms and conditions of the licence.

In 2003, the TRAI issued a direction to all service providers that disconnection of interconnection was not desirable and payment disputes should be settled through mutual agreement and if mutual agreement was not possible, the aggrieved party could approach the TRAI for determination. This was challenged successfully in the TDSAT, which held that the power to settle disputes is not vested with the TRAI. And finally, in a tariff Order when TRAI reduced the ceiling IPLC tariff by 70 per cent in 2003, the TDSAT stayed the Order citing breach of transparency and natural justice.

These judgements (both the earlier High Court judgement in 1998 and recently those of the TDSAT) were based on a strict interpretation of the statute and had a similar ring. Despite the fact that the new Act assigned TRAI the power to fix terms and conditions of interconnection, the TDSAT interpreted the statute to mean that for licences issued before the year 2000, the only power the TRAI had, was to bring these conditions at par with licences issued after 2000.

As described earlier, timely and fair interconnection provision and availability at fair terms is perhaps the most important instrument in promoting competition in the telecom sector. Tariffs and interconnection are items that are part of the licence conditions but are also subject to frequent review based on sector evolution. It could not have been the legislative intent to preclude these from the regulatory review if indeed the intention was to lift the quality of telecommunications in the country to world class levels. Therefore, the interpretation of the High Court in 1998 and the TDSAT in 2003 were both wrong and based on a very narrow reading of the statutory language.

Not for a moment should this mean that the regulator's decisions should not be subject to judicial review; on the contrary, the more power the regulator has, the more important are transparent administrative procedures and opportunities for judicial review. In fact the TRAI has appealed many of the decisions of the TDSAT in the Supreme Court with a view to clarifying its powers under the Act.

However, even within the existing statute, outcomes of the regulatory process could have been different if the institutions involved in policy and regulation had demonstrated more coordination among them. Specifically in the current context, greater coordination between the TRAI and TDSAT will send correct signals to the regulated entities. Outcomes in the telecom sector, already a talking point will show further improvement.

Some of this may be emerging if the recent judgement of the TDSAT in the IPLC case is any indication. Reversing its earlier judgement, the TDSAT declared in November 2005, that the TRAI is an 'expert body' and its tariff fixation exercise for IPLC met all the principles of natural justice and transparency. In another decision that seemingly restores the TRAI's role and legitimacy, the TDSAT has declared that the government must make public its reasons for rejecting recommendations from an expert body like the TRAI.

This is indeed welcome. As a general rule, one should not expect courts to become heavily involved in the details of complex technical issues that are supposed to be addressed by expert agencies. This would just create a second layer of regulation. The telecom industry is highly capital intensive and its returns, vastly sensitive to regulation. If the costs of litigation are small compared to the gains that can be had from perpetrating the status quo, litigation can be used effectively as a short term entry barrier by service providers. Both private and public sector operators have successfully used this process. The recent decisions of the TDSAT would certainly make operators think seriously whether to use the judicial process to delay reform.

Conclusion

The creation of the new regulatory agency was a significant event in the need to establish an institutional framework capable of achieving the objectives of NTP 94, which recognized that India's interest lay in allowing private capital to relieve the constraint of public investment in the telecom sector. With the creation of the TRAI, the DoT surrendered its regulatory role, although it retained policy making, licencing and operations. In 2000, BSNL was created out of the DoT, separating the policy maker from the service provider. However, there is a feeling that BSNL is not completely free of political pressure. In this scenario, BSNL is in a position to influence state policy and may not actually positively seek to transform itself from being a national monopoly into a global player. In any case, it is unlikely to do so i.e. become a global player while remaining under the State's restrictive tutelle for all sorts of reasons.

One characteristic of India's telecom reforms—and cause of many of the problems attending it—is that major reform measures like private entry into services were attempted in haste, without the policy having been thought through. The TRAI Act 1997 which established the TRAI in January 1997 came three years after the announcement of NTP 94. Even after the regulator was established, its role and legitimacy were questioned by the government itself.

In the early phase of reform, the disputes that occurred were between the TRAI and the Central Government whether in exercise of its powers to regulate 'service providers' it could regulate the functioning of the government as a licensor and whether it was mandatory for the government to seek its recommendations with regard to matters covered in the Act. After amendment in the TRAI Act, once again the role of the regulator has been questioned by entrenched vested interests.

On the other hand, a serious attempt has been made to benefit from the lessons of the first few years of 'independent' telecom regulation. The difficulties of the TRAI, severe as they were, were by no means unique to India. Other countries, including developed countries, attempting the transition to competitive telecommunications were experiencing or had experienced the same frustrations. As long ago as 1994, the World Bank's telecommunications policy team noted, The single most troubling issue in recent reforms has been the slow progress in developing regulatory capabilities. All major reforms have been predicated on the expectation that effective public regulation of the privatized monopolies...can be implemented fairly quickly. Yet building regulatory institutions in countries with little or no regulatory tradition in any sector is an arduous and slow task.[23]

[23] World Bank. *Telecommunications and Economic Development*. Baltimore: Johns Hopkins University Press, 1997

Annex I

Main Functions Entrusted to Telecom Regulatory Authority of India

a) To ensure technical compatibility and effective interconnection between different operators and service providers
b) Regulate the revenue sharing arrangement between different service providers
c) To lay down and ensure time frames for making available local and long-distance DoT circuits between service providers
d) To protect consumer interests through monitoring of service quality standards
e) To ensure compliance of licence conditions, universal service obligations and the stated overall pricing policy by all operators and service providers
f) To levy fees and other charges and to make regulations in that behalf
g) To settle disputes between service providers
h) To fix tariff for telecom service and ensure price regulation
i) To render advice to the government in the national context on technology options, service provision and other allied matters concerned with telecom
j) Any other matter referred to it by the govesrnment

The TRAI is to exercise recommendatory functions on the need and timing for introduction of new service provider and the terms and conditions of licence to a service provider.

In the exercise of its powers and the performance of its functions, the TRAI shall be bound by directions on questions of policy given by the Government.

The TRAI is vested with judicial authority and powers. Appeals against its decisions will lie with the High Court.

Source: TRAI (1997)

Annex II

Concessions to CMSPs when limited mobility was permitted [WLL(M)]

a) The amendment dated 25 September 2001 to the old CMTS licence agreement, permitted the CMSPs to provide 'Fixed Phones' based on existing GSM cellular network infrastructure in their licensed Service area.

b) Under the unified licensing regime, the above mentioned CMTS licence conditions need to be modified to the extent that the choice of the technology is left to the service provider.
c) The Cellular Mobile Service Providers were also permitted to use mobile PCOs.
d) The annual revenue share licence fee, which was higher for mobile services, was brought down to level of Basic Services i.e., at 8, 10 and 12 per cent for Category C, Category B and Category A Circles respectively.
e) The CMSPs were allowed to retain 5 per cent of the long distance call charge.

Concessions to CMSPs when Full mobility was permitted [WLL(M)]

a) 2 per cent concession in revenue share for 1st and 2nd CMSP in each service area for 4 years starting from financial year 2003–04.

References

Mody, Bella, Lai-si Tsui and Patricia McCormick, 1993, 'Telecommunications Privatization in the Periphery: Adjusting the Public-private Balance', *International Review of Comparative Public Policy*, 5, p. 257.

Communication Convergence Bill (2001), available at *http://communicationbill.dot.nic.in*.

Department of Telecommunications (DoT), 2000, *Guidelines for Issue of Licence for National Long Distance Service*.

_____, 1994, *National Telecom Policy*.

_____, *Annual Report* (various years).

_____, *Annual Telecom Statistics* (various years).

_____, 2001, *Guidelines for Issue of Licence for Basic Telephone Service*, January.

_____, 2000, *Guidelines for Issue of Licence for Cellular Mobile Telephone Service*.

_____, 1999, *New Telecom Policy*.

India Infrastructure Report—Expert Group, 1996, *Policy Imperatives for Growth and Welfare*, New Delhi: NCAER.

International Telecommunication Union (ITU), 2002, *Asia Pacific Telecommunication Indicators*, Geneva.

_____, *World Telecommunication Development Report* (various years).

Joskow, Paul L., 1998, 'Regulatory Priorities for Reforming Infrastructure Sectors in Developing Countries April 1998', Paper prepared for the Annual World Bank Conference on Development Economics, Washington, D.C., 20–21 April.

Planning Commission, India, 2002, *Report of the Steering Group on Foreign Direct Investment*, August.

_____, 1999, *Ninth Five Year Plan*.

Telecom Regulatory Authority of India (TRAI), 2004, *The Indian Telecom Services Performance Indicators Jan-March 04*, June.

_____, 2004, *Consultation Paper on Revision of Ceiling Tariff for Domestic Leased Circuits*, June.

_____, 2004, *Consultation Paper on Unified Licensing Regime*, March.

_____, 2004, *Consultation Paper on Fixation of Ceiling Tariff for International Private Leased Circuit (half circuit)*, April.

_____, 2004, *Consultation Paper on Spectrum related issues*, May.

_____, 2004, *Recommendations on Intra-Circle Mergers & Acquisition Guidelines*, January.

_____, 2003, *Consultation Paper on IUC issues*, May.

_____, 2003, *Recommendations on Unified Licensing Regime*, October.

_____, 2003, *The Telecommunication Interconnection Usage Charges Regulation, 2003 (4 of 2003)*, October.

_____, 1999, *Consultation Paper on Introduction of Competition in Domestic Long Distance Communications*.

_____, 1999, *Telecommunication Tariff Order*, March.

_____, 1999, Register for Interconnect Regulation (No. 2 of 1999).

_____, 1998, *Consultation Paper on Framework and Proposals for Telecom Pricing*, September.

_____, ORDERS 1997–1998.

Telecom Regulatory Authority of India Act, 1997.

Melody, William H. (ed.), 2001, *Telecom Reform—Principles, Policies and Regulatory Practices*, Technical University of Denmark, Lyngby.

World Trade Organisation (WTO) Reference Paper *www.wto.org*.

_____, Annex on Telecommunication, *www.wto.org*.

World Trade Organisation, Telecommunication (WTO) Services, 1998, Background note by the Secretariat, December.

World Bank, 1997, *Telecommunications and Economic Development*, Baltimore: Johns Hopkins University Press.

12

Issues in Government Intervention, Black Economy and Governance in India

ARUN KUMAR

Introduction

In present times, the quality of life of citizens depends crucially, but not solely on the role of the government and the quality of its governance. This is even more true in the case of developing countries, like India where a large number of people are marginal to the market and its processes. In India, the larger picture is deeply vitiated with vast numbers living in fairly primitive conditions (see Kumar, 2006 for India's international ranking in some key social indicators). There are any number of things that are wrong with our society and the nation so one can ask whether they all have a common cause or are they all different phenomena that have to be separately understood and remedied For instance:

Conditions of existence for a vast majority of the people are deplorable. Poverty remains at high and unacceptable levels and disparity is increasing. Corruption is rampant. Institutions of democracy are under severe stress. Environmental degradation is getting worse, and, criminalization is increasing and terrorist and Maoist movements are spreading fast.

There is something drastically wrong for so much to be wrong 60 years after independence, so focusing on the smaller or individual aspects of the problem seems to be pointless—that may only result in non-solutions and non-viable policy options. Hence in this paper,

Sections of this paper are based on Kumar (1999) and Kumar (2001)

the focus is on the larger picture to identify the common cause underlying all this.

When thinking about government and governance (as stated above, they are crucial to society's well being) we need to ask ourselves, what is the meaning of a law or a policy? Should it be seen as it is formulated on paper or as it functions in society? Clearly, in India, there is a substantial gap between the two. This gap represents society's and the state's inability to implement its will. This gap needs to be understood but this is not possible in purely economic terms.

Most economic models trying to capture such complex phenomena, like the black economy are not very relevant because non-economic factors are perhaps more important (like honesty) but are ignored in economic analysis. There is a methodological problem which needs to be resolved.

This paper looks at the larger issues involved in the understanding of the efficacy of economic interventions by the government in the shape of regulations and controls for social functioning. The problem is situated in the context of the state and the failure of policy so as to provide an analysis of the poor governance and the tremendous waste and inefficiency in the country. It will help understand issues related to the retreat of the state and the likelihood of the success of New Economic Policies. It is clear that today these issues cannot be understood without taking into account the black economy so this issue will be centrally located.

The issues listed above have a historical background, are rooted in the current politics and have an institutional setting. But usually, the analysis of the black economy, governance and illegality is ahistorical and apolitical (Allingham and Sandmo 1972 or NIPFP 1985). The paper tries to rectify this failing. Finally, it presents an outline of the possible solutions to the problem.

Need for Government Intervention in the Political Economy

The Political Economy of Government Intervention

Why is the government held responsible for the mess that exists? Implicitly it is accepted that a) government intervention is essential in an economy and b) individuals cannot obtain many of the essentials of a civilized existence on their own enterprise and initiative. The direction of modern day economy is set by the macroeconomic parameters and what the individual can achieve depends on these parameters so any failure can be laid at the doors of the government. At the macro level the government is inescapable. Government intervention in the economy may take many forms, like investment, development, controls and regulation. In economics there are two overarching views regarding the need for government intervention in an economy: a macro and a micro view.

1. The Macro View: Resource Creation

A nation has a given resource base at any time. For optimum growth these resources have to be mobilized and utilised optimally and this can not be done by individuals in isolation. The government is needed for achieving the optimum. This is the macro view.

The world economy went through a deep depression in the late 1920s and the early 1930s. After trying various traditional approaches to get out of it,, it was realized that government intervention was essential to take the economy out of the depression. President Roosevelt introduced the New Deal in the USA in 1934. He initiated massive public expenditure on infrastructure to boost demand. At the same time, Keynes in England and Kalecki proposed their theories of boosting demand through government intervention. All this gave a fillip to the idea of the welfare state.

The government was given an active role in boosting the growth rate of the economy and the building up of the social and physical infrastructure (like health care, highways and railways). This led to a liberal view of the state as it got involved in affirmative action and mitigating economic hardships, like unemployment, both through creation of jobs and through payment of dole when there was unemployment.

2. The Micro View: Market Failure

The micro view is based on the neo-classical understanding that an economy faces market failure and the government is required to take the economy to its optimum level (Pareto optimum frontier). At the time of market failure, the economy when left 'free' gets stuck at a sub-optimal level. Only government intervention can take the economy to the optimal point. Further, the markets fail to achieve the socially desired level of equity by themselves so the government has to intervene for this reason as well.

Markets fail in a wide variety of situations. First, in the case of public goods like, defence and law and order. Second, when there are externalities like pollution. Third, when there are merit goods like, education and health. Fourth, in the case of increasing returns to scale like a zoo, a rural road and utilities. Finally, in the case of fiscal federalism.

In brief, both the micro and the macro views suggest that to achieve optimality, there is need for government intervention in the economy. In India, given the level of poverty that prevails, most are by and large not able to take care of their economic needs in a market situation so that government intervention becomes necessary. With this understanding, not just in India, government intervention has increased the world over, right through the twentieth century (Kumar 1999: 294).

3. Notion of 'Free' Markets

The traditional neo-classical theory does not suggest that markets be left 'free'. In fact, in the construct of the market, there is nothing like a 'free' market.

A market is an institution for the exchange of goods and services. Exchange is via an explicit or an implicit contract. There has to be an agency to enforce the contract when there is a dispute amongst the parties to the contract. This is the role the government has played. It has traditionally guaranteed safe passage to traders who otherwise were under threat of being looted. Thus, markets cannot function unless the government sets the rules and enforces them. If the government has to perform its role, it needs resources and so it has to tax. In brief, there cannot be a market without a government so that there is nothing like a 'free' market.

Where does the notion of 'free' market emerge from? In the neo-classical tradition a distinction is made between the 'first best' and the 'second best' theories. In the first best theory the government only need intervene where the markets fail and the rest can be left to the devices of the market to achieve optimality. But this is a hypothetical situation since the world is not first best but second best. In the second best, when one market fails then all the markets tend to fail so that they need to be taken over to achieve efficiency. Thus, in a more realistic situation, the world is much more complex and 'free' markets do not work by themselves to achieve optimality.

Not only is there a need to lay down rules for the efficient functioning of a market and an agency to enforce them, there is also a more generalized requirement. There is a need to oversee/evolve the rules of social functioning and an agency or agencies or institutional set ups to oversee their implementation. For instance, under pressure from the state, caste system is transforming and the inequity associated with it is undergoing change, even if slowly. Reservations were introduced to take care of its worst effects. Setting and overseeing rules in the form of laws is where administration is required both in a formal and an informal sense. The informal actions of citizens and civil society groups also work in an institutional setting and are not a free-for-all situation.

Governance is the broader aspect of societal functioning and administration; controlled by the state is the instrument society uses to carry out governance. However, often governance is used more narrowly as signifying the conduct of policy and the affairs of the state. State intervention has gone through different phases. Just before the World War II with Roosevelt's New Deal, government intervention began to be viewed in a positive light and the welfare state emerged. Then in the next phase, from the late 1970s, Reaganism and Thatcherism became the ruling ideology with the understanding that the state should retreat and markets should dominate.

Globalization and the Strategic Retreat of the State

The neo-classical understanding was supplemented by another neo-liberal philosophy in the late 1970s that policy also fails to deliver so the government should intervene little and the markets should be left alone. This has led to the idea of the strategic retreat of the state. Namely, the government should do everything to help the market function (this form of intervention is legitimate) but retreat from all other forms of economic interventions.

The advent of Reaganism and That cherism in the USA and UK in the early 1980s marks the beginning of the phase of strategic retreat of the state. The decline of the Soviet system in the early 1980s and the weakening of the Third World because of a loss of an alternative at the global level added to the worldwide pressures to move in the same direction. Economic globalization has meant adjusting to the structures in the dominant economies and the deeper penetration of markets into social relations. The pressures from the IMF, the World Bank and the WTO are all in the same direction.

Global capital desires to have the freedom for itself and does not like those forms of government intervention in the economy that limit its scope. It is using globalization to capture markets and expand itself. Where the state comes in the way of that, it must retreat. The requirement of the IMF for a reduction in the fiscal deficit while cutting taxes for the well-off, is a recipe for reducing the role of government in the economy (Kumar 1994a). Not that public sector units cannot be efficient but the principal problem for capital is that if the public sector operates in some areas, it creates difficulties for the entry of the private sector in that area. The size of the market decreases and the chance of making super profits declines (Kalecki 1971). Hence the moves for the privatization of the public sector. The markets in India always respond positively to the news of privatization of PSUs. Often these units are obtained at throwaway prices as was done in Russia in the 1990s, and yield large profits to the buyers.

For instance, if there are first class public hospitals like the All India Institute of Medical Sciences (AIIMS) in Delhi then the private hospitals find it difficult to charge higher prices. When public hospitals deteriorate in quality, the demand for private hospitals rises. If there are first class universities and IITs, cutback in their funding threatens their quality so that they either come under private sector influence or private institutions can come up.

With globalization, nation states are competing with each other to attract global capital. For this they are competitively offering concessions and losing control over their resources. In India, this led to the fall of the tax–GDP ratio after 1991 so that the government's capacity to intervene in the economy was dented (Kumar 1994a). Not only nation states but different regions of a country compete to attract capital by offering concessions. For instance, Karnataka, Andhra Pradesh and Maharashtra may compete for capital in the IT sector and give concessions, as each one tries to upstage the other. In the process the states have less control over their resources and the government has to retreat from the economy (Kumar et al. 2005).

In spite of the strategic retreat of the state, the world over since the late 1970s, the most important actor in any economy remains the State. In spite of the growing domination of the Multinational Corporations (MNCs) and the impression that they represent supra-national entities, the nation state is a reality. Its sovereignty may have been dented but most of its elements remain intact. For instance, in the WTO dispute settlement mechanism, it is the nation state that can appeal and not an MNC. The MNC has to be rooted in a nation to protect its interest. For instance, Lakshmi Mittal appealed to the Indian government in the Arcelor merger case. Similarly, the Enron fraud detection and prosecution took place in the USA. In the literature, the idea of the retreat of the state is supplemented by the notion of the minimalist state.

Notion of the Minimalist State

The quality of government intervention depends on its capacity to govern which in turn requires an instrumentality, the administration. The effectiveness of a state depends on the quality of its governance. A state may attempt a lot but if governance is wanting, it will achieve little.

It has become fashionable to propagate the idea that 'that government is the best which governs the least'. This is taken to mean that the government should intervene in as few areas of social activity as possible and have as few rules as possible. It is taken to imply strategic retreat of the state.

The above mentioned phrase can be interpreted rather differently. It goes without saying that government should be where it is needed and not (unnecessarily) where not required. The question is who decides where it is needed? If a builder is asked she/he would argue that there should be no zoning or building bylaw. However, no sane citizen would want unplanned cities (like Indian cities have become) and buildings of poor quality (such as those which collapsed easily in Kutch and Ahmedabad in the earthquake of 2001). There has to be a social consensus on these matters. It cannot be decided by a ruling clique alone.

However, the important thing is that whatever be the rules and regulations in a society they should be voluntarily followed. This minimizes the need for administrative action. A policeman cannot be posted along with every citizen to see that no illegality is committed. The larger the number of citizens who voluntarily follow the law, the fewer is the number of regulators required and the more efficient the administration becomes. It is in this sense that least governance is applied: involuntary compliance and the need for least government action. It does not mean that even where government is needed it should abdicate its responsibility to the citizen, such as in the fields of education and health or poverty removal.

There is no doubt that for the effective functioning of a society, most things in a citizen's life should be self-regulated. For this, society needs norms which should be widely acceptable to the citizens. This is difficult for societies in transition or those having large inequality. Old values like implicit agreement amongst citizens on how to function are in the process of being given up and new values have not yet evolved so agreement is difficult. A conflict develops between the old and the new or the gainers and the losers. Self-regulation slowly gives way. Experimentation takes the place of set patterns and citizens tend to do what suits them. The definition of what is legal is stretched and the divide between legality and illegality is blurred. In the process many illegalities get committed and the task of governance becomes difficult.

What was formerly considered illegal becomes acceptable. For instance, gold brought into India until 1992 was considered to be smuggling but in 1992 after the law was changed, importing gold became legal. In retrospect, smuggling does not seem to be a crime. If taxes were evaded in the past, through schemes like VDIS in 1997, past sins were washed clean. Tax evasion became legitimate and the honest taxpayers felt cheated since if they too had evaded taxes they might have benefited.

For good governance, the citizen needs to be committed to the rules and policies and to the tasks set by the government. This requires a consensus over policies, otherwise violations occur. For voluntary compliance with rules citizens need to believe in society and should not be alienated from it. Thus existing alienation of the citizens needs to be countered. When there is alienation and the citizen behaves like an automaton, incentives are the motive for action/work. Under the circumstances, if breaking rules gets greater gains then that would become the ruling norm, as in India (See Alingham and Sandmo 1972 in the context of tax evasion). Punishment comes as a device to raise the cost of breaking rules and lowering the return. However, voluntary compliance may not follow punishment since the latter may not be implemented due to corruption. As soon as the opportunity presents itself, as is likely in a dynamic society, the law is violated since there is no urge to comply. Thus, a vicious cycle of crime and punishment builds up. Voluntary compliance through commitment to society is the only solution. This is what Gandhi believed in.

For voluntary commitment to society, citizens should feel that there is social justice. Thus, norms of public action and functioning have to be very high. Not only should justice be done but also seen to be done. Some widely acceptable principles of public functioning have to be jointly evolved so that they have widespread acceptability. This is missing today and especially from public life. Leaders do not command respect since they are seen to be some of the worst kind of people who easily resort to half-truths. For instance, statements given on camera are flatly denied, or promises at election time are promptly forgotten.

Social justice requires the system to be transparent and accountable so that it appears to be fair and the citizen can trust it. The political and bureaucratic classes in India have used the classic British ruling class technique of divide-and-rule and opaqueness. That is why many believe that in 1947, power simply passed from the white sahibs to the brown sahibs. While the British were not particularly interested in people's commitment since their objective function was different, that cannot work within a system of self-governance that is supposed to be democratic.

With weak transparency, accountability and social justice, commitment to the society is suspect and therefore, governance tends to be weak. The government apparatus continuously expands and even then policies tend to fail. This brings about a sub-optimal state of society. Retreat of the state to cater to the idea of the minimalist state can then only be in favour of capital which gets the freedom to do what it likes and at the expense of the rest in the society.

One-way Globalization and Administration in India

The present phase of globalization may be characterized as one-way globalization since India has little influence on its direction. India is adjusting to the economic influences emanating from the advanced economies. In the process, there is loss of control over policies (Kumar 1996). Policies have to be adjusted to what is required by the global markets even if that goes against the interest of a vast majority of Indians (Kumar 1994a). This is hardly the recipe for getting the social commitment of the citizens.

For instance, today employment generation cannot be the principal focus of policy since globally, industry is moving towards more capital intensive technology, and displacing labour (ILO 2003). Maintaining international credit rating is more important than helping the poor in drought-affected areas or giving food subsidy to help the poor ward off the pressures of inflation. If the WTO requires that agriculture be opened up and reservations for the small-scale sector be virtually eliminated then even if hundreds of millions are adversely affected, this has to be done. Policies are increasingly being determined by external factors. Government has become less responsive to the needs of the citizens on the grounds that it has to fulfil international obligations to attract capital.

Our administration has come under increasing influence of foreign agencies. This phenomenon has markedly increased after 1991. The lure of jobs in the IMF, the World Bank, WTO, ADB, etc. has increased not only because of the high salaries offered there but also because they are seen to be the super bureaucracies controlling policy in India. As national policy loses its importance vis-à-vis the global, what is the value of national commitment of the administration? For instance, if the financial architecture in India has to follow the blueprint given by the World Bank, then it is better to be in the World Bank than in the Ministry of Finance.

With the weakening of the idea of the nation, setting of the national agenda by outside forces and atomization of the individual under the growing influence of the markets, the individual's commitment to the nation has also weakened. This is also true of the individuals in administration. Thus, many in administration are today serving the interests of the private sector or of foreign agencies. Many of the children of senior bureaucrats and politicians are working for MNCs and foreign agencies, and a *quid pro quo* is suspected. Bureaucrats and personnel of defence forces after retiring (or taking early retirement) serve the private sector and other agencies. For this to happen, a nexus is developed before retirement.

Such a shift in the agenda of those in the administration has weakened their acceptability to people and society and therefore affected governance and administration. For the alienated ruling elite, progress does not mean one more primary school in Bastar but it stands for, say, the next trip abroad or sending their child abroad for education. The elite's emotional attachment with the nation has weakened and with that the commitment to nation building. This underlies policy failure.

Cause of Black Income Generation: Illegality around Laws

The black economy represents the size of illegality in the society and is the principal cause of the failure of policies and the inability of the society to deliver to the citizens (Kumar 1999). Since black economy is significant and has serious macro economic consequences for the society, it follows that action is needed to curb it. To act, the cause(s) of the problem need to be identified. As with other aspects of black economy, there is confusion here too. Often, if black incomes are found to be generated in some activity then this activity (source) itself is taken to be the cause and the solution suggested is to eliminate it (source) (NIPFP 1985 and Gupta 1992). Say, if a tax is evaded to generate black incomes, that tax is taken to be the cause of black income generation. Obviously, if that tax is eliminated it cannot be evaded. But can this be a solution?

Traffic police is supposed to enforce discipline on the roads. However, if it uses the law to make money, it brings the law into contempt. Successfully bribing policemen to escape punishment for jumping a red light or for encroaching on pavements, is a cue, especially to the well-off, that they can continue the abuse of law. The existence of laws cannot be the cause of their being violated (Kumar 1999). The cause lies elsewhere.

Traffic police is oblivious to the convenience of the public and this makes following rules difficult—traffic lights are placed behind electricity poles or trees, yellow lines are placed without a break, turnings are badly designed, bus stops are poorly situated, etc. The indifference of the lawmaker and the enforcer with regard to the rules makes obeying them difficult.

Traffic rules establish the right of way for all forms of traffic. Violators of rules try to take precedence over others and encroach on their rights. A conflict over the right of way develops. Those in power lord it over others through the use of red beacon lights and stoppage of traffic; then come the trucks and buses, the motorized smaller vehicles, the mechanized forms of transport, and finally the pedestrians. The pecking order has become more important than the rules so that social functioning is inefficient.

Clearly, when those responsible for maintaining rules violate them or are indifferent to them, there is a feeling of injustice leading to increased conflicts and difficulties in social functioning. This is also true of the black economy. Rules or having too many of them are not the cause for their violation. By eliminating roads or rules or the police, the problem is not resolved; it just becomes worse.

Scams and corruption cases are hardly ever resolved. In the Bofors case, it is clear that money was made but years after it was unearthed, it is still not known who made the money. Businessmen, politicians, bureaucrats and investigation agencies, all know that havala channels are active in India. But the Jain case (1991) has ended without prosecution even though at least one politician admitted to having received money, and colleagues of another admitted that he received funds for the party. Evidence was found that it was also used to channel funds to terrorists. The state seems unconcerned about its own rot and the ruling group is incapable of action in their own self-interest. The cause of the existence of the black economy is at once both simple and complex involving the entire system.

In brief, existence of laws is not the cause of their violation. The cause lies in the growing sense of social injustice in people, poorly designed rules and indifference amongst the law makers towards the implementation of the laws so that they can themselves get away with violations for their own ends.

Laws, Social Needs and Black Economy

It is widely believed that controls and regulations are responsible for the generation of black incomes (NIPFP 1985). It is popularized by the terms 'license-quota-permit' raj or the 'inspector' raj. Kabra (1982) saw the issue as a part of the wider drive to 'remove-controls reduce-taxation'. He has stated that 'controls and taxation are necessary to curb certain activities in the economy. They themselves by no means create or help black economy. It is illogical to hold the laws governing economic activities themselves as constituting the reasons why people violate or evade the laws' (p. 162).

While the distinction between controls and regulations is not sharp, one may distinguish controls as economic laws that limit an economic activity while regulations may be thought of as laws that define the way an economic activity is to be carried out. So while urban land ceiling law may be thought of as a control which limits the use of urban land by some, a zoning law may be thought of as defining how construction may be carried out in a city. As is clear from this example, the distinction is not sharp. Urban land ceiling may also be thought to be defining how urban land is to be used (so as to minimize its waste) and zoning, by defining what cannot be done (say setting up offices and shops in residential areas) maybe thought of as a control. Consequently, even though in the literature a distinction is drawn between controls and regulations, no such distinction is drawn here. They are treated as economic laws.

That controls have a history, needs to be stressed. Uncontrolled speculation or price fixing by industry and trade has often resulted in public pressure on policy to institute controls. For instance, there have been demands for controls on the functioning of the share market or the prices of onions. With the growth of the black economy and opening up of the economy, the potential for unscrupulous manipulation of the markets has grown. Even industry and/or trade have demanded controls and regulation in many instances. George Soros, the high priest of international finance, has been demanding controls on international capital flows.

Rules and laws have not emerged in the abstract. They have a historical specificity as situations emerge. With time, society has become more complex and more laws are required. Since no law is perfect, especially in the beginning when many loopholes are discovered in practice, they are violated. To plug these, more laws are brought into the statute books and a complexity develops. This complexity has two sources, one in the social developments and the other in the human ingenuity of atomized individuals who want to take advantage of every situation for their narrow gains.

In India regulations and controls need to be understood in the wider perspective of the nature of the state. Policies designed to achieve wider national goals like, equity have not met with national consensus more so amongst the ruling classes. Consequently, sectional interests have viewed policies either as so many impediments to be overcome or as tools of economic gain. The black economy emerges as the natural corollary of this process of subversion of national policies and the state connives in this process.

Such a hypothesis implies that the state is neither neutral to classes nor does it represent a stable set of sectional interests. Kabra (1982) while recognizing the intra-class conflict amongst the ruling elite, nonetheless suggests a political conspiracy to fool the masses as an explanation for non-implementation of policy and the emergence of the black economy. This need not be so. A non-conspiratorial hypothesis might also suggest that in an unmitigated pursuit of narrow sectional interests, the burden of adjustment would necessarily fall on the unorganized and the weak.

Further, it cannot be denied that vested interests have developed around controls and that they can be under-cut by removing controls (See Dagli Committee Report, GOI 1979). However, the critics of controls need to recognize that mere removal of controls not only does not eliminate the need of sectional interests to maximize their incomes but also helps them do so openly and legitimately. One cannot make a general case for or against controls. The concept of social accountability must not be thrown to the winds, especially when it may lead to greater inequity in a very poor society like India's.

In fact, if there is a law, its violation results in illegality and incomes associated with this activity are generated as black incomes. Corruption is a part of this phenomenon. Illegality can end if the rule of law is either followed or abolished. But, the latter amounts to eliminating society itself and there is little left to discuss. Laws define the parameters of social functioning and need to be based on what is socially desirable.

Subversion of Laws: Roots in the Political Process

Proliferation of controls and regulations result in a complexity in laws and a difficulty in administration especially if they are violated with impunity. They become something other than what they are on paper; ill-defined and dependent on the whims and fancies of the administrators and the rulers. Flouting of controls and regulations in the economy to generate black incomes is not a random process but involves developing specific mechanisms.

The difficulty of establishing any link between the degree of controls and regulations in the economy and the size of the black economy lies in the inability to represent the former as a composite. It is far easier to see the link in the case of an individual activity which may be subject to 'controls and regulation'. In the case of the sugar industry, various degrees of controls have been imposed on its production and distribution for a long time. Yet, an analysis of the data did not show a link between the degree of control and the size of black incomes generated (see NIPFP 1985).

Real estate has also been subject to various controls, like, the Urban Land Ceilings Act, 1976. It has been argued however, that it led to an acceleration of price rise in urban landed properties because of freezing of excess land. It is well known that a rapid rise in land prices leads to an increase in black income generation. However, an analysis of the data for Delhi shows that from the mid-1960s to mid-1970s, the average price of land increased from around Rs 15 to Rs 250 per square yard while the rise in the next decade took it to around Rs 3,000 per square yard and then to around Rs 35,000 per square yard. Thus, the rate of increase in land prices cannot be said to have accelerated after the imposition of the Urban Land Ceilings Act, 1976. The problem of dramatic land price increase is linked to weak governance and policy failure. It is a result of corruption, rampant speculation unchecked by government policies, inadequate property and wealth taxation. It is also the result of improper policies with regard to employment generation and creation of infrastructure in rural areas resulting in concentrated urbanization due to huge migration of people from deprived areas to a few urban areas (Kumar 1987).

Controls and regulations, supposed to give powers to the politician and the bureaucrats, can be and are, misused to extract a rent. For instance, anyone who has tried to construct a house in India knows how much harassment he has faced. Delays are used to extract a bribe. Usually the flouting of a rule is associated with some economic gain and the advice for this may even be given by the concerned official himself. However even when rules are not flouted, a bribe may be given simply to save time and trouble, by way of 'speed money'.

The administration extracts a rent by agreeing to ignore the violation of the law or for using its discretion to grant a favour. To extract a rent, a surplus must be generated in the activity from which the rent is extracted. In other words, the bribe paid is typically a fraction of the benefit accruing or likely to accrue from the twisting of the law. The experience of businessmen and the police 'hafta' narrated in Kumar (1999) bear out this conclusion.

The discussion, therefore, raises three questions. First, why have laws become complex? Second, why has administration become ineffective and demoralized? And finally, how can the flouting of rules persist over a period of time in spite of the checks and balances in a democracy?

A legal structure may become complex because of rapid changes in society. As new situations arise, new solutions are called for. Yet, the earlier social structures do not disappear all at once and the laws relating to them continue to be required. Sometimes, the old laws remain in the statute books long after they have lost their relevance. In addition, poor administration of the law increases the complexity of the situation.

No law can be perfect since it cannot cover all contingencies. Thus, a law has to be administered both in letter and spirit. A corrupt and inefficient administration either implements the law rigidly or not at all. The flexibility or the initiative required to deal with a dynamic situation does not exist. Thus, a large number of loopholes are evolved by the ruling groups bent on taking advantage of the law. In response to such situations, legislatures keep modifying laws to plug their loopholes in an ad hoc manner, and in the process, make them more complex.

The other two questions will be taken up later since they relate to the prevailing political process.

Reduction in Controls after 1991

The experience of the post-1991 period calls into question the hypothesis of a link between controls and the black economy. Gupta (1992, pp. 80–3, pp. 93–4) argues on that growth of black incomes will be curbed by the new policy measures since controls are being relaxed or reduced. But, later he argues to the contrary when he says that NEP may not succeed because '... we may say that the reasons for persistent policy failures (including the new policies) to curb black income generation and unearth black money must be sought in the rampant ... corruption in the country ...' (p. 174).

When controls are removed an illegal activity may become legal. Does the tag 'legal' or 'illegal' matter? Take the case of gold imports mentioned earlier. It is not so important that gold can now be brought in legally whereas it was illegal to do so earlier and was called smuggling. Gold was put on the banned list of imports since in a poor and capital-short country it constituted a drain of resources. Gold import, ceteris paribus, still creates BOP problems since it constitutes a drain on the official reserves. The economic impact of the activity through the BOP, drain of savings and lowering of productive investments in the economy continues; only the illegality has reduced. In fact, ceteris paribus, economic problems have increased since now, five times more gold is flowing in than in 1992 so the loss of precious savings for a poor country has only increased. The rapid build-up of foreign exchange reserves in the recent period in spite of this outflow is due to other reasons. In fact but for this increased activity, the build-up would have been larger.

Suppose various laws are eliminated. By definition then, incomes would become white and illegality and corruption would reduce. What difference would it make? Tomorrow, due to an inability to curb theft, suppose it is legalized, would it generate security for the citizens because its illegality has declined. Can laundering of drug money and its use for criminal activities be legalized? Hence, what matters is the nature of economic activity and not the tag of 'white' or 'black'. If certain laws are needed for social functioning then their elimination can only disrupt social functioning.

Lower customs duties across the board may mean less smuggling but even greater importation of the same goods, leading to loss of foreign exchange and setback to indigenous producers of those goods. Lower direct tax rates will mean continuing adverse movements in income and wealth inequalities and the shrinkage of the market size in the medium run. Also, under the present regime it would mean lower rate of growth of public investment and social sector expenditures, redefining the state's responsibility to society. Is all this based on a new consensus in society about tolerating greater inequity? Has this followed a change in society's priorities? There is little evidence for this but the elite is pushing for it in its own narrow interest.

The real question in the context of the rapidly growing black economy is why does the Indian ruling elite resort to flouting the rule of law on such a large scale? This has little to do with the amount of government regulation or controls. Illegality can be high even if there are few controls and may not occur when there are a large number of them. Controls are only the means of generating black incomes. They are the means and not the cause (which is illegality) (Kumar 1994b).

The stock market, regulated or unregulated, has been a major conduit of black incomes. Illegal construction is proliferating in metropolitan India even though it is unrelated to the control of land. Zoning laws, essential for the efficient functioning of cities are being flouted by the builders and the rulers, leading to a breakdown of Indian cities. The crux of the matter is additional profits, over and above that which can be legally generated. This has not changed post-1991.

After 1991, controls and regulations have been greatly diluted. The MRTP and FERA have been done away with, small-scale reservations have been greatly diluted, imports have been liberalized, etc. Whatever was on the wish list of Indian businesses and MNCs has been implemented. Yet, the size of the black economy continues to increase (Kumar, 1999) substantially negating this hypothesis.

Controls and regulations are not the basic causes of black income generation and only represent the necessary condition for the generation of black incomes. In other words, if a tax or a law did not exist there would be no question of its evasion but it does not follow that if a law exists, its violation is automatic. Hence having a tax or a high tax rate does not mean that evasion will follow. Similarly, it is not that controls necessarily result in black income generation; they are only a source of generating black incomes.

Triad as the Cause of Black Income Generation

Lack of commitment to society has led at one level, to individualization—retreat of the individual into her/his shell—and at another level, to conflicts amongst groups. Individuals have strengthened their traditional ties to their region, caste, community, etc. and they hope to derive benefits from the system through these kinship ties. All this has led to growing conflict in society and a lack of consensus over social functioning. There are no stable long-term interests to act on. In economic terms, this has led to the fostering of the black economy to making gains over and above what can be made legally. The size of the black economy has grown and it has become the cause of much systemic inefficiency (Kumar 1999).

Indian politics governed by conflict is playing havoc with institutions. It is conflict which has weakened commitment to society and made illegality acceptable to the propertied. The black economy as the means of making additional economic gains by cheating the system and the subversion of democracy is a natural corollary of this. Today in India, many of those in power violate any law they can, whether it is a building by-law, rent control regulation, industrial licensing, tax laws, child marriage, child labour and minimum wages laws, traffic rules, environmental and industrial safety regulations and so on. Courts are overflowing with pending cases and full of corruption. It needs to be explained why there is this state of anarchy. Conflicts among the propertied, illegality, black economy, subversion of democracy and poverty are mutually interlinked and feed on each other. This social phenomenon needs to be examined carefully.

Laws, more specifically, controls and regulations can be violated and cause black incomes to be generated. Thus, illegality is the cause of black income generation and the source can be the violation of any specific law (Kumar 1999). Where there is lack of consensus and there is conflict or a feeling of lack of social justice, laws are violated more. Let us take the example of taxation. Countries with high rates of taxes may have lower amount of evasion while those countries, like India, where the rates earlier were much higher, evasion remains rampant in spite of much lower rates. In fact, tax rates have declined but the size of the black economy has only increased (Kumar 1999).

Complexity of laws may make it easier to violate them but this is not in itself the cause of illegality. Actually, India is mostly under-regulated in areas, like industrial regulation, pollution control, environmental regulation and urban zoning.

The system for the generation of large amounts of black incomes is based on the existence of a Triad. It is not that black incomes are generated on some days and not on others. It is not accidental but is based on a system in place. Laws have to be violated systematically so that all those involved in the preservation of the system have to be involved and requires the involvement of the political, business and the executive classes (consisting of the bureaucracy, judiciary and the police). Criminal elements in society have entered this nexus and often control it. Once all this is in place pretty much any law can be violated.

Possible Solution

Policy failure, poor governance and uncivilized living conditions of the citizens is linked to the growing black economy and illegality. This paper has tried to establish that this is not a consequence of government intervention in the economy whether in the shape of controls or regulations. The cause of the growing illegality is in the political process and the weakening of democratic processes in the country.

Not a Narrow Technical Problem

To improve governance, the credibility of the administration has to be restored and the causes of alienation of the individual addressed. The sense of social justice has to be revived. The problems of governance and administration are second order problems to the attitudinal changes needed and not merely technical ones. Mere setting up of commissions to suggest technical changes, like downsizing the government, increasing salaries, hiring people on contract, going in for citizen's charters or for greater use of IT, etc. will not help since the issues are not merely technical. Many committees have been set up from time to time to go into the problems and they have suggested technical changes which have been incremental in nature. Since the problems are irresolvable at the micro level, the recommendations have remained on paper and the reports have merely gathered dust.

Many committees have also gone into the issues pertaining to the growth of the black economy and have made suggestions to curb it. These have not addressed the integrated nature of the problem and so have not been a part of the basic reform required. Their suggestions therefore, have remained ad hoc in character and failed even when implemented. Some of these suggestions may have worked as a part of an overall package but ad-hocism has discredited these suggestions and they may not be tried for a long time to come.

Specific technical suggestions are unlikely to succeed because of the widespread failure of governance. Generalized causes have to be sought and remedies to these systemic failures sought and implemented. It is in this spirit that some suggestions are made below based on the analysis of the systemic failures.

Need to Strengthen Democracy

The basic attitudes of the Indian elite were shaped during the British rule. These need conscious reassessment. They have to analyse themselves critically to discover their weaknesses and boldly reformulate their priorities and be willing to take risks. The idea that accelerated economic development means following the path set by the West, has proved to be an erroneous one for India. The task of governance and administration cannot be limited to putting the country on that illusory path. A society is a historically-conditioned entity and cannot just transform itself by waving a wand.

The Indian ruling elite has to be receptive to ideas even when they go against its short-run interests. They have to develop the habit of being self-critical rather than self-laudatory and defensive about their shortcomings. If basic changes are made, the rulers may face severe criticism for what they are and what they have done. Assuming that they are interested in the long-term interest of the country, this has to be accepted and acted on objectively. Today, they react to criticism with defensiveness and act to marginalize their critics. Ideas should not be treated as subversive and dissent is not a malaise to be suppressed. Ideas must be encouraged rather than seen as a challenge to society since they are the principal source of dynamism in society.

A policy of divide-and-rule and offers of inducements (like positions, projects and committee memberships) are held out to those who are critical. The attempt is to co-opt or marginalize the critics but this blunts the nation's creativity. What the rulers have to realize is that the threat to them is a global one and to face it they need a strong and dynamic nation, not a weak one which is not able to deliver because of weak governance.

Alienation of the individual has to be addressed so that the citizens may be able to contribute their maximum to social development. This is possible if the individual feels that the system is responsive and that there is social justice. The government and the administration should be responsive to the needs of the people and should be seen to be fair. This is only possible if democracy is strengthened at every level and decentralization and centralization are dovetailed so that the micro and the macro do not stand in contradiction to each other.

There needs to be genuine grass roots consensus over policies. This is a prerequisite to good governance and administration. It can then have a single goal and deliver without appearing to be partisan. When there are hidden agendas transparency and accountability are the first casualty. There can be transparency and accountability only when there is consensus over policies.

There is need to implement the Right to Information at all levels of administration. The newly-introduced format for this is inadequate. The implementing agency is probably headed by some bureaucrat who has spent a lifetime evading rules and keeping information away from the public gaze. Now he would be expected to do the opposite. There is a danger that the top man would tend to be a pliable person or be part of a coterie. Further, the implementing officers in the departments may also be bureaucrats who would have sympathy with their own colleagues. We know that there are vigilance officers in each department to check corruption but they have been ineffective in controlling it and the same is likely to be the fate of the new set of officers appointed to access information. Basically, unless the mind set of the rulers changes, little can be achieved and it is possible that this right will be accessible to only a few determined people.

Very few things need to be kept secret. Currently, secrecy is grossly misused to subvert policies and generate black incomes. Those from whom secrecy needs to be maintained are able to use corruption to get all the relevant information so that the secrecy is to exclude the citizen only. It becomes a means to disempower the citizen. Decision making has to be decentralized and rules simplified so that they are easily accessible and understandable by even the layperson. Finally, Gandhi's principle 'last person first' must be followed all the way down the line in administration.

In a poor country the administration has to be non-elitist in functioning. The example has to be set at the highest levels by cutting down on the huge amount of waste. Gandhi remains relevant even today. The functioning of the bureaucracy should be such as not to awe the people with its power but to make them feel comfortable and they should be able to feel they can have a relationship of trust.

These changes would be painful for the administration used to functioning as an elite body but it would lead to good governance over a period of time. It is not that the nation cannot afford what it is spending on the bureaucracy but the important thing would be the change of attitude that would be involved in an administration shorn of its show of power. Did not the leaders of the Independence movement identify with the people and was that not the cause of the success of the movement? How simply Gandhi lived and how effective he was!

The task of administration in India should be to enable equal opportunity to all citizens. This would bring about a sense of social justice in society and reduce the individual's alienation from society. If a sense of social justice prevails in society, an income policy would be feasible (otherwise not). In a globalizing economy, without an income policy, the sense of social justice is eroded by the income disparities that arise when some draw salaries comparable with international standards while others draw what the Indian per capita incomes allow.

The conflict between the specialist and the generalist has to be settled once for all. As issues become more and more complex in a globalizing world, the role of specialists becomes more critical. They must be the formulators of policy while the generalists should be the implementers. In international negotiations and representation the role of specialists is critical and that of the generalists is marginal. Both these groups while answerable to the political leadership, should be able to take a stand before them rather than becoming subservient to them. Appointments by contract would undermine the capacity of the administration to take a stand against violations of the policy.

Administrative rules need to be simplified and made transparent so that everyone can understand them. The government should intervene effectively where needed. The question is not more or less of government intervention but the right amount as dictated by a national agenda based on consensus. India's problem is not that there is too much of government intervention in the economy but that whatever rules exist, are violated. There is considerable lawlessness in the country that adversely affects governance.

There is an urgent need to break the Triad. This would strengthen democracy. An independent national agenda would give a mooring to administration and to the national leadership which is missing today. The Right to information, transparency and accountability would go a long way in weakening the functioning of the triad. Accountability means fixing responsibility and setting time limits for tasks.

Conclusion

The paper argues that governance in India is poor because there is a substantial black economy. The cause of the existence of the black economy is shown to be illegality and not controls and regulations (as argued in the literature, like, NIPFP 1985). In turn, illegality is the result of a lack of commitment of the ruling elites to Indian society. They tend to break most rules and regulations (black incomes are concentrated in the hands of 3 per cent of the population) in their own narrow interest to earn incomes over and above what they are able to earn legally. It is argued here that in a poor society, like, India, government has to continue to play a large role since a majority are marginal to the markets. The notion of the minimalist state should not be interpreted to stand for a retreat of the state but a self-governing state where rules and laws are voluntarily obeyed by the citizens so that a minimum of governance is required. Unfortunately, capital is using this idea in the former sense in the current globalizing world to push its own interest to the detriment of the larger interest of society.

A nation is defined by the set of the rules it agrees to govern itself by and the culture in which the citizens operate and work. When these change or are violated (due to illegality and the black economy) the nation itself changes. The gap between what 'is' and 'should be' grows and the capacity to achieve goals is circumscribed.

Failure of governance and public administration is largely the result of a growing black economy and lack of a national perspective on its current problems. It is not that the Constitution is inadequate or that the rules are flawed and the two are in need of drastic changes. The implementation is flawed and the intentions are suspect. The roots of the crisis lie in the societal processes which have led to a narrowing of horizons and a loss of value for ideas. Consequently, the problems faced by public or private administration in the country whether in the corporate sector or the NGOs are the same. Hence these have not been discussed separately. The solution lies in a change of consciousness of the ruling groups. This can happen only if there are movements which change the consciousness of the citizens and enable democracy to take deeper roots in the country. The movements have to be sustained since often after laws are brought on the statue books, the movements die out and the laws remain unimplemented. The Right to Information is an example of this. As it is, very few are able to use it and there are already pressures to dilute it. In a nutshell, democracy has to be strengthened through adopting Gandhi's principle 'last person first'.

References

Allingham, M. G. and Samdmo, A., 1972, 'Income Tax Evasion: A Theoretical Analysis', *Journal of Public Economics*, 1.

GOI, Ministry of Finance, 1979, *Report of the Committee on Controls and Subsidies.*

Gupta, S. B., 1992, *Black Income in India*, Sage Publications, New Delhi.

Kabra, K. N., 1982, *The Black Economy in India: Problems and Policies*, Chanakya Publications, New Delhi.

Kalecki, M., 1971, *Selected Essays on the Dynamics of the Capitalist Economy*, Cambridge University Press, Cambridge.

Kumar, A., 1987, 'A Perspective on Urbanization and Urban Land Policy', *Nagarlok*, January-March.

_____, 1994a, 'Proposals for a Citizens' Union Budget for the Nation for 1994–95; 'An Alternative to the Fund Bank Dictated Union Budget for 1994–95', Mimeo presented to the Citizen's Committee on 12 February at GPF New Delhi organized by Preparatory Committee for Alternative Economic Policies.

_____, 1994b, 'Corruption as the Source of Black Income in India. Book Review of Black Income in India by S. B. Gupta', *The Indian Economic Review*, July-December, pp. 229–32.

_____, 1996, 'New Economic Policies, Instability and Policy Ineffectiveness', *Economic & Political Weekly*, 23 November, pp. 3061-70.

_____, 1999, *The Black Economy in India*, Penguin, New Delhi.

_____, 2001, 'Public Administration and Governance in India: A Critical

Look', Mimeo for the National Commission for the Review of the Working of the Constitution.

———, 2006, 'Union Budget 2006–07: Growth vs. Equity', *Bhartiya Samajik Chintan*, vol. IV, no. 4.

———, S. Chattopadhyay and S. A. Dharan, 2005 (eds.), 'Fiscal Policies. In Alternative Economic Survey Group', *Alternative Economic Survey 2005*, Danish Books, New Delhi.

NIPFP, 1985, *Aspects of the Black Economy*, NIPFP, New Delhi.